Children and Television

For all children of the television era, and
especially Anna, John, Jenny, Cathy, Christine,
Kara, Karena and Katya

Children
and Television

A Semiotic Approach

Robert Hodge and David Tripp

Stanford University Press
Stanford, California
1986

Stanford University Press
Stanford, California
©1986 Robert Hodge and David Tripp
Originating publisher: Polity Press, Cambridge
  in association with Basil Blackwell, Oxford
First published in the U.S.A. by
  Stanford University Press, 1986
Printed in Great Britain
ISBN 0-8047-1352-9
LC 86-61517

Contents

Introduction   1

1 **The double face of Fangs**
   Myth, ideology and the content of children's television   14
   Introduction   14
   Reading a cartoon   17

2 **'You sorta listen with your eyes'**
   Decoding children's responses to television   41
   Models and methods of analysis   41
   A child's-eye-view of *Fangface*   50
   Different codes, different messages   61

3 **Television and the mind of the child**
   A development perspective   73
   Theories of development: a semiotic synthesis   75
   The growth of children's perception and thinking   77
   Television and mental growth   85
   Gender and constructions of reality   93
   Social class and structures of thought   95

4 **'God didn't make Yogi Bear'**
   The modality of children's television   100
   The fantasy-effect: problems or solution   100
   The many markers of modality   104
   The development of children's reality constructs   119
   Modality, age and class   126

5 **Society and the viewer**
   The construction of meaning   132
   Social context and modality   132

Black viewers and reality   138
Sex, power and the negotiation of meanings   142

6 **Television and schooling**
   The hidden curriculum   159
   Television and scholastic performance:
      the evidence from research   160
   Television and the teachers' curriculum   166
   Television and the hidden curriculum   171
   Television as teacher   178

7 **The violence debate**
   A crisis in media studies   189
   A Kuhnian perspective   189
   New models for old   199
   Classic texts revisited   201

8 **Conclusion**
   Ten theses on children and television   213

   References   219
   Index   227

Introduction

This book is about children and television. This is a topic that poses a dilemma for many people in western society. In countries such as the USA, Great Britain and Australia, television is all-pervasive: up to 98 per cent of homes have a television set, and children are dedicated consumers of television. Day in, day out, 20–25 hours per week is an average rate, and heavy viewers manage a 40-hour week or more in front of the box. Such universality would seem to suggest a general social acceptance of television. However, there is also a widespread unease that is voiced by parents, teachers and other educators (Schulman, 1973; Postman, 1979; Winn, 1977); there is a feeling that television is possibly very dangerous, and ought to be controlled. These doubts are especially interesting because most parents do not act upon them. Surveys show (e.g. Australian Senate Inquiry, 1978) that a majority of parents feel that they do not control their children's viewing sufficiently, that the content of television is trivial or even harmful; but yet, if they really believe that, why do they not prevent their children from watching it? Such a paralysis of the will, such a contradiction between actual practice and avowed belief, is an unhappy state. But the situation is even more cloudy than that. The belief that television is a bad influence is for many an unstable, insecure one. Certainly it is often hard to sustain in the face of the apparently robust and healthy enjoyment of television by one's own children.

The belief that television is probably bad is in some cases highly conservative, part of a rejection of contemporary society and technology in favour of earlier, often idealized social and cultural forms. Such people nostalgically evoke a pre-television world where children read books, played vigorous games, dreamed rich dreams, and talked (or were talked at by their elders and betters) at the family meal. There is also a left-wing form of hostility to television. These critics cannot believe that a medium owned and controlled by big business could be other than insidiously ideological and manipulative (see Bonney and Wilson, 1983). A belief that is shared by both radicals and reactionaries looks a powerful one; but this is a strange alliance, and it is opposed by a much more pervasive but unacknowledged belief, one that is embodied in the practice of the multitudes of children who enjoy television and watch it, and parents who watch it themselves without seeing insidious signs of self-degeneration. Is the condemnation of television a mere ritual, without real force? Or is the toleration, if not acceptance, of television a great betrayal of the young of a whole generation? To answer these questions it is essential to leave popular opinions aside to seek a firmer basis for judgement.

There is no doubt, however, that people are absolutely right to be concerned about television and children. Anything that occupies 20 per cent of children's waking hours cannot be ignored. The worries parents have are basic ones. Not to ask questions about the effects of television on children would be irresponsible. So parents and legislators look to experts for some answers; and that is where the dilemma turns into a miasmic and oppressive cloud of uncertainty – for although the experts have turned out study upon study for decades, the result has seldom been a progressive clarification, an increasing certainty and confidence about what is or is not so. Rather, the opposite is the case: there are only conflicting results and conflicting interpretations, reservations and qualifications that increase as the scope and force of the conclusions decrease towards zero. All we can be certain of is how little we actually know.

However, we are not unduly pessimistic about this situation. The problem, we will argue, is that these 'experts' have been trying to answer the wrong questions in the wrong order, with theories and methods that have been overly partial and inadequate. In view of the remarkably inconclusive and contradictory results obtained over the past three decades from so many industrious experimenters, it becomes clear that the demand for so-called objective proof, and an almost obsessive preoccupation with 'effects', are premature and misguided. It is folly to attempt to prove something which is not understood in the first place. Most of these researchers have operated with a naive and inadequate notion of how 'effects' operate in the mass media. The very term 'effects' raises problems because most of the so-called 'effects' of television, if they exist, are self-evidently not effects of the same kind as that of a bat hitting a ball. Balls don't think: children do. Television sends out messages, which are interpreted and acted on by social agents responsible for their actions. Television communicates meanings. It does not pick children up and send them rampaging through the streets. If television affects behaviour, it can only do so very indirectly via meanings, beliefs, values.

From this it is clear where we need to look for the necessary background for understanding children and television. We need to know how television carries meanings; how different minds will interpret and use these meanings, particularly children's growing and developing minds; and how such meanings are likely to be enacted in the real world of the child viewer. This world is not composed of carefully cross-matched small groups watching television in a sound-proofed room, but social beings whose world is always constrained by a complex of social forces. So the disciplines or fields of knowledge that the researcher must be acquainted with are semiotics, or the study of meaning; psychology, or the study of mental processes; and social and political theory, or the study of social agency. Just one or two of these fields is not enough, since the phenomenon we must understand – children connecting television with the rest of their life – is a single complex phenomenon in which these different aspects are inseparable. Our diagnosis of the problems of this area of research is that very few researchers draw on a sufficiently broad background. Too often they do not even draw on a whole discipline, but just one school within it, a particular brand of psychology, sociology or (more rarely) semiotics.

However, interdisciplinarity on its own is not enough. Our own work is also guided by a number of principles – basic convictions we started with which our research has only seemed to confirm. One was that children's response to television is typically a complex cognitive act, not the enemy of reading and thought as so widely feared, but so closely akin that it makes good sense to talk of 'reading' television. Allied to this is a conception of children as not solely passive and helpless in this transaction, but active as well, creating and using meanings in their own lives, for their own purposes.

Our own work must be regarded as a specific intervention, an attempt to contest some tendencies in the field and to align ourselves with others, so it will be appropriate for us to indicate briefly how we see the present state of the study of children and television, and how our own work is situated in relation to it. We apologize in advance for being too schematic to be fair to the value and diversity of the work that has been carried out: we shall go into greater detail in the rest of the book. Though we make no claim to pure objectivity and even-handedness, we gladly concede that the former is not possible, and even-handedness is not always a virtue in diagnoses.

Broadly speaking there are two dominant traditions in the analysis of the television message itself, which are currently very influential.

The first of these is literary criticism. This tradition is difficult to assimilate into a scientific account of children and television, because it militantly opposes the whole experimental approach. So it seems not to affect the vast bulk of articles in scholarly journals, which aspire to the traditions of science. Literary criticism cannot be ignored, however, because it it still so influential in its own sphere and influences public opinion powerfully in spite of being so 'unscientific'. Most teachers of English, in countries such as England, America and Australia, have been trained in literary criticism. There are different schools in literary studies, but over many centuries there have evolved some intuitive but effective ways of reading literary texts, that bring out some complex and subtle meanings in them. The same practices of reading could have been deployed, suitably modified, on children's television, and on the whole field of popular culture and the visual media; but in general, mainstream literary criticism and the educational establishment have not taken this route. In practice they have tended to be elitist, opposed to popular texts that are enjoyed by children, and hostile to any cultural form that seems to threaten the dominance of the written word (see e.g. Thompson, 1964; Bigsby, 1976). Because children's television does not seem to have the same kinds of meaning or ways of being meaningful as literature – especially 'great' literature, written by adults for adults – television is dismissed as meaningless, or worse: as a threat to the meaningfulness of literary works, and the culture of literacy.

This approach is hard to rebut in a scientific scholarly way, because it is not usually offered in a scholarly form. However, it acts through the influence of teachers, pre-eminently English teachers, who form a powerful and effective interest group, shaping the attitudes of parents and students alike, and agitating at government inquiries into children and television on behalf of a specific conception of children and their needs. We do not wish to minimize either the importance or the potential of this approach. On the contrary, we believe that the attitudes and abilities of teachers are a crucial dimension of the nexus between children and television; so much so that we devote a whole chapter to the topic. If teachers in general had a different orientation to television and children, it would profoundly influence the 'effects' of television on children in contemporary society, and even on the meanings which had those 'effects'. We believe that some such deep shift is already under way. We also feel that it still has far to go.

The other dominant approach to the meaning of television for children seems at first sight to be at the opposite pole to literary criticism. Content analysis has developed to be as amenable to quantitative, 'scientific' analysis as literary criticism is resistant to it. Content analysis breaks up the meanings of a programme or programme type into countable units. After they have been counted, these units of meaning can be subjected to elaborate statistical treatment, seeking correlations, employing complex factor analyses. Since statistical significance is the dominant form of proof in the social sciences, some kind of content analysis is basic in much of this field of research, and as computer programs develop there is likely to be even more such work. We have no *a priori* objection to counting, or correlations, or the use of the computers, but the computer operators' label 'Gigo' is to the point here. 'Gigo' ('Garbage in, garbage out') is a salutary reminder that all further computing operations, however sophisticated, will be no better than the quality of the data input.

Correlations between violence and behaviour, as the outstanding instance (see e.g. Gerbner et al., 1977; Murray, 1973), depend for their value on the researchers' ability to specify just what meaning 'violence' has, or what is really regarded as violence, by those they are studying. Goldsen (1971, quoted in Edgar, 1977) effortlessly lists more than 40 kinds of violence which are impossible to evaluate in terms of any context-free impact rating. For instance, is hitting someone over the head with a stick a similarly violent act in a western serial, a family soap opera and a cartoon? Is it a more or less violent act than degrading a person by verbally exposing them to public ridicule? Is that rendered more or less violent by being a deserved retribution or maliciously unjust? If meaning were a simple, surface matter, easily identifiable by any normal person, then content analysis as it is customarily carried out would be sound enough. However, meaning is not at all a simple, surface matter. It refers to the results of immensely complex operations that take place out of view, inside minds, sometimes outside of consciousness. We shall argue that only with a due sense of the complexity of meaning processes can anyone hope to do justice to children's television. Only after, and if, this recognition proves possible, can the counting and the correlations begin.

Some recent work shows a much more sophisticated sense of how meaning works in the television image (see e.g. Salomon (1979) in the USA; Baggaley and Duck (1976) in England; and Noble (1970, 1973, 1975) in Australia). For this trend to achieve its full potential, however, we believe that researchers on children and television must address themselves seriously and systematically to current work in the field of semiotics, as the study of meaning systems and processes. We need to say something about semiotics here, partly because this is likely to be an unfamiliar word to many of our readers, and partly because our own approach draws so heavily on semiotic theory.

It is precisely because we lay such emphasis on theories of meaning and on semiotics that we need to be clear about limitations of semiotics, and equivocations in our own relation to it. We don't want to suggest that Semiotics (capital 'S') has just discovered the key to the universe of meanings, and has only to be applied to children's television for all problems to be resolved. 'Semiotics' as a recognized field is relatively new, but it also has long roots. The work that established it as a distant field was carried out in the postwar period, with important contributions by Lévi-Strauss, Barthes and Eco, who in different ways extended the achievements of structuralism in linguistics to cover the full range of sign systems used by humans. But semiotics developed out of linguistics, and linguistics must still be seen as a subdiscipline of semiotics. So the work of thinkers like Jakobson, Chomsky, Halliday, Bernstein and Labov is often labelled linguistics or sociolinguistics but comes within the general field of semiotics. In addition to this structuralist tradition in the study of language and sign systems, there have been other important traditions concerned with the study of meaning, including the philosophy of language (where Locke in the seventeenth century can be credited with the invention of the word 'semiotics'), anthropology (e.g. Malinowski and Bateson), psychology (e.g. Freud, Piaget, Kelly and Skinner), and sociology (e.g. Berger, Luckman, Durkheim and Goffman). This list is far from exhaustive, but it makes the point that a concern with systems and processes of meaning is very widespread, and crosses a whole series of disciplinary boundaries and factional allegiances. We would not wish to exclude this diverse range of work from semiotics, as though the achievements of a self-conscious discipline of semiotics had rendered all previous and concurrent work obsolete.

We adopt a very broad concept of semiotics in order to avoid getting caught up in such forms of imperialism, for openness, flexibility, and breadth of sympathies are essential for understanding the problems in the particular area of children and television. Some semioticians dispute with one another in order to try to align the same 'semiotics' with one particular brand of it. General readers, we presume, do not want an illusory unity of semiotics imposed on them, but nor do they want yet another academic squabble dumped in their laps, in place of some clarification of the important issues that they have every right to expect. So we will try to be careful and explicit in our use of work in this area, not appealing to 'semiotics' as such, as though it had some absolute coherence and authority, but drawing on specific methods and concepts that seem to us to be well-grounded and relevant to the study of children and television.

One finding of contemporary semiotics that is certainly of importance is its demonstration that the messages potentially carried by the humblest television show for children are formidably rich and complex. As Fiske and Hartley (1978) point out, television fare is deliberately ambiguous, so that, because society contains so many different groups and views different people will be able to read different things into it. Thus, a television show is not a single stimulus, it is a vast meaning-potential complex, an interrelated set of verbal and visual meanings. But this potential is only abstract until there is someone to realize it. Interpretation is an intensely active process. Meaning is always constructed, or reconstructed, by the interaction of a set of signs with an overall code.

If a different code is used to interpret something, then different meanings will be seen in the same 'message'. The written word 'gut', for instance, means a part of the anatomy for an English reader, but to a German it means 'good'. What if children's codes, or their versions of adult codes, are so different from adults' that they represent a different language? What if children 'read' a different meaning from what seemed the same message? 'Children's television' is not simply shows made for children. It is the sense children make of whatever they watch. Almost invariably children's shows are made by adults, and children's television viewing equally invariably includes shows that were made for adults.

To account for complex structures of meaning in television, especially for children, we need a suitably complex account of the structures and processes of the minds that can create such meanings; and that account must be developmental. Too much of the research in the 1960s and 1970s concentrated on aspects of 'scientific' method (size of sample, statistical procedures, experimental method, etc.), rather than complex developmental accounts of mental processes. A major shift in the field, especially in America, has been an interest in cognitive theorists such as Piaget, Bruner, Kelly and Vygotsky. These theorists all see the operations of the mind as so complex and subtle that they might be missed in a crude survey approach, or in an artificial laboratory situation. They also recognize that children's ways of thinking may be qualitatively different at different stages of their development. Researchers with this background have also developed a wider range of themes and concerns. The unproductive obsession with violence, as the one significant but elusive 'effect' of television, is gradually giving way to a more open concern with television as it interacts with the growing child – positively as well as negatively – leading to new kinds of learning, new kinds of discrimination, as well as to new opportunities being missed by television producers. (As exponents of this development, see Wartella and Delia in America, Noble in Australia.) Our own work strongly endorses this new tendency, which we regard as a welcome breath of sanity in a field whose narrow concern with the possible pathological effects of television on children was itself in danger of becoming pathological.

There is, however, another important tradition in psychology that so far has hardly been deployed on the issues of children and television: that of Freud and his numerous progeny. In Anglo-American psychology departments there tends to be somewhat of a stand-off between 'psychology' and psychoanalysis (i.e. Freudian theories). But Freud had an account of messages and minds, language and discourse processes, which simply cannot be ignored. He also had a developmental theory, and a theory of social being: neither of them wholly convincing, or beyond criticism, but nonetheless not without interest. Psychologists have looked askance at Freud because he was not sufficiently 'empirical'. Marxists have criticized his work because it lacks an adequate social theory. Both criticisms have justice, but still leave much that is of value in the Freudian tradition. We have drawn on it for our own work on children and television.

Children watch television as part of their social existence, and this is another dimension that cannot be ignored. In some respects the social dimension has not been neglected, because it is as a social problem that television has presented itself as demanding research. Classic sociological method finds it easy to segment a populace, to see the different effects of television on different groups in terms of class, sex and sometimes race or self-esteem. Correlations have been found, between quantity and type of television programmes viewed and specific sub-groups in society. For instance, there is a general pattern of higher viewing in lower socioeconomic class (SEC) groups, and in low self-esteem groups. However, these findings, though useful as far as they go, seem hardly able to explain any of the important issues of children and television on their own, without a wider understanding of social processes. One research tradition, which has been called the 'uses and gratifications' tradition, emphasizes the different uses of television that different viewers might employ (see Katz et al., 1973). If viewers are not only active, as this research suggests, but active in different ways, then crude correlations will not tell us much of what we want to know.

The uses and gratifications tradition connects television viewing with social life generally, and this is clearly what must be done if we are to understand how television fits into the whole pattern of children's life. To do this in any coherent and systematic way we need to look at theories of socialization and education, theories of ideology, culture and acculturation. In England especially, there has developed a tradition often called the 'cultural studies' approach, which analyses the contemporary media using Marxist theories of society and the state, allied to various forms of structuralism (see for example, Williams, 1974; Hall, 1980). We regard our own work as very much within this tradition, as a contribution to a common enterprise. That tradition has so far tended to focus on adults and not children; on the ideological product and its presumed effects, rather than the ideological process and its stages and moments of risk. Our work is complementary, taking up the 'cultural studies' story a little earlier than they normally do. Yet we also find that the story is slightly different from what had been envisaged: more complex, and also in some ways more hopeful, because children turn out to be totally formed, or formable, from birth for their prescribed ideological role.

What we have found in our study challenges many widespread beliefs, shared by the public and by some experts. We argue, for instance, that young children, below the age of 6, interpret television so differently that they not only prefer different shows – that much has been obvious – but prefer them because they 'read' those shows and others differently. The *bête noir* of lobby groups, the cartoon, which has been stubbornly supported by generations of children, turns out, when analysed by different methods, to be a healthy form, ideally adapted to children's growing powers. For instance, far from the fantastic nature of cartoons causing confusion between fantasy and reality, the largeness of the gap is helpful to young children in building up precisely this capacity to discriminate.

Similarly, much of the concern about the effects of television violence turns out to be more than a little misdirected, because it is based on a misunderstanding of how children are interpreting different aspects of the shows which cause most concern. It is not that television violence of all kinds is benign for all ages and kinds of children. What we argue for is an understanding of how qualities of content, like violence, interact with a sense of reality and with more general social attitudes and relationships. 'Violence' is not a simple fact about a television programme, which acts as an irresistible cause of enactments of violence by viewers. It is part of a complex structure of meanings, which are interpreted, mediated and acted on in very different ways.

We also question another common fear of parents and teachers, that television watching is' an inherently passive and low-level intellectual activity, which will turn the growing brain to mush. Children watching television are not zombies. They are learning important and complex structures of meaning, and developing capacities for thinking and judgement that are a necessary part of the process of socialization. What they learn from television does not enter and remain in their heads as a self-contained and erroneous body of knowledge. As we see later, most schools systematically disparage and exclude this learning, where it might be better to acknowledge and integrate it.

In other ways the influence of television learning is exaggerated and misunderstood because it is seen as a separate entity in isolation, not as an integral part of a complex communication situation. Meaning is constantly negotiated. Interpretation and re-interpretation are part of a continual process, and in that process other social agencies play a decisive role. Individuals are not helpless victims of whatever they see on the box, but nor are they isolated and autonomous beings. The ideological content of television programmes would have no force if it existed in a social vacuum. Among the determinants of ideological formation, television plays an ambiguous and often passive role because it carries no sanctions, only gratifications, to enforce its meanings.

The topic of children and television is one that interests many people. We have tried to write in a way that readers with many different backgrounds will find clear and accessible. However, we also believe that the dominant form of study of this whole area rests on a number of fundamental misconceptions and that the current orthodoxy is in a state of crisis from which it will not re-emerge without radical change. There is not a single consensus view, accepted by ourselves and all other reputable authorities, which we can simply present in readable form. Readers will rightly wonder how our work relates to a research field which we agree is undergoing change. So we have devoted a chapter to the state of the field as we see it, partly as background to our own project, but partly because crises and revolutions in academic fields are relatively rare, and have their own interest to people concerned with the contemporary conditions of intellectual life.

Our book has another purpose, however, and another audience in view. We are writing for a range of people who are concerned in a practical way with the issues of children and television, whether as producers or parents or educators. We want to address the fears and aspirations of such people directly and constructively, saying which fears we believe are groundless or misunderstood, and what could be done about the real bogeys. So we finish this book with a brief charter: a list of ten principles which we hope will be useful and practical guides; flexible enough to stimulate a range of responses; clear enough to provide a firm basis for judgements.

In this book we are sometimes critical of the methodologies of others, so it is only right that we declare our own procedures and debts. The book is based on the findings of a 3-year research project, which ultimately involved more than 600 children. Semioticians have often been criticized, with some justification, for disparaging empirical methods of enquiry. Although we have been sceptical at times of mere quantification, of 'number crunching' for its own sake, we did not want to fall into this semiotics trap – not least because of its implicit elitism. A semiotics that does not listen imposes its own neat certainties, or complex uncertainties, on a silenced audience; and the rewards of listening to the unmanageable, unpredictable diversity of children's responses more than made up for all the neat conclusions we had to scrap on the way, and the tedious hours of processing and collating and interpreting the data.

Yet in spite of the number of children we used, it must be said that most of our individual studies do not constitute proof of our conclusions. That was a decision of principle we made early on, in the light of our sense of the needs of the field. After the plethora of failed and partial 'proofs' of the 1960s and 1970s, we felt the time had come for an emphasis on discovery rather than proof, exploration rather than demonstration, suggestiveness rather than certainty – though these distinctions are not absolute. In general, we devised experiments and determined the size of groups in such a way as to confront ourselves with the diversity of children's responses, rather than try to show, within the bounds of statistical probability, that a particular phenomenon or 'effect' was always at issue. We carried out too many experiments with too few subjects from too many different points of view to make a watertight case in any one. However, we believe that this approach was the correct one for us at the present stage of knowledge in the field. The different experiments and the different children's responses shed light from so many different angles that we felt we had a better sense of the fascinating process of children's responses to television as the multifaceted whole that it is, and there was no other way we could get at this whole.

Complementing our empirical work was a wide-ranging theoretical enterprise. Our greatest theoretical debts are to those in psychology, sociology, linguistics, literature, communications and anthropology who have either worked in a semiotic framework themselves (e.g. Halliday, Jakobson, Lévi-Strauss, Barthes and Saussure), or whose work lends itself to semiotic interpretation (e.g. Freud, Vygotsky, Piaget, Bateson, Chomsky and Bernstein). These debts become apparent in the text, and so need no further mention here. For a more systematic and technical exposition of the theoretical model that underpins the present work, see Hodge and Kress, forthcoming.

Not so apparent, however, are our great debts to those others who were involved with the actual research project in one way or another. First, the project was made possible by generous funding from Station TVW7, Perth, over the full 3-year period. It is important in thanking our sponsors to point out that the kind of open-ended discovery approach that we took was only possible because TVW7 were prepared to offer funding with no strings attached on the basis of our having a task, a general direction and a method of procedure, rather than a closed set of hypotheses of the kind derived from existing findings, and generally demanded by any public body funding academic research. Among other things, this funding enabled the team to employ four research assistants, at different times: Peter Cook, Adrienne Walker, Susan D'Amelio and Anna Carr, whose efforts and expertise have become part of the fabric of the study: pervasive, indispensable and beyond local acknowledgement.

Murdoch University and the Mount Lawley campus of the WA College of Advanced Education (WACAE) supported the research in a variety of ways, providing facilities and equipment, but most of all, personnel. The ideas in this book grew out of weekly meetings and debates, over a period of more than 3 years, with major contributions from Peter Jeffery of Murdoch University, Mike Grant, Jean Collins, Brian Shoesmith of WACAE and other helpful criticism and support from Russell Perry of TVW7, Michael Davis, Viv Howard, Colin Shiva of WACAE, Michael O'Toole of Murdoch University, and Susan Argard of the Australian Broadcasting Tribunal.

Over 600 children have been involved in the project, mostly from schools in Western Australia, courtesy of the WA Education Department, and a number of School principals and teachers, and we gratefully acknowledge their help. Then, at an important stage in the life of the project, we received invaluable criticism and advice from Ellen Wartella, of the University of Illinois, and Grant Noble, of the University of New England, who battled for a whole week with an overluxuriance of neologisms and the proud parents of what was then something less than a coherent set of ideas. The final stages in the preparation of the text benefited greatly from the positive but critical perspective provided by John Thompson of Cambridge and Polity Press. Our grateful thanks to all.

Chapter 1

The double face of Fangs

Myth, ideology and the
content of children's television

Introduction

When adults look at children's television it seems simple stuff: too simple even for children if anything. Similarly, as they listen to children talk, or half-remember what they thought as children, it all seems so familiar and unproblematic as not to merit close attention or analysis. Analysis can show, however, that the apparent simplicity is an illusion. Language and art are immensely complex achievements which distinguish humans from all other species. Capacities for language and other forms of expression are laid down so early in life, and operate so powerfully and unconsciously, that they are extremely difficult to study, but that only makes them more important.

The first problem we face concerns the 'content' of television. In one sense, television 'content' is only patterns of light and sound. This content, however, only becomes interesting because of the meanings it gives rise to. Meanings are constructed by minds, minds which bring other systems to bear on these physical systems. The systems, and the meanings they produce, are locked inside brains. They are not directly open to inspection. We cannot even assume that they are available to consciousness. Like Molière's M. Jourdain who discovered in middle age that he had been speaking prose all his life without being aware of it, we act as though we have a knowledge that we cannot put into words or even into clear ideas. If this is true generally of the content of television (and other complex message systems) then children's television raises especially acute problems. Television programmes are made, sold and judged by adults. It is generally agreed that child viewers in some important ways are quite different from adults (Greenberg, 1974), and yet in other ways they seem so similar. Everyone would acknowledge these obvious truths; but it is not enough simply to say that in some ways they are the same, in other ways they are different: we also need to find a principled, systematic way of explaining the differences and similarities and their consequences.

Modern semiotics has begun to evolve some powerful methods for analysing narratives, and as children's television programmes are essentially narrative structures that is where we begin. Seminal work has been done by Lévi-Strauss on myth in primitive cultures (1963, 1969, 1972). For applications to television see Newcomb, 1978). He has shown how seemingly simple, inconsequential, even bizarre narratives can code highly important meanings for a culture. His method of analysis brings out not just meanings, but a whole set of codes that constitute a system which is a kind of logic of the culture, a way of making sense of the world. At this level of analysis he found that much of the apparent diversity of stories in different versions became comprehensible in relation to an underlying principle. With the materials he studied over a range of cultures, he found a recurring feature in the content of myths: they seem to be situated on boundaries. Myths deal with aberrations, with 'monsters', deviant beings, transgressors. They reflect rather than display in a direct form the logic of a culture, the primary systems and categories that organize thought and behaviour in the society which creates and maintains that culture. Principally they explore the culture's limits, its problems, its contradictions. The biblical Samson had immense strength, for instance, but he also had long hair; he was a hero of Israel, but he also showed a distinct preference for non-Jewish wives. The codes by which people were expected to live in that society were thus problematized rather than exemplified in Samson. Semiotics is important because it provides the possibility of a method of analysis which can deal with the messages of myths, and in so doing it can throw light on the meanings of television for children.

The method we developed specified a number of stages of analysis. We started with a single programme made for children, a cartoon entitled *Fangface* which we analysed along semiotic lines. What this gave rise to was a rich repertoire of possible meanings and an account of the codes by which these meanings were projected. We did not suppose that all these meanings and codes existed for children, however. On the contrary, these were postulated simply as what would be true for children if they were using our (adult) forms of code and structures of meaning. So the next stages were crucial: to use what we knew or believed about children's forms of thought and experience to provide hypotheses about alternative possible structures of meaning and interpretation, then to observe children in order to see whether children seemed to respond in the ways we would expect from our hypotheses.

The main problem with the method was how to check on whether our semiotic analysis was relevant to child viewers, because the sheer power of the method constituted its main danger – the danger being the tendency to impose our adult meanings on children. Whatever the checks, however, it must be stressed that there is no way of totally avoiding such a problem. In the case of this research we sought empirical substantiation of our analyses; but what constitutes adequate empirical evidence is itself often debated, and our work is as yet still essentially at the pioneering stage.

For instance, we analysed only one television programme in detail, which will seem an absurdly small sample to scholars trained in some of the more statistical of the empiricist-oriented branches of the social sciences. But that one programme was not the only data we drew on; we used it as a focus, not as a self-contained text, for our primary target was not that particular story, but the system which determined its significance. To establish the system's codes, a large number of texts are not necessary if the language is already known. A single sentence of English, for instance, will exemplify many of the primary structures of the system: the main sounds (or letters), the main parts of speech (e.g. noun, verb, etc.) and at least some of the rules of combination (e.g. subjects preceding verbs). Even when the system is only hypothesized, one page of typical sentences can provide more than enough material on which to base a reconstruction of the basic grammar of the English sentence. Similarly, as someone goes about decoding even a single television programme, all the major systems can slowly emerge, and as they are tried out on more examples of different kinds, the hypotheses about the underlying systems will be abandoned, modified, reformulated and new ones added, but they will also become stronger and richer, confirmed and elaborated. So the quantity of text we chose (one cartoon) and the number of 'native speakers' of the language (42 children) we worked with are not as small a sample for a semiotic kind of research as they might be for some other research paradigms.

What we do in the remainder of this chapter is to present, as an example of our analysis, the reading of a cartoon. Because the aim of this reading is to show just how complex cartoons actually are, it follows that our reading itself is necessarily detailed and complex. We ask readers to bear with us in this, for the sake of this demonstration.

Reading a cartoon

Cartoons are a long-standing target for the critics of children's television, and at the same time a firmly entrenched favourite viewing category for younger viewers (Comstock et al., 1978; Edgar and Callus, 1979). It therefore seemed the obvious choice of programme on which to begin our analysis. Since we needed to test the show on viewers who had not seen it before, we used a 20-minute cartoon entitled *Fangface: 'Heap of Trouble'*, which had not been released in Western Australia, where we did our research.

At this point, if this were a talk, we would show the cartoon, whose characters, plot and every detail are now deeply graven into the memories of our research team. For this book a summary will have to suffice. The cartoon is one of a series which focuses on the adventures of four characters. The central character is Fangface, a werewolf, who is the transformation of Sherman Fangsworth (Fangs), an adolescent whose three friends are Kim, Biff and Pugsie. In the episode that we analyse, a monster called The Heap attacks professors and steals scientific equipment. Fangs and his gang go to the last professor in the faculty who has not been attacked by The Heap, Professor Boyd, and attempt to guard him. The Heap, however, abducts the Professor in spite of the efforts of the group. Fangs and Pugsie track The Heap to his hideout: a cave in the mountain. They find out that The Heap is really Professor Arnoss, another professor in the university who was expelled from the faculty and has discovered a ray that transforms men into monsters. Fangface releases the Professor who is held prisoner there, but The Heap escapes, carrying off his invention. Fangface and Pugsie give chase, The Heap is turned back to Professor Arnoss by Kim and Biff using the captured ray, and at the end Arnoss is led off into captivity.

Where does a semiotician start, with a text like *Fangface*? Because many different features of the text lead to the same point, to some extent it does not matter, but since many readers will not be familiar with semiotics we will proceed from basic principles. Fundamental to all semiotic analysis is the fact that any system of signs (semiotic code) is carried by a material medium *which has its own principles of structure*. In the case of television the message is communicated by both visual and aural means: the visual image carries marks in space, both pictures and writing; the sound track carries sounds in time: speech, music, sound effects, and in this case, canned laughter. Each of these is a different code, organized according to different principles, carrying

Illustration 1

Illustration 2

potentially different messages. We need to be aware from the start of this multiplicity of codes (and as we shall see, the further subcodes) so that we can guard against too limited a sense of the sheer quantity and complexity of the meaning content of the text.

The next question to ask of what seem to be the main codes – in this case the sound track plus the picture – concerns the building blocks of the message. What kinds of elements are there, and how are they related to build into meanings? What are taken to be elements, relations and codes depends upon the assumptions and purposes of the method of analysis. Semiotics, in common with all other methods of analysis, has its own system of priorities and assumptions which have been developed in terms of the requirements of the method. Perhaps the most basic semiotic distinction is between paradigmatic and syntagmatic structures. These may be distinguished in a number of different ways. Paradigmatic structures may be seen, for instance, as the conceptual structures of the elements; syntagmatic structures as the relations between them when they are combined in a message.

	Subject	Verb	Object
	The man	opened	the door
PARADIGMATIC	The woman	opened	the door
DIMENSION	The man	closed	the door
	The man	opened	the tin

SYNTAGMATIC DIMENSION

Figure 1

Perhaps the distinction is best made by illustration from an example in language (figure 1). With these structures represented as two different domains or *dimensions*, in a simple *subject/verb/object* sentence such as 'the man opened the door', the *order* of the parts of speech is the syntagmatic dimension, because it is the system of combination. The same elements could be combined in a different way, such as *object/verb/subject* to give 'the door was opened by the man', which would be a change or 'transformation' at the syntagmatic level. At the paradigmatic level there has been a selection of elements to fill the slots made available by the syntagmatic structure. The subject could be *man, woman, child, horse*, or any other elements chosen from the paradigmatic set of possible agents. Similarly, the verb could be *opened, closed, hit, fought*, and the object could be *door, box*, or *wound*, for instance. The important point is that both syntagmatic and paradigmatic dimensions carry meanings separately and in combination. The use of the passive ('the door was opened by the man') is itself significant, because the emphasis is placed on the object rather than the subject. Similarly, the elements selected contain their own articulations and relationships, as is evidenced by the fact that one chooses *man* rather than the more general *person* or the more specific *policeman*; and the notion *man* is itself constituted through its relationships to what has not been chosen: *woman*, *child*, for instance.

So our most basic technical terms are syntagmatic structures or *syntagms* (how elements combine in the text) and *paradigms* or paradigmatic structures (classes of element and their structures). The full meanings of these two fundamental terms will become clearer as the argument develops, but we will take syntagmatic structures first, because these are the natural point of entry into any text. We can identify a number of syntagmatic types, categorized according to three variables: *space*, *time* and *continuity*.

In order to do that we need to introduce some more terms, to cover syntagms existing in the same time (*synchronic*), different time (*diachronic*), same space (*syntopic*), different space (*diatopic*). Combinations of these give us four possibilities which are best illustrated with examples.

A   *Synchronic/syntopic syntagm:* shot of a child playing near a fire. The syntagm suggests that the child is in danger from the fire, since they are both present together in the same time and the same space.

B   *Diachronic/syntopic syntagm:* shot of a child playing beside a fire which has only just been lit and therefore looks safe: followed by a shot of the child playing in front of the fire which is now roaring and dangerous.

C   *Synchronic/diatopic syntagm:* split frame, one side showing a child playing on floor by fireplace where fire is roaring, other side showing oblivious parent on phone in another room.

D   *Diachronic/diatopic syntagm:* shot of child playing in a room where the fire is lit but rendered harmless by an adequate guard; followed by a shot in which a child is in another room on another occasion, playing next to a fire which is lit and unguarded.

With regard to place conventions in modern media, in practice the majority of synchronic syntagms are also syntopic, the common exception being the 'meanwhile back at the ranch . . .' combination.

In that case, with regard to time, it could be said that within the time dimension of the action of the film the shots are synchronic, but as perceived by the viewer they are diachronic; but because we are dealing here with the way in which they are presented and perceived, we must call such shots diachronic. To cover cases such as the presentation of two entities in the same medium at the same time (child and fire) or different aspects of the same message carried by different mediums at the same time (speech and gesture, action and music), we use the term synchronic, because they must always also be syntopic. We will only refer to the syntopic/diatopic dimension where there is an exception to the synchronic/diachronic labelling, or where place is important.

These four variables are further complicated by the possibility of the way in which the connections between the shots may be presented to the viewer. All the examples given are illustrations of *continuous syntagms*. Each element (shot) is immediately conjoined to the next element, so that the combinations occur between adjacent elements. However, in many forms of communication, including television, there are *discontinuous syntagms*: that is, two shots are related to each other but other shots intervene. To give one example, there could be a shot of a child playing in front of a fire which has just been lit; that is followed by a shot of the child's parent on the telephone in a bedroom; which is followed by a shot of the fire roaring dangerously with the child still playing next to it. The syntagm which communicates the idea of the growing fire threatening the child is no longer continuous in that the shot of the parent ('meanwhile back at the ranch . . .') has been placed between the two fundamental elements, to create the message that the child is in danger from the fire, *and* the parent does not know.

Finally, it should be apparent from this last example that what is taken to constitute a syntagm depends upon the level of analysis. At one level the elements of the plot of a story constitute a diachronic syntagm; at another level the instant of a single spoken word followed by a visual gesture constitutes another synchronic syntagm. The term syntagm is therefore a conceptual unit of analysis for which there are no set dimensions of complexity or duration. One could therefore break up the last example into a discontinuous diachronic syntopic syntagm if we deal only with the first and third shots, or a continuous diachronic diatopic syntagm if we deal with all three.

Returning now to the question of children and television, we need to distinguish these different types of syntagm because they present different problems for the decoder. Every syntagm carries a meaning, however trivial and obvious or obscure and ambiguous. The juxtaposition of two elements makes up a new meaning. Some are intrinsically more difficult to grasp (such as the passive construction in English), and it is therefore likely that younger children will not perceive them so readily, or if they do perceive them they will tend to forget them. Large-scale structures make heavier demands than small-scale structures, though only up to a point: clearly very small-scale structures which are too small or too quick will be hard to distinguish. Discontinuous syntagms will be harder to decode than continuous syntagms because of the separation of elements, and diachronic syntagms will be harder than synchronic syntagms because of the extension in time.

Such points are not new: the work of Collins and his associates (Collins, 1979) suggests that second- and third-graders do not perceive the main plot of a filmed drama as well as eighth-graders. In semiotic terms this suggests that the scale of the syntagmatic structures that the younger children could perceive was smaller. Collins also found that they had more difficulties than older children with discontinuous syntagms: i.e. when subplots and other material come between elements of the main plot. The potential effect of such differences is clear: meanings carried by the main plot which could be seen as the main meaning by adult or older viewers were invisible to younger children.

It may seem no great matter that younger members could miss the main plot of a show not intended for them anyway; but the plot is shadowed by another kind of meaning which is much more important and problematic: the social message, as some would call it. Maybe we prefer the term ideological content. The category 'ideology' is notoriously slippery (see Williams, 1976; Thompson, 1984) yet we believe it is indispensable to an adequate theorization of the way the media carry social meanings with social effects. We define ideology as a coercive and general version of social reality, originating from a specific site in society. In structuralist-semiotic terms, an ideological formation involves both syntagmatic and paradigmatic structures in a tight functional relationship. Within an ideological formation there is typically contradiction, which is managed through systematic paradigmatic transformations. For instance, a version of class society in Britain can equally be underpinned by representations of (decent) working people celebrating the birth of a son to Charles and Di (the good working class) as by representations of (thuggish) miners engaged in a lengthy strike (the bad working class).

In addition to this set of specific syntagms, an ideology has another syntagmatic dimension: the syntagm of its interface with individuals and groups in society. In Althusser's (1971) terms, an ideological form 'hails' or 'interpellates' individual subjects. Without this syntagm of interpellation, ideology would miss its characteristic effects. But 'interpellation' implies a totally one-sided process. In practice the syntagm of the interface potentially allows struggle, negotiation and resistance from those who are prospective ideological subjects (Giroux, 1983); thus the possibility of paradigmatic categorization and transformation on both sides.

There are a number of reasons for our preferring a term such as ideology, for all its difficulties, over 'pro-social' (or anti-social) messages. The most important is that it problematizes the value systems at issue; so if children below a certain age cannot see that beating up and shooting a criminal before due process of trial and conviction is unacceptable (Collins's example, essentially) then their genuine innocence in the face of this ideological construct is not automatically to be deplored. Our concept of ideology sees it as cognitively very complex in its full ramifications, and inherently so: not a gratuitously buried message which some viewers might not get down to, but a major, pervasive but equivocal dimension of interpretation with stages of development that deserve to be carefully mapped. So throughout this book we will regard ideology as including a complex set of meanings carried by television, and a structuralization of the processes of production and consumption of meaning on the part of viewers.

Turning now to our text (the cartoon *Fangface*) we find it falls into two main parts: an opening sequence of 50 seconds, with the title and credits, plus some background on the Fangface myth, followed by the story proper, lasting just over 19 minutes. The opening sequence itself breaks down into a number of episodes. All these are syntagmatic structures of different scales: some small-scale, others larger-scale. We can see a sharp distinction, then, between the two major syntagmatic elements – the opening and the story. The opening lasts 50 seconds. It is highly compressed, using rapid, small-scale syntagms. Once the series went into regular transmission (as it now has in Western Australia) this segment was repeated with every story. We could suspect that like advertisements it will become very well known – the most salient memory children have of *Fangface*.

This two-part structure is a well-established convention for adult as well as children's television series. In effect, the opening gives, in a highly compressed form, the meaning of the series (which is a more general category than the particular show), to be followed by the particular instance of the actual programme. In the case of *Fangface*, and this is typical, we are given not simply the background to the character Fangface, plus the essential significance of the myth; we are also shown compressed incidents from other stories in the series. It is interesting to note that just as Lévi-Strauss (1963) required the semiotician to take a series of myths as the primary unit for analysis of meaning, not an individual story, the makers of *Fangface* also seem to recognize this point: they present the series, or a transformation of it, as an obligatory introduction to every programme.

So whatever else we analyse as semioticians, we cannot ignore the opening: only 50 seconds long but dense with meaning. We will start our analysis with the sound track, the dialogue and sound effects during the first hundred shots, since these features are easily presented in written form.

Introduction
'Every 400 years a baby werewolf is born into the Fangsworth family, and so when the moon shined on little Sherman Fangsworth he changed into "Fangface".'
[Howls, music in.]
'A werewolf! Only the sun can change him back to normal. And so little Fangs grew up and teamed up with three daring teenagers, Kim, Biff and Pugsie, and together they find danger, excitement and adventure.'
[Music and sound effects continue.]
'Who can save the day. Who can run the race and right the wrongs. None other than "Fangface"!'

The verbal language here accompanies a visual text which is much richer in that there are many more images than words. But the verbal language affects the interpretation of the accompanying visual text. One important thing it does is to assign names. These label some images and ought to make them easier to recall and use in verbal language, giving them salience, and imposing specific interpretations on them. Barthes (1977) calls this function 'anchorage', by which he refers to the function of verbal language in limiting and tying down the ambiguity and multiple meanings of visual signs.

Verbal language also communicates abstract concepts such as '400 years', 'the Fangsworth family', which are not present in the visual images. Words can convey concepts like time and causality more directly than pictures; but if we look closely at the words of this text we find some interesting illogicalities. The verbal text falls into three segments. In the first we have the account of the werewolf background.

Knowing what werewolves are in myth, we might be surprised at 'And so little Fangs . . .' in the second paragraph. 'So' suggests causality, but what is the causal connection between being a werewolf, and growing up and having adventures with 'three daring teenagers'? Clearly the word 'so' here is an example of pseudo-causality. However, this fact only becomes obvious if we have the text written out, as here. The written form is a continuous synchronic syntagm, but in the actual programme these clauses unfold in time (diachronic syntagms), and they are juxtaposed with competing visual images. Although these images themselves are synchronic syntagms, they separate the verbal syntagms from each other to form at a micro-level, discontinuous syntagms. So although most of the words are simple, the overall meaning of this text is actually very difficult to interpret. If its larger structures are perceived at all, they will be seen as contradictions. However, there are strong pressures against this contradictoriness being perceived. Even for adults the overall message will tend to decompose into a chaos of apparently unrelated fragments, a series of rapid and discrete small-scale syntagms. Children, we can hypothesize, will hardly bother to 'read' the larger message at all, and its contradictory elements will float together in their memories arbitrarily and without recognition of their lack of coherence.

The phenomenon we have illustrated here is very widespread in television shows, those made for children as for adults. We can call it *functional irrationality*. The verbal text of a children's television programme, far from offering a rational framework which anchors the chaotic multiplicity of visual images, in practice may defeat a single rational schema, while concealing the degree of the-irrationality. In *One-dimensional Man* (1964) Marcuse criticizes an analogous feature of the language of the mass media, whereby contradictory qualities are so fused in a single phrase that criticism is rendered impossible ('clean bomb'; 'missile harmony'). He called this 'one-dimensional discourse' leading to 'one-dimensional thought'. A fused contradiction is a synchronic syntagm, whereas what we are looking at is a discontinuous diachronic syntagm, yet the effect seems similar.

The sound track, of course, does not exist alone. We also need to analyse the visual dimension of the show. As semioticians we need methods for 'reading' such texts. We will start by giving a shotlist of the first sequence.

1. Lightning.
2. 'FANGFACE' (title).

3. CUT Fangface, wearing red hat. Licks lips and smiles. Freeze.
4. Lightning, high angle shot of house.
5. Zoom in on house.
6. Zoom in on baby in nappy, in bassinet.
7. Clouds pass over moon, zoom out to reveal baby at window, spins rapidly, turns into werewolf in nappy.
8. Zoom out from picture of sun on packet of soap powder to Fangface turning back into baby.
9. Dissolve – baby to teenage boy.

This translation into words does not explain the meanings of this stretch of film: on the contrary, the film is a key to the meaning of the words. To get at the meaning of these images the only method is to take a syntagmatic structure and see what paradigmatic categories constitute it. Paradigmatic structures (the options of possible elements) are often represented as binary oppositions, pairs of opposites such as man/woman, old/young. When these options are laid out one can see how they move from very basic and general choices to highly

```
                        ⎧ older    –   Biff  ⎫
                ⎧ Male  ⎨                     ⎪
                ⎪       ⎩ younger  –   Pugs  ⎬  Three daring teenagers
Character  ⎨            ⎧ older    –   Kim   ⎭
                ⎪ Female ⎨
                ⎩       ⎩ younger
```

Figure 2

complex and specific ones. Sex, age and character, for instance, provide the choices shown in figure 2. To illustrate, we will just take shots 1–3. The word 'Fangface' has before it a flash of lightning, and after it a picture of an animal with a single prominent tooth protruding, wearing a red hat with the peak turned round to the back. The obvious reading of the juxtaposition of word and image is that 'Fangface' is the name of the animal. We are in fact given in general terms the *paradigmatic categories* that make up this synchronic syntagm: word (or name) and image (or thing that is named). The picture itself is a syntagm, consisting of a face of an animal with a hat. How do we categorize the two elements, to make up a meaning? Or what categories are implied by meanings that we assign it? The hat looks odd, on Fangface's head. To express the oddness, we can point to the animal nature of Fangface and the human, cultural quality of a hat.

The baby werewolf wearing a nappy looks odd, too, and for the same reason. In the paradigmatic dimension the options are a pair of categories *nature/culture* (or *animal/human*, which is a more specific instance of the broader pair), which is the source of the image's meaning. We can translate this meaning into words – Fangface is both animal and human, representative of both nature and culture. This meaning, of course, also underlies the concept of a werewolf. Fangface's hat is odd in another way: it faces backwards. Here one paradigmatic set of categories concerns the position of a hat. This pair *backwards/forwards* constitutes a single structure. Forwards signals, among other things, conformity, normality; backwards, therefore, signals the opposite: abnormality, non-conformity.

Again it is important to stress that as decoders we do not simply work from categories such as *backwards/forwards* to deduce the meaning: we simultaneously register a meaning and discover the paradigmatic categories which are the basis of that meaning for us. Nor is that meaning a necessary and invariable one: it applies only for those it exists for, those persons who assign those paradigmatic categories to that syntagm. There might, for instance, be a culture in which hats are always worn with the peak backwards. That would give an exactly opposite reading to the one we have just given. Nor is our reading exhaustive. We have not considered Fangface's single tooth, which is big (signifying old, powerful) yet single (non-powerful, and perhaps young – reminiscent of the first of the adult teeth, which come at about 6 years old). Nor have we considered that the hat is red, which forms a significant contrast with other primary colours (like blue), and non-primary colours (like brown).

As these examples show, it is doubtful whether there can ever be such a thing as an exhaustive semiotic analysis, not only because there is so much to analyse, but because a 'complete' analysis would still be partial because it would still be located in particular social and historical circumstances. Nevertheless, a real if provisional under-standing of the kind of structures used to encode meaning is gained from such an analysis, and it is essential as the basis of hypotheses about children's interpretation of the messages. However, although the shots we have been discussing last less than a second, and the reading we have given is basic, nevertheless the analysis immediately raises problems concerning the processing of the message. Could an adult, much less a child, pick up all these meanings in so short a time? Do they exist as a potential set, from which a viewer would pick meanings at random? Or are some meanings reinforced, so that they go from a state of latency to become, at some level, dominant meanings?

If we consider this set of shots we see one factor which would help a decoder: the title and images of Fangface are repeated frequently during the cartoon, and the viewer has many opportunities to see all the features we have analysed. They *are* Fangface, his defining qualities. Every repetition of the message is technically surplus, a redundancy, but redundancy is highly functional in communication. It ensures that the message does get across, and it can emphasize some parts of the message as especially important. Paradoxically, however, massive redundancy can also mask a message from consciousness. Like breathing or the ground beneath our feet, information is taken for granted, or is not talked about or reflected on, unless suddenly it is difficult or is no longer there.

Redundancy is not confined to systematic aspects of particular messages that recur. There is also redundancy of paradigmatic structures. To show how this works, we will continue our analysis of the first nine shots. The sequence 4–5–6 goes from lightning to the house seen from the outside to a zoom on the baby, inside the house, in a bassinet. The sequence is clearly organized by a movement from outside to inside, from nature (as a dangerous, threatening force) to culture, the house and the bassinet, and the baby protected within by both. In shot 7 the movement is repeated, starting with a shot of the moon (outside, nature) then showing the baby at the window (not threatened by nature). The baby then spins rapidly, like a whirlwind (nature) or like a machine (culture) and turns into a baby werewolf (nature). However, this werewolf is not a threatening figure. It has a cute expression, and wears a nappy (human, culture). Then, with the sound track saying 'only the sun [nature] can change him back to normal', we see a picture of the sun with alongside it the words 'Sunshine Laundry' (culture). A zoom out reveals that this picture of the sun is on a packet of soap powder in a kitchen. The 'sun' that controls Fangface, then, is not the natural sun, but a commercial appropriation of the sun, tamed for domestic purposes. In the cartoon that follows, Fangface's metamorphoses are always triggered by photographs or pictures of sun and moon, either seen accidentally by him in a kitchen or other domestic space, but more often shown to him by one of the 'three daring teenagers' who thus control him.

The pattern throughout this sequence is built up of different arrangements of primary oppositions: nature–culture, human–animal. The result is not a single consistent message about the relations between the two. Sometimes nature is seen as threatening, sometimes as compatible with culture. Fangface is the focus of both ambiguity and ambivalence. He is both animal and human. Not only does he wear the red hat and, as an infant, a nappy, but he also stands upright, and his body is ambiguously both human and animal. He shares this ambiguity with other cartoon animals, who typically occupy an indeterminate space between human and animal. Fangface speaks (human) but also howls (animal). He is ambiguous in age: his voice is normally deep (adult), but he has a (childlike) obsession with food, and a single tooth (baby). His relative size also changes: sometimes he is larger than the teenagers and at other times he seems no bigger than a largeish dog.

In terms of other qualities, though Fangface is basically presented as a force for good ('who can save the day . . .') there are other contrary suggestions. The forces he represents (lightning, wolves, darkness and destructiveness, the forces of the night) are presented as safely tamed and controlled, but nevertheless those are still the forces he contains. If goodness needs a Fangface to 'right the wrongs', then goodness (the sun, light, culture) is acknowledging a dependence on these primal potentially amoral and destructive forces of nature. Lévi-Strauss (1963) found that mythic figures typically were ambiguous: monsters, liminal figures, transgressors. Fangface is that kind of figure. So are other cartoon heroes: Bugs Bunny (a modern descendant of the trickster figure so common in primitive myth: see Lévi-Strauss, 1963), Yogi Bear, Tom and Jerry, even the almost human Mickey Mouse.

The rest of the opening sequence introduces the main cast list, who are shown in typical adventures. In the first shot they are shown climbing a stairway in a cellar at night. Fangs (in human form) goes up first, followed by Pugsie, then Kim, with Biff in the rear. Fangs and Pugsie form a pair. They are distinguished from the other two by clothing (more scruffy informal clothes, indicative of lower social status) and voice (lower-class accents). Kim, the girl, has a darker-coloured face. It is ambiguous whether she is meant to be black or not, but in every other way she is respectably middle class. The four meet a monster covered entirely in bandages at the top of the stair – a Mummy – and they run down the stairs in reverse order, Biff the middle-class male leading the way. Kim shows Fangs a picture of the moon. His face is shown close-up, different parts of it going in and out like a machine, then he whirls and turns into Fangface, who grasps an end of the bandage of the pursuing Mummy, which collapses into a heap.

We then see, in quick succession, six monsters, black, blue, green, yellow, plus two others. The blue one is The Heap, the monster of the story we will look at. Another is a large armour-plated female with Egyptian clothing. The final shot sequence shows Pugsie, pursued by a monster, jumping into a rubbish bin. Fangface (while the voice-over says 'who can run the race and right the wrongs') presses his foot on the ejection pedal. Pugsie shoots into the air, and is caught by Fangface in two huge slices of bread. Fangface opens his mouth as though to eat Pugsie, then converts the action into a kiss, and smiles towards the audience.

This brief summary gives us the outlines of what is an authoritative transformation of the series, authoritative in the sense that it is done by the makers of it. First, the plot structure reduces to three elemental moments: humans seek monster, monster chases humans, good monster (Fangface) defeats bad monster. In this summary it is clear that a bad monster is as indispensable as the good one, even though it will be a different bad monster each new story. The opposition human/monster, then, is primary for the series. It generates not only Fangface, who is both, but also his opponent.

The cast list has a significant structure. As we have seen, Kim and Biff go together, and so do Pugsie and Fangs, signifying middle class and working class respectively. The elemental social world of the cartoon has the paradigmatic structure shown in figure 3. So the working class are represented as without females. However, the relationship between the middle-class Kim and Biff is cool and proper. Kim has more interaction with Fangs (whom she keeps turning into a monster) than with Biff. Pugsie and Fangs interact more intensely, if more aggressively, and they have appetites (Fangs often eats, and Fangface is dominated by his desire for food). There is also the quick last shot in the opening sequence, of Fangface kissing Pugsie. A very discrete hint of a homosexual relationship with the macho Pugsie?

$$
\left\{
\begin{array}{ll}
\text{Middle class} & \left\{ \begin{array}{l} \text{male (Biff)} \\ \text{female (Kim)} \end{array} \right. \\[2em]
\text{Working class} & \left\{ \begin{array}{l} \text{dominant (Pugsie)} \\ \text{subordinate (Fangs)} \end{array} \right.
\end{array}
\right.
$$

Figure 3

The underlying structures determining the main characters can be seen in the cast of the story that follows. The middle-class Kim and Biff have as their transformational equivalents the good Professor Boyd and his daughter Sally. There is also a group of three scientists shown – two males and one female – plus a couple in a restaurant. The leading scientist has a face which seems coloured, like Kim's, and a lady in a restaurant likewise. Such repetition confirms the analysis. The other main character is Professor Arnoss, and his alter ego, The Heap. This human/monster is recognizably a transformation of

Fangface/Fangs; but whereas Fangs is low in the social hierarchy, Arnoss comes from near the top – a professor, even though he has been sacked. The world of the cartoon as a whole, then, can be seen to be derived from a simple set of elements by a small number of transformations. The principles plus the transformations are a kind of formula for the series. Lévi-Strauss saw a formula of this kind, grasped as a generative principle, as what he called 'understanding' the myth. Understanding in this sense would mean that someone could predict plot developments, or appreciate the ingenuity and significance of novel but valid twists of characterization or plot.

However, 'understanding' can take us wider afield than the Fangface series. Fangface has structural similarities with Scooby Doo, a popular cartoon dog which also goes on adventures with three 'daring teenagers' and which likewise has humanoid qualities. Scooby does not metamorphose, and does not have super powers, but the similarities are close enough for us to see Fangface as a partial transform of Scooby. The Heap is, similarly, a recognizable transform of another popular character, The Incredible Hulk, who metamorphoses from the scientist David Banner. Only the colour (blue not green) and the valuation (bad not good) are different. Fangface, given his transformational relationship to The Heap, is also a transform of The Hulk. His derivation from the werewolf myth is made explicit. His name, and his one prominent tooth, probably evoke the vampire myth, and his obsession with eating is a transform of the vampire's obsession with sucking, though again there is a transformation from bad to good: vampires suck, people eat.

If *Fangface* were a literary text, some schools of criticism would see this set of connections as an example of intertextual meaning, an enrichment of the meaning of a specific text by its interaction with (including its contestation of) meanings of other texts, even of a whole tradition. Another school of literary criticism would talk of influences, stressing ways in which the author of this particular text was affected by other works, and was to that degree unoriginal. Both these kinds of judgement are as appropriate to this text as to a work of high literature, even though *Fangface* is only that despised form, a modern cartoon for children. What a semiotic analysis adds to the purely literary approaches is a recognition of the status and structures of the meanings at issue. Any one of these characters carries a rich set of meanings which are bundles of paradigmatic oppositions, representing categories which are basic to a cultural logic, thus giving them their continuous appeal.

The effect of seeing a range of different versions of this figure is not so much to gain an entirely new but particular meaning, but more, as Lévi-Strauss saw, a greater understanding of the transformational possibilities of a matrix of meanings: a greater facility in manipulating the powerful but problematic categories of this logic. This kind of 'understanding' is transformational power, the capacity for a major intellectual and cultural activity. It raises the question of whether, or when, or who among children can perform such operations on a show like *Fangface*, and whether humble television fare like this can stimulate the growth of these capacities. This view suggests, of course, that cartoons, far from being trivial forms that stunt the growing mind, have a positive cultural value and as important a role in emotional and intellectual development as Bettelheim (1976) demonstrated for the humble fairy tale.

Our analysis so far has barely touched the meanings of the particular story, 'Heap of Trouble'. We have suggested that the meanings of a cartoon like this are very rich, highly *polysemic* (polysemy is when a number of different meanings coexist in a single signifier), but also highly redundant. We will illustrate these qualities in the first episode of 'Heap of Trouble'. We will start, again, with the sound track at the point when Professor Boyd is about to demonstrate his new invention, a very complex looking machine:

> [Scary music in, with low breathing.]
> 'After four months of work, my invention's finally perfected. You're all going to have the honour of being the first to witness . . .'
> [Panting, growls, howls, screams.]
> 'Stay away! Get back!' [Climactic music – discordant.]

Again, we can see that the plot is barely carried by the dialogue. This time we have no voice-over giving narrative information. The verbal language is precise ('four months', 'my invention'), but seemingly irrelevant. The soundtrack carries three distinct main codes which form a significant structure: music, speech, and animal sounds. Speech is opposed to howls as culture is to nature, human to animal. Music is between the two. It is a product of culture, yet also allied with the emotional, the physical, the animal side of man. Unsurprisingly, the professor speaks human language, and the monster merely breathes heavily and howls; but significantly the scientist, when confronted by The Heap, breaks off this verbal discourse and screams, thus returning to a more primitive nature. Part of Professor Arnoss's evil plan, we will be told, was to 'turn the whole faculty into hulking monsters'. Causing professors to break down into a scream achieves that as much as smashing complex machines, though in a different way.

Again it is the shot list that carries more information. Here is the opening sequence:

31. Pan around buildings, night-time clock shows nearly midnight. Zoom into sign.
32. 'State University' sign on wall. Blue hands grab top of wall.
33. Ground on other side of wall, blue feet land, walk on.
34. Pan with feet to sign 'Science Building'.
35. Back view of man at window. Naked muscular back, long blue hair, trousers with ragged bottoms.
36. Interior of lab, three scientists inside in white coats.
37. Leading scientist at machine, turns.
38. The Heap bursts through door.
39. [Close up] Heap's face – menaces.
40. [Close up] leading scientist, scared.
41. Heap walks to machine, picks it up.
42. Heap with machine above head, walks out.

The first shot is a pan from above and outside a building at night, just as in the opening credits. The sweep of the camera picks up a sequence of buildings (in neoclassical style) and grounds: an alteration of high culture and cultivated nature. The basic colour tonality is blue, the same colour as The Heap and the 'inventions' which we will see in the laboratory. So blue establishes an equivalence between The Heap, night, and machines: both nature and technology, evil and good.

The camera picks up a clock which redundantly shows that the time is after midnight, a somewhat strange time for the professor to demonstrate his new invention, but one which links technology, including even the machines of good professors, to the forces of evil (the witching hour) and darkness. But the addition of the clock does have a further significance: it is a cultural object, a machine confirming the message communicated by the colouring, that it really is the time of darkness, evil, and nature. The opposition nature/culture is repeated in a strong form with two sequences: first a yellow sign 'State University', with the blue hands grabbing the top of the wall, then a pan from bare blue feet, with muscular legs and a glimpse of ragged trousers, followed by the sign 'Science Building'.

A last comment we will make on this sequence concerns The Heap's hair. The first full-length shot of The Heap, from the back, shows his dark blue hair going half-way down his back. Long hair is a signifier with a long and complex history. At some points in history long hair has signified female, short hair male. It has also signified the luxuriance, energy, even the rebelliousness of youth, or nature generally. The figure of Samson is a famous example of the second. Long hair is an ambiguous signifier, and thus ambiguity is a current fact about contemporary Western culture. Discussions about hair length, and hair care, by parents and children, and by children among themselves, are often heavily laden with significance, and particular instances are explicitly taken as symbols of general culturally important attitudes. Children, we might expect, will pay close attention to hairy meanings. The Heap's long unkempt hair contrasts in a number of ways with Professor Arnoss's bald head ringed by short smooth grey hair. The hint of sexual ambiguity in The Heap is repeated, incidentally, with some of the monsters in the opening sequence. The bandaged monster would be familiarly referred to as a 'Mummy'. Another monster was a very masculine Egyptian lady.

A reading like this picks up innumerable small messages. The terms of these messages are highly redundant – the same paradigmatic pairs repeated in different structures. There is also considerable repetition of messages, since once the set of paradigmatic terms is established it generates a limited set of possible syntagms. There is also, however, considerable contradiction between the messages. Just taking the terms nature/culture, nature is sometimes seen as opposed to culture, sometimes as compatible with it; sometimes benign, sometimes hostile; sometimes human, sometimes opposed to human; sometimes associated with female, sometimes with male; sometimes active and powerful, sometimes weak and passive. Contradictions exist between shots, within shots, even within single characters or objects. If the short sequence we have analysed – far from exhaustively – contains so many, it can be imagined what a cornucopia of contradictory messages around primary themes a 20-minute cartoon will offer its viewers. It will not matter whether an individual child sees only one tenth of them. So great is the redundancy that any random sample will be much the same. There are, however, two factors that could affect this: one is that the selection is not random, or not random for some kinds of children; the other is that there are also overriding controls on the meaning structures of a cartoon or other show (controls which may be external to the cartoon), which reduce the ambiguities and contradictions of individual meanings to a unitary significance for a whole class of viewer. We must therefore go on to explore how that kind of unification could take place.

One kind of meaning has special importance here. This is the message carried by the story as a whole. The opening sequence, as we have seen, gives a schematic shape for this large-scale syntagm, and it may even be an aid to learning the syntagmatic structure of a full narrative. We previously said that the structure given there is: teenagers seek monster, monster chases teenagers, good monster defeats bad monster. In 'Heap of Trouble', we find that this formula applies at a number of levels. A more accurate account of the structure has the two kinds of chase alternating with one another, always resolved by an intervention from Fangface, but only the last intervention leads to the unmasking and defeat of the monster. We can represent the structure schematically as shown in figure 4.

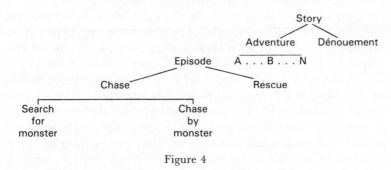

Figure 4

So far in our analysis we have discussed the structure of the cartoon in terms of paradigmatic and syntagmatic dimensions. Now we want to consider for a moment two different ways in which these structures are themselves structured. We have already shown how paradigmatic structures can be considered as binary oppositions, each pair derived from a more general option. We can term that kind of structure *hypotactic* because each pair is subordinated by the more general option. Thus male/female are subsumed by sex, man/boy by male, old/young by age, for example. Another kind of structure we term *paratactic*, because the options exist alongside each other. Their structure is of a 'this *and* that' variety, and, of course, the possible number of '. . . and . . . and . . . and' may be infinite.

Again we can most easily illustrate the terms in language. In the description 'he wore a cap that was red, and peaked, and made of cloth', each element of the description is simply linked on to the previous one. We could then add any other adjectives we might wish to, such as 'round', or 'new'. This would constitute a typical paratactic structuring of a syntagm. Hypotactic structures, on the other hand, are closed-ended structures in which the order is always determined to some extent. These differences in features mean that paratactic structures are simpler and hence more easily grasped than hypotactic structures. But hypotactic structures are a more powerful type of organization, since each successive level reduces elements at a lower level to a unity. Simple sentences in English are always hypotactic structures. For example, 'The monsters are frightening the children' is a hypotactic structure organizing 10 syllables, or 28 distinct sounds, which would be difficult to remember as random nonsense syllables or isolated sounds. Only through hypotactic organization could a story be said or understood to have a single meaning or 'point'. Without hypotactic structures a 'story' would simply be an endless succession of '. . . and then . . . and then . . .'.

Applying the notions to our analysis, the story must have both an adventure and a dénouement, and so it may be seen to be hypotactic because it is a structure with subordinate elements (figure 4). The dénouement is an element of 'story', and is fixed in its relation to the other elements by the superordinate 'story'. Paratactic structures, on the other hand, do not involve subordination. In the cartoon a sequence of episodes is a paratactic structure if they could equally well be present or absent, or in a different order. For example, there could be a car chase followed by a foot chase, or vice-versa. The chase could go through a forest then across a river, or vice-versa.

In the development of language it is clear that hypotactic structures take time to evolve (Brown, 1973; see also chapter 3). Similarly with regard to television, we have mentioned Collins's findings that younger children do not so readily grasp the key elements of the main plot, or the main plot itself, and this is consistent with the view that a grasp of hypotactic structures of television programmes is still evolving at age 10–11. Collins's (1979) stimulus was an hour-length action-adventure show. The scope of this is greater than the 20-minute cartoon we have taken, but it is less than a 2-hour feature, which may present further problems of organization. Sheer length, of course, is not the only criterion. Paratactic structures can be quite long as in, for example, a magazine show, or an episodic narrative. One would expect different cartoons to be more or less hypotactic, and we found, for instance, *Tom and Jerry* to be more paratactic than *Fangface* in its organization (O'Toole, 1981). The plot of cat chases mouse, mouse beats cat is repeated several times in each cartoon. The interest lies in the variety of situations (cat chases mouse with knife in kitchen, cat chases mouse in hosepipe) not in the cumulative development of the series of situations.

A general recognition that a paratactic structure will present fewer problems of interpretation for younger children seems to be reflected in the typical format of programmes made for them: smaller in overall length, and with a serial organization in which one thing simply follows another (cf. also Huston-Stein and Wright, 1977, reported in Salomon, 1979). More important, it follows that when a capacity to organize a mass of material, such as 20 minutes of cartoon or an adult drama, has not been developed, the material will be interpreted as though it were organized paratactically, which is as a random string of individual messages, not as a single complex whole. The issue that Collins's work has raised is what is the distinctive content and function of the highest-level meanings in a hypotactic structure, and what might be the effect if a certain kind of viewer does not grasp them, or grasps them too weakly?

In order to fix the larger structure of 'Heap of Trouble', we need a description of its ending, the dénouement. In the final episode Fangface and Pugsie pursue The Heap, who is carrying his ray gun. The Heap evades Fangface, and chases Pugsie. Fangface grabs the ray gun, and he and Pugsie leap into an elevator. Fangface blindly carries the elevator on to a rocket which shoots off into space, with The Heap outside the elevator attempting to get at Pugsie and Fangface. The elevator falls off the rocket, and lands balanced on the point of a radio tower. As it sways The Heap falls off, grabbing Pugsie as he goes. Fangface holds on to Pugsie, and almost falls out too. He manages to support himself and the other two by his toes, but is slowly losing his grip.

Meanwhile the ray gun has fallen and been caught by Kim in a car driven by Biff that had been tracking the rocket from below. She falls over after catching the gun, but is still able to hand it over to Biff, who turns it on to The Heap. The Heap immediately turns back to the lightweight body of Professor Arnoss, and Fangface is able to pull the three back into the elevator. The final scene has police putting Professor Arnoss into a police van. Professor Boyd and his daughter, Sally, with Kim and Biff, stand in a group. Fangface threatens to eat Pugsie, but Kim turns him back into Fangs. The final shot is a long shot, from behind the two middle-class couples, standing arm in arm as Pugsie chases Fangs into the distance, their laughter merging with canned laughter on the soundtrack.

This ending falls into two parts: the end of the adventure, and the end of the programme. Each has its own structure, which we can represent as shown in figure 5. The principles of this hypotactic structure are essentially the same as the larger structure we saw before. They are homologous in structure, and equivalent in content, so that if the largest level of structure is missed its message might still be seen at other levels. However, there are a number of significant differences.

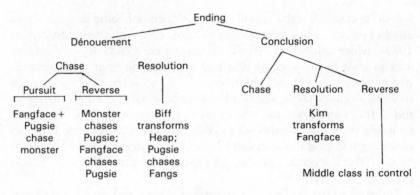

Figure 5

In the rest of the plot Fangface, usually accompanied by Pugsie, saves the other two, whereas in the dénouement it is the two teenagers who save Fangface, by transforming The Heap back to normal. In the conclusion, the only monster left to threaten humanity with his uncontrolled appetites is Fangface; but Kim turns him back to normal, too, and viewers are left with an image of that normality in the final tableau. The tableau is a synchronic syntagm, which may be read in at least two different ways. In one the middle class are a majority, forming a cohesive group, male and female, young and old harmoniously united in laughter at Fangs and Pugsie. Camera position, plus the canned laughter, invite the audience to take a particular class point of view, from which the representatives of the lower classes are seen as ridiculous, self-divided, self-cancelling, disappearing from the scene. They are too involved in satisfying their immediate appetites to ask for any reward or any recognition of their role in capturing The Heap and restoring the world to normality: a normality which is dominated by the middle class in every way.

Another reading would emphasize the parental (rational, controlled, thinking) aspect of the group in contrast to the immature childishness of Pugsie and Fangs. So we can see that a number of different meanings are carried by the ending. Not only does crime not pay: being lower class or childish does not pay either. Nor does being a monster, or abnormal in any way, in spite of a brief period when Fangface seemed to be valued and The Heap feared. These messages are heavily ideological. They only exist, however, as hypotactic structures, which establish for each viewer able to perceive them a hierarchy by prioritizing particular messages from among the whole set of messages of the cartoon. However, if, as we have suggested will be the case for very young children, the hypotactic structures are not perceived, especially those at the highest level, then the story will be interpreted as a paratactic structure; as a relatively unordered string of messages each of equal validity. We can say, then, that anyone who is not oriented towards hypotactic messages will miss most of what some researchers call the 'pro-social content' (such as that crime does not pay), and at the same time will also miss the ideological content, such as that middle-class adult norms define reality. We can see, therefore, that in practice the terms hypotaxis and parataxis define not simply different types of content, but also different perspectives and different valuations.

For the viewer oriented to paratactic structures the story will not exist as a unity. If there is a single meaning that is seen as *the* meaning of *Fangface* for the paratactic viewer, it is likely to be a repeated syntagm, or a repeated paradigmatic structure: especially a densely coded meaning carried by a repeated synchronic syntagm. Of these, the most pervasive is the central character: in this case Fangface/Fangs. The meanings carried by this complex syntagm are, we have seen, ambiguous, contradictory and ambivalent. The non-hypotactic meanings, then, are the site of contradiction, subversion and contestation. We cannot even postulate an either–or, because paratactic meanings are primitive and powerful, accessible as an alternative content even for someone who can interpret hypotactic structures. What we have, with *Fangface* and with children's programmes generally, is a double set of possibilities of different meanings. Different types of show could rely on different proportions of the two types of structure, or children of different ages might give different weighting to the two types of structure.

Conclusion

The purpose of this chapter has been to introduce some principles of semiotic analysis, applying them to a cartoon in order to demonstrate the enormous complexity of what is often taken to be a very simple and straightforward message structure. An incidental purpose was to familiarize readers with the cartoon which we used extensively in our empirical work. We have so far only prepared the ground for an exploration of children as television viewers, by elucidating some of the messages which are at least potentially perceivable by them. We also foregrounded the diverse kinds of messages that are carried by different forms of structure, drawing out hypothetically what the consequences would be if children are more oriented to one kind of structure rather than another, or if they typically fail to perceive and 'need' certain kinds of structure that are important in an adult reading. However, the questions that really matter concern what actually happens when children watch television: which of these meanings do *they* see? How do they organize the meanings they see; how do they make sense of television messages? These are the questions we attempt to address more empirically in subsequent chapters.

Chapter 2

'You sorta listen with your eyes'
Decoding children's responses to television

Models and methods of analysis

A semiotic analysis of content, like the one in the previous chapter, invites a crucial three-part question: how do these meanings exist, for whom, and how can we know? Many adults suppose that television viewing is a simple, passive, mindless process. One 9-year-old child we interviewed, however, had a much more powerful and subtle account of the viewing process, which he encapsulated in the graphic phrase: 'You sorta listen with your eyes.' Research strategies should be at least as complex and semiotically aware as that child. Having shown in the previous chapter just how complex and problematic the content of television is, we must do the same with the 'content' of the response. The meanings of television come via different media (visual, verbal) and these media carry different codes. This multiple set of messages is then decoded according to an internal set of rules. Following the analogy with rule systems in verbal language we will call this a 'grammar'. Only after meanings have been encoded and decoded is there a 'content' that matters; but this 'content' still lies deep inside the mind of the viewer, so how do we know what children are really thinking?

Many parents worry whether their children are thinking at all, when they stare at the screen for what seem incredible lengths of time and show no signs of physical or mental activity. Is a face that scarcely flickers the sign of a zombie? Not necessarily: university students concentrating on a difficult text, or microsurgeons severing tissue, display a similarly intense impassivity. Simple observations of expressions do not tell us enough. The obvious way of finding out what someone thinks in response to television is to ask them. However, as most of us are aware, there is as large a gap between what we can put into words and what we think as there is between what we can do and how we can explain it. What we say is itself a set of meanings, which may or may not be what we really understand – and we may well understand more than we are ever conscious of. Television messages pass so quickly that we only retain a small part of them for recall; yet that does not necessarily mean that the ones we do not retain are meaningless or irrelevant. What we say must be interpreted in its turn by someone who understands our language and shares our grammar. We may say nothing to someone we do not know or trust, or we may deliberately deceive them, or we may communicate by non-verbal means. Turning a television set off, or avoiding a question, are not merely acts; they are acts which carry meanings, and are thus messages.

To bring some order into this complex picture we will represent the process in a diagram (figure 6). This shows the key phases of television communication. The message encoded by production is reproduced on the television set which is perceived by the viewer (receiver), who makes meanings from it, meanings which affect the viewer's behaviour in terms of thought, attitudes, actions and relationships. The model we are suggesting meets the demand of semiotics to take specific account of both sight and sound: different content is encoded in the different media, thus requiring different 'grammars' for decoding the mesage. Each box labelled 'grammar' therefore contains at least two and possibly more functionally interrelated systems.

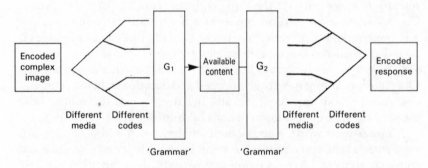

Figure 6

In more detail, in decoding the media the grammar first produces significant content (which may be different from what the sender intended). The receiver then assimilates what has been understood to a whole set of other experiences, meanings and desires. The viewer then may or may not encode into internal mental and, via the media, external physical behaviour the understandings created from the decoded physical signs. It is merely the overt signs produced by this last stage which we may observe: all our understanding of, and theories about, the other stages have to be posited on these very indirect, limited and often ambiguous indications. Naturally, according to this model, as observers we employ the same sequence of processes (though with different grammars) to decode, understand and write about the viewer's encoded overt responses.

We will see later that this model is still too simple in some respects, and will have to be modified. In the meantime we can point to some important consequences of adopting this model for research on children and television:

1. The significant content of television is not merely the *product* of the process of encoding, but is also a product of a process of decoding, that is of interpretation: meaning is not a self-evident property of the image itself.
2. Any message sent as a 'response' is itself a communication, which needs to be decoded in its turn.
3. Just as the television message is transmitted by different media and codes, so responses are communicated by different media and codes.

A crucial term in this model is 'grammar'. Following Chomsky (1957: 65) we use this word in an extended sense to refer to the complete set of rule systems which interpret the full range of signs of a language. A grammar in this sense is like a theory of how language works, a theory on which everyone's competence as a speaker is based, yet it is mostly unconscious. In our conception a grammar consists of four components: a set of rules which produce a system of options (*paradigms*), a set of rules for combining those options into structures (*syntagms*), and changes to and permutations of these options and combinations (*transformations*), together with ways of situating messages in relation to an ostensible reality (modality). Two speakers with different 'grammars' will fail to understand each other. Eco (1976) has argued that this kind of communication gap, which he calls 'aberrant coding', exists between senders and receivers in all the mass media. The producers of advertisements recognize this in their specification of a 'target audience', often a relatively small subsection of the whole audience at any one time. Of course where the senders are middle-class American adults, and the receivers are working-class Australian children, the possibilities for aberrant coding are so much the greater. As researchers we must recognize that the same problem exists when it is children who are the senders, communicating their responses to us, highly educated, middle-class adults.

As a great deal more is known about the grammar of verbal language than about other kinds of language, an obvious strategy is to examine its implications for other grammars of the kind that we suggest exist for television viewers. As a starting point we can begin with Chomsky's influential theory of language in which he posited an underlying process for the acquisition of syntax (1965). He originally suggested children were born with an innate capacity to abstract a complex set of rules from what they hear around them – an arbitrary and sometimes incorrect corpus of examples. Although Chomsky's original idea of a 'language acquisition device' has been seriously challenged, he still sees the child as a proto-scientist, a system-builder, who goes through successive 'grammars', each of them self-contained and rule-governed, each closer to the adult 'grammar' (cf. Brown and Bellugi, 1964). The main points are that this process is not seen to be greatly influenced by grammatical instruction from adults, and it remains largely unconscious. The child and adult effortlessly use a grammar whose full complexity is not fully understood by professional linguists today.

Another major linguistic theorist, Jakobson, has argued a similar case with children's acquisition of the sound system (the phonology) of a language. According to Jakobson (1968: see also Hodge, 1981), children in all cultures acquire the adult sound system in a systematic fashion, making only major distinctions such as vowels and consonants first, then using analogous distinctions to build up the full set of sounds in the system. So a child's repertoire of significant sounds is based on a structure of distinctive features. No-one tells the child what these features are – how could they, before the child has acquired the sounds of the language needed to comprehend speech? The child abstracts both features and structure long before it is capable of saying what a feature is, or what a remarkable intellectual feat it has performed. The test for whether a child has acquired a feature is whether the child produces or recognizes significantly contrasting sounds (e.g. says both '*p*ark' and '*b*ark'). The test for whether the structure has been acquired is more abstract. The full phonological structure is strongly hypotactic. So if the structure as well as the features have been grasped, children who produce a lower set of features in the schema should also know higher features.

A third, and quite different, approach to the problem is that of Halliday (1978). He offers a social theory in which he sees the child as driven to communicate, not only by informational needs, but by the desire to act in and upon social situations. In this view the child constructs meanings first, and in seeking to express them develops a personal language which progressively conforms to adult language in order to be better understood, and for the child to express more complex social meanings in a variety of situations. Halliday's theory is important precisely because it places primacy upon social relationships and meanings, rather than cognitive processes or information-processing strategies in isolation. Television is a personal interaction of a special, some might say aberrant or unnatural, social nature. In some children's relationship to and use of television one is reminded of Luria and Yudovich's (1971) study of twins whose very closeness to each other meant they needed to relate very little to adults, so that they continued to develop their shared private (proto-)language rather than learning to conform to the language of adults. The importance of Halliday's theories is that they give due recognition to the influence of social context on meaning construction.

There are two implications for the study of children and television for us to address here. One is that there may be an additional kind of 'content' that children might be acquiring from television. In addition to the abstract deep content which Lévi-Strauss called 'understanding the myth', children may be acquiring the basic grammar of the medium: an abstract set of rules which enable complex meanings to be understood and possibly produced. Second, the linguistic methodologies suggest ways of discovering this content, a content which is so important both in itself and in its determining effects on how other content will be understood.

Essentially this method relies on hypothetico-deductive reasoning allied to close observation of a small number of subjects who are set specific tasks that elicit the relevant behaviour. Grasp of a feature is an either/or matter. In most cases there is a stage when it seems clear that the child has not acquired a certain feature or syntactic rule, followed by a fairly brief stage where the feature or form appears with approximations or occasional errors, after which the form stabilizes (Brown, 1973). There may still be performance errors, but the individual knows that they are errors, and consistently interprets according to the real rule. Non-appearance of a form is not proof that the form has not been acquired (Chomsky, 1965). It might exist at a latent level: *understood* but not *produced* for some reason. However, as soon as the form appears even a small number of times for an individual or class of individual, that is strong evidence that the form is now part of the grammar. It becomes redundant to accumulate large numbers of examples, since such accumulation will normally simply replicate the initial judgement. Working in a different tradition, Piaget (1952) independently evolved a similar strategy, relying on intensive observation of a relatively small number of children as the basis for the generation of his most powerful hypotheses. It may well be the only way to gain an understanding of deep and inaccessible mental processes.

Chomsky, Jakobson and to a lesser extent Halliday, worked mainly with verbal language, but television communicates by verbal and visual media, and we cannot simply assume that the 'grammar' of verbal language is the same as a visual language, or that there is only one grammar of visual language. Again, there are a number of different theories which attempt to relate to both these assumptions. For instance, McLuhan (1964) strongly contrasted what he called 'hot' media (high-definition, low-participation media: e.g. print, film) and 'cool' media (low-definition, high-participation: e.g. radio, or oral forms). 'Hot' versus 'cool' does not correspond to visual versus oral (e.g. he classified television as a 'cool' medium), but visual media allow for greater resolution than aural. Cross-cultural studies have suggested the effect of different 'senso-types' (i.e. the sense that is the predominant one) on the kinds of thinking that characterize different cultures (cf. Berry and Dasen, 1974). Bandler and Grinder (1979) have seen similar differences of senso-type affecting how people in American culture think. Salomon (1979) has stressed the role of what he calls the 'symbolic modes of presentation' of television compared to reading in developing different cognitive abilities.

Such theories make it clear that we cannot assume that children have only one 'grammar' that they use to decode both visual and verbal television messages, or to send their own. However, we would not want to rule out the possibility that there is a 'meta-grammar', a higher-level grammar that integrates messages in the different 'languages' (cf. Bateson, 1973). If a 'meta-grammar' exists (as it must, if people derive a single sense from television programmes, as they seem to do at least some of the time) then it becomes important to ask what this system is like, how is it acquired and when, and what the consequences are if it does not develop. If, in the words of the boy we quoted earlier, 'you sorta listen with your eyes' as a competent watcher of television, then what happens for the visually or verbally illiterate, or those who cannot integrate the two?

This leads to a further complication that we must introduce into our model. Freud (1960, 1971) has shown that some messages have a composite form, as though the surface form is a fusion of meanings that come from different aspects of the psyche, so different and contradictory that they sometimes seem like different selves within the individual. Freud labelled the three different selves as *ego, superego* and *id*. The meanings of the id are closer to those of an infantile self, while superego meanings come from an introjected parent figure, and the ego meanings represent the individual's sense of reality. Transactional analysis has developed a form of analysis of communication, usually between two people, which identifies the level from which a message comes or at which it is received. Berne (1968) labels the three selves *child* (id), *adult* (ego) and *parent* (superego). In any exchange, an individual may be transmitting or receiving messages on behalf of more than one 'self'. These messages may be different or even contradictory. They may be simultaneous, and either fused in one medium or code, or distributed among different codes, verbal and non-verbal. The meanings carried by the verbal channel are not necessarily the most important, and their relationship with other levels of meaning is often essential for understanding the full meaning of an exchange.

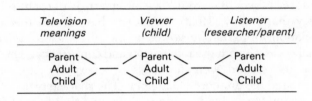

Figure 7

Figure 7 represents the possible messages in the communication chain as viewers (including children) tell of their responses to listeners (including parents, teachers and researchers). In this scheme the television meanings are classified as 'parent' (i.e. moralistic, ideological messages), 'adult' (i.e. information) and 'child' (i.e. subversive pleasurable meanings) with these meanings layered together, not necessarily integrated. The child viewer may respond to ideological meanings by incorporating them ('parent' response) or subverting them ('child' response) or treating them as information ('adult' response). Any meanings may be selected or excluded, but whatever meanings are received, by the different selves, different kinds of listener will be likely to receive different selections from or packagings of the complex response. In so far as parents interact with their children primarily through their role as parents, there is likely to be a systematic skew in the kind of meaning that will be foregrounded by the children.

Teachers often occupy the same structural position, and researchers may well be similarly classified by children. The scheme described by Berne was designed to describe communication between adults, and it would have to be modified to describe the developing structures of children. In spite of some reservations in detail, we found the Berne model a salutary reminder of a dimension of child–adult communication that is too often left out of models of research. In particular it brings a number of important questions to our attention. How do the different 'selves' in children interpret, integrate and use the different kinds of meaning of the televisual messages? What is the effect of the complex structures of televisual messages on the developing structures of a child's psyche? Finally (crucial questions for the would-be decoder of children's responses), how do we recognize the different strands in their communication about television, and how can we be sure we have a comprehensive sense of the different components of their response?

As a start towards developing ways of distinguishing these different kinds of self in the flow of children's discourse, we looked for markers in their speech form that would be characteristic of each 'self' in the same way that Labov (1972) and others have found that different pronunciations of particular vowels mark differences of social status and social occasion with great precision and consistency. The markers we came to rely on were loudness or energy, rising or falling intonation, and the presence of laughter. The characteristics of energy, falling intonation, and laughter are motivated signifiers of a 'child'-utterance. These characteristics tend to go together, typically marking a child's point of view – in transactional terms: hedonistic, subversive and amoral. The opposite characteristics – low energy, rising intonation, and no laughter – typically mark parent discourse. These markers therefore suggest when phrases and judgements are likely to be internalized quotations of a parent or authority figure, and hence opposed to a 'child' view. It is possible to code every transcript in these terms, to represent visually the stratifications of the children's discourse. We will give examples indicating the value of this kind of analysis in this chapter and in chapter 5.

Within the verbal channel, sociolinguists studying English and many other languages recognize a broad difference between two codes, which have been labelled *high* (H-form) and *low* (L-form) respectively (Fergusson, 1959; Fishman, 1972). Because the H-form is a high-status, more educated form, it is associated with high-status speakers on more formal occasions; and the L-form, having lower status, is associated with lower-class speakers and/or informal occasions.

Halliday (1978) has developed the related but stronger concept of *register* which associates specific types of situation with a mode of discourse, plus a kind of subject matter and a set of role relationships. H-forms are usually a super-posed form, which young children will not have fully mastered, and which working-class children will find more alien than middle-class children. One would expect, therefore, that such children might have some difficulty in understanding what is being said to them when it is said in an H-form.

However, more is at issue with H- and L-forms than comprehension. As Halliday points out, there is a nexus between codes, subject-matter and situation. Intimate meanings, including child meanings, are felt to be inappropriate in H-forms, and superego meanings are inappropriate in L-forms. With some situations, characterized by formality and relations of dominance and inequality, L-codes and child meanings tend to be suppressed. The extent to which these meanings will be under-represented in the discourse will be a function of the social situation.

Researchers can make serious errors of interpretation if they fail to see this. For instance Labov (1972) illustrated the importance of this principle for interview strategies in his work with black children. He found that lower-class black children interviewed by a black interviewer in a formal setting were almost silent, apparently inarticulate and incoherent; but when the situation was changed, with the interviewer sitting on the floor, joking and using L-forms, the talk had a totally different character, because many children could only communicate fluently and effectively in L-forms, and in situations where L-forms were felt to be fully acceptable. Thus if one wants to know what children think about television, one cannot ask them academically precise questions or hand them a questionnaire form to fill in. Every act of communication is fundamentally a social act, affected in some way by the nature of the social relationship that constitutes it – even if researchers sometimes appear to believe that impersonality and objectivity put them outside or above the interaction (Tripp, 1983).

From this discussion we can abstract a number of principles to guide a semiotically informed research strategy into children's television:

1. Decoding children's responses to television requires a prior and powerful theory of how television has 'content'.
2. The theory must take account of different levels of message, and different codes and media.

3. The theory must also project abstract grammars of the languages of the media in such a way that differences between different codes, or between different kinds of viewer and sender, can be explored and tested.
4. Hypotheses must be empirically checked by reference to children's responses at different levels and in a range of codes and media.
5. The social dimension of children's responses must be taken into account, so that its effects on the response can be allowed for.
6. Responses should include, where possible, responses in another code or medium: verbal responses should be recorded to include some non-verbal cues, and similarly non-verbal responses should be supplemented by verbal commentaries.

From these principles we get an inventory – far from exhaustive – of types of material to use as data (figure 8). This schema gives us five kinds of data to collect, each with both verbal and non-verbal messages in tandem. We do not see the full range as essential for every research project, and we did not use all types of data in our own work. A spread of data-types ought to provide a more reliable basis of judgement than only one or two, but what matters most is the six principles we have enunciated.

- Responses
  - verbal
    - (i) monologue
    - dialogue
      - (ii) child-led
      - (iii) adult-led
    - (+ non-verbal cues)
  - non-verbal
    - (iv) enactments
    - (v) drawings
    - (+ verbal commentary)

Figure 8

A child's-eye view of *Fangface*

After these preliminary words of caution we turn again to *Fangface*, and our opening question: how much of our analysis is relevant to children? As a start towards an answer, we set up a number of interviews with children, in which we showed the first 5 minutes of the cartoon, then discussed it with them in groups of five or six. The total number of children interviewed was 42. They came from six different schools, from different socioeconomic areas, though there was no other attempt to ensure a spread of social class. All groups were mixed sex, with a total of 23 boys and 19 girls, and all groups were aged between 8 and 9 years except for one group of 11–12-year-olds. The interviews were all conducted by the same person: a skilled interviewer and an experienced teacher, who was acquainted with semiotic theory. She attempted to conduct the discussions in as relaxed and informal a manner as possible. She and the children sat together on the floor; the children knew each other well, and conversation flowed smoothly in all groups. However, she was an unfamiliar person – an adult in a position of authority – and the discussions were held in a studio, with cameras visible. We failed in our attempts to have adequate-quality video recordings of interviews in less artificial situations.

The transcripts we used took far more time to transcribe than to collect or to analyse. To get down exactly what people say – including all their hesitations, repetitions, errors, half-swallowed asides – is much more exacting than most people appreciate. Even with studio recordings, sometimes six or seven listenings are required to decide exactly what word a child said, and a non-verbal transcript is even more demanding. The non-verbal transcript has to cover all the children in the group. Only one child speaks at a time usually (though not invariably), but all of them continuously communicate non-verbally, and that communication is often decisive in interpreting the verbal dimension, as Birdwhistell (1972) points out. If one child says something and the rest nod approval, the single utterance has the status of group assent; but if a child says something and the others are all looking away, that indicates their distance from the utterance, though not necessarily their dissent. Laughter is another important though ambiguous and complex indicator. Sometimes it indicates that the statement is completely ridiculous, and is disowned by the laughter. Sometimes it signals great enjoyment and endorsement of what is said. However, precisely because of its ambiguity it must be recorded exactly: who laughs at what, and who they are directing the laughter at.

One of our concerns in these interviews was to see how far children aged 9 have come in what Lévi-Strauss called 'understanding the myth', by which we here mean their grasp of invariant formulae underlying different episodes or versions of the story. Our data suggest they have an impressive grasp of it. The cartoon immediately mobilized children's acquaintance with the relevant genres. Two children whispered 'Scooby Doo' early on, while they were watching *Fangface*. Most groups referred to *Scooby Doo* as a relevant programme, and all groups compared The Heap to The Incredible Hulk, and many children even got The Heap's name wrong, calling him The Hulk. This occurred eight times in the series of interviews – the largest number of 'errors' we recorded. Thus it is clear that Levi-Strauss and the producers are right to see not simply the series, but the genre, as an important unit of meaning because children decoding a new example of a cartoon go from the general to the particular, from genre to series to programme, following major transformational routes.

'Understanding the myth', then, does not appear to be an abstract and late stage of decoding, but an important and early stage, which is activated afresh with each new item. The hours of what many parents think is 'wasted time' that go into the normal child's viewing development can be seen in this account, to build up a kind of cultural knowledge which, if it is active in new learning, will also affect attitudes based upon the kind of social understandings outlined in the previous chapter.

In this experiment we showed only the first 5 minutes of the cartoon in order to judge how well children could use their 'understanding' to predict how the story would end. Children were all emphatic that good would triumph, and that The Heap would be caught (e.g. 'They catch them. They always do.' Other children nod agreement). Most groups believed that the monster would be unmasked; that is, they projected him as a character with a dual identity. Children in four different groups guessed that Professor Arnoss would turn out to be The Heap, or be responsible in some way. One boy from the 12-year-old group had this to say very early in the interview:

Gordon: I think – I've worked out what, what – who's Fang – I mean um The Heap, er, or whatever it is, um, you know, that man who got discharged from the University or or something most probably he's he's dressed up or something to just ah scare the men that, yeah.
Interviewer: Did anyone else think that might be something to do with it? [General noises of agreement] What about you, Kara?
Kara: Oh I just thought that I reckon that, um, that they'd catch him and then they'd get off his mask and pull it off. They always do.
Mabel: Yeah, like in Scooby Doo.

Equally interesting was one mistaken prediction Gordon made a little later, that the 'good' professor would be revealed to be The Heap.

A mistaken prediction like this (cf. Smith, 1973 on 'virtuous errors') reveals the underlying processes more clearly than a correct one. This boy is employing a transformational model which is powerful enough to throw up not only right answers, but also wrong answers of the right kind: professor transformed to The Heap is mind transformed to body, good transformed to bad. He has grasped the principle of metamorphosis, in terms of which the category of 'professor' is destabilized, and becomes ambivalent, so that both monsters and professors, good and evil, are seen as different sides of the same coin. He is actively interrogating the text for evidence with which to substantiate his hypothesis. Another of the 12-year-olds, a girl, also suspected the 'good' professor. None of the 9-year-olds made so interesting an error, so this level of transformational understanding may be beyond them, although they could certainly grasp the substantive metamorphosis from professor to monster, mental to physical power, good to evil.

Further evidence of children's ability to grasp the myth was that most groups showed a generative grasp of the cast list: that is, they remembered the structure as well as the individuals. The typical pattern of recall had The Heap then Fangface as the most salient. Everyone listed these two characters, usually first, and most discussion revolved around them. All this is unsurprising. At the other extreme in memorability were Biff (the 'good' teenager) and Sally Boyd, daughter of Professor Boyd, the 'good' professor. No-one in any of the groups mentioned Sally. There were two errors of recall associated with Biff: two boys in different groups got the colour of his hair wrong, calling it blond when it was dark brown. It was, in fact, good Professor Boyd, and his good daughter Sally, who had blond hair. Two girls changed Biff's sex, seeing the group of teenagers as made up of two girls. We have two observations to make about this. One concerns the transformational equivalence of the 'good' characters in the minds of the child viewers, particularly Biff and the professor. Second is their apparent unimportance in children's perception of the programme. With regard to the first point, as has also been found elsewhere (Durkin, 1985), the children were articulate in their descriptions of the ideology underpinning these stereotypic characters, and how it would be realized in a programme. One boy coined the distinction between 'goodies' and 'goody-goodies':

Interviewer: What's the difference between goody-goodies, and just plain goodies?

Chris: Well, the goody-goodies real good-good. [Loud
                laughter from whole group.]

'Goody-goodies' in this cartoon were then identified as Kim and Biff,
and the judgement was made:

Alan: The goodies might not solve the problems – the goody-
                goodies would. [Whole group laughs.]

The laughter here is an important signal: it seems to indicate first
that the group endorses Chris's and Alan's explication, second that
there is a subversive force to this comment. There is a simultaneous
recognition and resistance of the ideological rules of the cartoon
universe: they know that the middle-class pair will be vindicated and
in control at the end of the cartoon but they also doubt, if not actually
repudiate, the values represented. There are a number of signals that
this is a 'child' utterance: the vocabulary ('goody-goody'), the laughter,
eye gaze (children look at each other, not at the interviewer as normal),
and intonation (a downwards intonation at the end, indicating
definiteness or confidence in their meanings).

   In spite of this laughter, the relevant rules were described in detail
by this group. One rule concerns who can drive cars. Alan put the
rule as follows:

Alan: The main characters do not drive the car. And the
                not so main characters do not – do. Ha!
Interviewer: Who were the main characters?
Alan and Mary: Fangface, Pugsy.

Behind this new distinction, between 'main' and 'not-so-main', is
the same recognition as with 'goody-goodies' versus 'goodies', that
the characters who are at the centre for the child viewer, offered for
identification and enjoyment, are excluded from power. On the role
of these not-so-main characters, opinions were sometimes mixed. Alan,
when asked whether Kim might drive the car, said yes, but Mary
disagreed. Others speculated whether Pugsie and Fangs (as the boy)
could have driven a car, but the consensus was that they could not. So
Biff emerges as the only one who can drive a car, with all that that
signifies about his power in the world. We can postulate from this and
other features of the cartoon that there is an underlying categorization
whereby Biff and Kim have the status of proto-parents, while *Pugsy and
Fangs* are children. But Biff is not a highly valued character in all respects:

Interviewer: The one that was driving. Mm. What sort of person
                was he?

Alan: Oh, a person that agrees with anyone. [Smiles; so
                 do other boys.]
Chris: Kind of a boring person. [Smiles; as do the other
                 boys.]

The smiles that accompany this comment (this time it is a male
consensus) again signal the subversiveness of the comment. This kind
of exchange brings out something that our initial analysis did not:
the 'good' middle-class characters are effective but unappealing.

The main focus of ambivalence, however, was The Heap. Many
of the boys identified with him, eight in all. In discussion everyone
mentioned two features: his colour (normally contrasted with The
Incredible Hulk) and his hair. Every group mentioned that his hair
was unusually long. Two children, one boy, one girl, in different
groups speculated that he might be female:

Alan: You couldn't tell if it was a boy or girl 'cos it had its
                 hair way down there. [Indicates point low down on
                 his back, and laughs. Another boy laughs.]

And in another interview:

Interviewer: What else did you think about him?
Ray: He had messy hair.
Phyllis: I thought he was a girl at first . . . when he um . . .
Interviewer: Did you? Why did you think he was a girl, Phyllis?
Phyllis: 'Cause he has long, um, hair.

In spite of this transient ambiguity, no girls unequivocally volunteered
the wish to be The Heap. We can see some of the forces at work from
the following exchange:

Interviewer: But you girls didn't want to be, uh, The Heap, Heap,
                 or you didn't want to be Fangface.
Kristie: I'd like to be Fangface, wouldn't mind being
                 Fangface. [Two boys look at her.]
Alan: The Heap's not for a girl. [The other two boys still
                 look at Kristie.]
Kristie: But um The Heap, well, it'd be okay, but everybody
                 would be out to get you. You'd have to be running
                 all the time, you couldn't stay in one spot.

Explicit pressure is being exerted here by the boys (with
encouragement from the interviewer) to exclude girls from identifying
with The Heap. It is Alan, who had initially seen The Heap as

bisexual, who now insists that girls must not be The Heap. In another group, boys were similarly insistent that girls must not be The Heap. But Kristie only renounces the role of The Heap because of The Heap's status as victim. She was happy to be Fangface, though we note that she changes her initial enthusiastic 'I'd like' to a more tentative 'Wouldn't mind'. (Two other girls nominated Fangface, while six opted to be Kim, the girl.) In this cartoon there is really only one female character for girls to identify with (Sally Boyd has too insignificant a role), and when pressed, girls do accept that role. However, one of the 12-year-old girls did so only with reservations:

Kara: I'd be that girl, but I would do more if I was her.
Interviewer: Would you? What would you do?
Kara: I'd find out mysteries and then all the guys'd think you were fantastic. [Laughs to girl friend.] Have a note [mimes writing] da! da! [imitates fanfare].

The surface form of the cartoon is unfair to girls in that it offers them only one option to identify with as girls, whereas boys have a choice of six characters and four types of character (good and bad monster, middle-class and lower-class male). Boys could explicitly identify with more than one of these, and a number of them did so, offering to be for example, both Fangface and The Heap, or, in one case, both The Heap and Biff. Excluded by the surface form from this range of choices, girls have two options: to rewrite the possibilities of the girl's role, or to covertly identify with one of the 'male' characters, transforming his gender. Both these options have to go against the grain of the cartoon itself, but the cartoon gives both options a point of entry. The Heap does have long hair (and bulging pectorals), and Kim is the controller of Fangface. She is the intellectual of the group (often shown reading) and, in a part of the cartoon that these children did not see, she captures the ray gun to save the day. That is, both these characters have an obvious significance in the cartoon, but there is also the hint of a very different significance, which children aged 9 are quite capable of seeing and making use of, though it remains difficult for them to make it public, in a situation like this. (See chapter 5 for a fuller account of the process whereby meanings are negotiated in a group of this kind. Here we wish to emphasize the reading process rather than the negotiation process, even though the two are often inseparable in practice.)

The attraction of The Heap was clearly that he represented unrestrained, forbidden aggressive impulses. A typical exchange is as follows:

Interviewer:	Why would you like to be the blue man? What would you do?
Michael:	Because I can carry people if something else – like when my friends try to hurt me, and I'm n'supposed to hurt 'em. I'll go bash 'em up, then I'll get the person, and I'll carry him to the hospital. [Michael smiles. Len laughs, and falls on back with legs in air.]
Interviewer:	I see. Would that be being good, or bad? [Children laugh.]
Michael:	Good. [Children continue to laugh.]
Interviewer:	That would be being good? Was the blue man good?
Phyllis:	No.
Michelle:	No.
Charmaine:	No.
Len:	No.
Michael:	Yes.
Ray:	No. – Yes. [All together.]

The ambivalent response to The Heap was typical. A number of children saw Fangface as both good and bad, too; but the contradictory judgements normally existed at different levels. All these children knew that officially The Heap was to be classified as bad, and they itemized the signs of badness (face, actions, colour). As in the present case, claims that The Heap is good (and that Fangface is bad) were normally accompanied by smiles or laughter, and said in a 'child' voice (high energy, downwards intonation). The reason Michael gives for wanting to be The Heap is a perfect fusion of contradictory motives: pro-social (carrying people, especially to hospital) and anti-social (putting them in a condition to need to go to hospital in the first place). The contradictions proliferate in his speech. It is friends, not enemies, who try to hurt him, and whom he 'bashes up'. The clause 'I'm n'supposed to hurt 'em' carries contradictions in a state of fine suspension. The negative (represented as 'n' ') is so swallowed that it's virtually inaudible. (Of five people who listened to the tape, two could not hear it, and the others only heard the slightest trace.) So the clause almost comes out as 'I'm supposed to hurt 'em', as though hurting friends is a duty imposed on him. But this complex statement is all delivered with a smile, and it's accepted as a joke. Len laughs, and even goes along with it by rolling on his back, as though 'bashed' by his friend Michael, The Heap. Michael's discourse is doubly determined by different kinds of meaning, 'child' and 'parent' meanings in transactional analysis terms, just as the cartoon is. Michael's language shows by its form as well as its content that he is easily able to cope with ambiguous messages at two levels.

In this group interview situation girls are not so readily permitted to produce such discourse, but occasionally they were able to express the same meanings.

Interviewer: And what about The Heap? Why would you like to be The Heap? He was a baddie.

Alan: Oh, I like being The Hulk. [All children laugh.]

Interviewer: [Laughs.] What would you do, if you woke up one day and you were The Heap, and you had to go off to school, what would you do when you got there?

Alan: I'd just go and anyone that teased me, I'd hit 'em. [smiles.]

Kara: [Looks at Alan.] Scare the teacher.

Alan: Yeah, scare the teacher out of her wits and then muck around in the classroom.

In this exchange, Alan has a similar fantasy to Michael's without any pretence at virtuous motives. It is legitimate for a boy, and he laughs, as do the girls. When Kara gives her fantasy, legitimated by the authority-figure's instructions to fantasize, and under cover of Alan's remarks, no-one else smiles. But she is heard, and Alan picks up her comment and extends it.

   A little later, the discussion had moved on to Fangface.

Craig: I like Fangface, too. He's good.

Interviewer: Yes. Is it possible to be good and bad, then?

Alan: Yeah, cos, um, say, uh, you were good at the start and say someone did something wrong to you and wanted to get your revenge. [Looks down.]

Interviewer: Yes.

Kara: And sometimes you can't help being bad.

Interviewer: Mm. Does that happen to you sometimes, that you can't help being bad?

Kara: Yes, when I beat up my brother! [Boys laugh.]

Michelle: Same here when I beat up my sister.

In this exchange, Alan is now speaking in a 'Parent-voice'. He finishes on a rising inflection, as though asking if he is right. He looks at the interviewer, then down, not relating to his peers. He is attempting to do justice to the complex moral proposition the interviewer has put to him. Kara's first statement is similarly earnest, with the same markers of 'Parent'. Her second statement, however, switches abruptly to 'Child'. She smiles, and the boys laugh. Her speech has energy and finishes on a downwards inflection. Although it is rare for her, and other girls, to express these meanings, when they do so they have the same form as the boys'. In this analysis we take it that characters like Fangface and The Heap perform the same functions and carry the same meanings for girls as boys, but with a higher level of repression. At a deeper level, both these characters are bisexual, or asexual, and both boys and girls seem to recognize the fact.

The last character to look at is the hero, Fangface/Fangs. His popularity was second to The Heap's among boys – six for Fangface, against eight for The Heap – but three girls also identified with him, giving him a nine–eight overall victory over The Heap. Fangface was present for a greater amount of time, and children mentioned all his significant features. His single tooth was mentioned by most children. It was seen as ridiculous. For example, in one interview there was this exchange:

Interviewer: Who thought that – who thought Fangface was like
               The Incredible Hulk?
Cheralyn: With one tooth!? [Laughs. Looks at other children,
               who exchange glances with her.]
Others: Yeah!

The one tooth was clearly seen as self-evident disqualification from monster status. Fangface was associated with appetite. The episode that children most often laughed out loud at was one where, in response to a 'food word' (Pugsie saying 'Go catch that turkey!'), Fangface swallowed Pugsie. This episode was also the one that was most frequently recalled, and Fangface's responsiveness to food and food words in general was normally mentioned. Most groups mentioned not only that the sun and the moon controlled his metamorphoses, but that it was done by pictures. One girl specified Kim's role in showing the pictures. In the same interview, one boy speculates that Fangs would not like being transformed. Fangface's hat, and the fact that he wore it backwards, was mentioned twice by the older children, where it was associated with dumbness:

Interviewer: How can you tell the dumb one?
Kara: 'Cos he's got the head, the hat back to front with the –
               he's got a long face. [Draws out her face downwards
               with her hand, and pulls a face.]

By 12, children can certainly read this sign, but although it was not mentioned by the 9-year-olds, there seems no reason in principle why it should not be part of their response too.

In spite of Fangface's exposure, there were some errors of recall. One girl misheard his name as 'Funnyface' – a revealing error. Children in two groups referred to him as a dog. One child said he was brown and white, rather than brown, thereby conflating him with Scooby Doo, who is a brown and white dog. In our analysis of Fangface we represented him as a fused figure, a composite transform from Scooby Doo and The Incredible Hulk. That analysis is confirmed by this tendency of the children to reverse one or other transformation, and see Fangface as either monster or dog. The instability of the transform is aided by the inconsistency in Fangface as shown in the cartoon. His relative size changes, and sometimes he is a formidable figure who might frighten even The Heap, while at other times he is cuddly, greedy, and as cowardly as Scooby Doo.

At this point in the study it might be useful to set out some hypotheses which have emerged. We note that these are only hypotheses, derived from only 42 children's responses, under specific conditions, to the first 5 minutes of a single 20-minute cartoon. But 42 children are better than none, so although our hypotheses need to be refined and clarified by further work, they can still reveal something of the competence of 9-year-olds (i.e. what 9-year-old children seem to be able to do in interpreting the content of television). Although we can assume that older children have access to the same competence, we still do not know how or when this competence is acquired, or what the competence of very young children is. With all these reservations, these hypotheses seem to us a useful provisional clarification.

1. By 9 years old, children decode television programmes with essentially the same 'grammar' as do adults.

2. A new programme is read by them as a transformation of a number of abstract types. That is, there is a unit of 'understanding' which is wider even than a series, and it includes a set of types of character, plot, situation and action which, though realized differently in each one of the series, are nevertheless to be seen as transformations of a single set of characteristics.

3. Children's grasp of the rules of a programme type is generative: that is, they can project new and correct versions of the programme type. It seems to be the case that by the age of 12, children's transformational grasp is powerful enough to project hypothetical counter-forms, as well as the ones that do actually appear.

4. The primary meaning is carried by the main characters as synchronic syntagms. These synchronic syntagms consist of a set of significant features, and some of these are ambiguous or contradictory, thus allowing different children to read them differently.

5. Both television content and children's responses to it carry meanings at two levels, sometimes fused, sometimes in contradiction with each other. Since the two levels of meaning coexist, children's statements cannot be considered in isolation as evidence for what they really think. Under different conditions they may well say one thing or its opposite, and actually mean both.

6. Of the two kinds of meaning – ideological (Parent) and subversive (Child) meanings – the emotional charge and attraction of the programme is invested in the subversive (Child) meanings.

7. Where the surface form undervalues a class of person (as here with girls), members of that group can compensate by a more extensive but covert transformation of that surface. Such viewers may have, at one level, an interpretation that is more like that of the dominant group than would be expected from analysis of the surface forms, or from a superficial view of what those individuals say.

Different codes, different messages

In our initial analysis of *Fangface* it seemed clear that the visual channel was much more significant to the viewer than the verbal channel. We noted that there seemed to be considerable redundancy between the two channels, but did not elaborate on the possibility that the kind of content carried by verbal and visual codes may be importantly different. Semiotically that aspect is crucial, so in our empirical work we attempted to explore the possibility in a number of different ways. First, we showed modified versions of the first 5 minutes of *Fangface*. One group saw the programme with the sound track removed. Another group heard a sound-only version, of the same length, with a verbal summary of the visual track. We could then compare their responses with those of the children who had seen and heard the full version.

The children who saw the visual-only version had a reasonable grasp of what was going on. They knew that The Heap was the villain, that Fangface was a wolf (some of the other groups called him a dog

even though they had heard him described as a werewolf). They noted
that it was a picture or 'photo' of the sun or moon which triggered
the metamorphosis. While watching, they were more intent than the
other groups but when it finished they relaxed and laughed, and said
they found it funny. Their description of characters and their clothes
was more precise than any other group's. As with all other groups,
Kim's clothes were more fully described – mainly by girls – than
anyone else's, but no other groups mentioned the detail of the orange
ribbon Kim wore. They got Biff's hair colour right, and also the colour
of his clothes – a feat of recall attempted by no-one else. The one
mistake was that he was attributed with an orange hat, whereas it
was Fangs who wore an orange hat, and that back to front.

However, their generative grasp of the plot was impaired. The visual
track did not contain references to the other professor. The phrase
'unauthorized experiments' was repeated by a number of the children
who had heard the soundtrack, as the most significant clue to the
identity of The Heap. All that the children who did not hear the
soundtrack could guess was that the police would come, and that The
Heap would be killed. One child also misread the significance of Pugsie
and described him as a 'robber' because Fangface ate him, though
the rest of the group were quite clear about what was happening. In
general, the grasp of individual incidents – including use of visual cues
as to who was good and who was bad – was equivalent to that of the
other groups and the recall was more precise, but the capacity to see
relationships, and to project larger patterns, was much poorer.

On analysing the cartoon it becomes clear that it is primarily the
verbal code which carried the necessary clues for 'understanding' the
plot as a whole. These children's failure is not due to chance. The
visual code works more efficiently through paratactic synchronic
syntagms (in juxtaposition within a frame, e.g. Fangface with his one
tooth), and diachronic syntagms which are short in scope (e.g.
Fangface seeing a picture and metamorphosing). In the case of
Fangface, the crucial plot information was carried not merely by verbal
language, but by an H-form of it: that is by Professor Boyd using
words like 'unauthorized experiments'. The H-form, we have
suggested, is likely to be more incomprehensible than L-forms to
children of this age, and for some it may have the same effect as having
the sound switched off at those points. Children have been observed
to pay greatest attention to television when other children are talking
(and probably using L-forms) (cf. Anderson et al., 1977). One group
which did not predict that The Heap was Professor Arnoss also claimed
to find Boyd's speech boring.

Interviewer:	Were there any bits that weren't funny?
Sasha:	Yeah, when they were talking about the man.
Interviewer:	Which man?
Manuela:	Uh – the pr – pr – professor. [Manuela and two others look at Interviewer. Others look away.]
Interviewer:	Mmm.
Sasha:	It was boring. [Two children look at interviewer, others look away or play with carpet.]

These children did not initially remember the names of Fangface or The Heap. Sasha's prediction for the end was:

Sasha:	Um, Fangface would have um, did something really silly, and they would have caught the monster somehow because . . . [Interviewer: yes?] that's how they all . . . cartoons end.

Sasha also endorsed The Heap's anti-intellectual bias. Immediately after his comment that it was 'boring' there was the following exchange:

Cheralyn:	Um, it's . . . not funny because of the Professors. 'Cause they make their machines and they get destroyed.
Sasha:	Ooh . . . poor little machines! [Smiles.]

Needless to say Sasha said he would like to be The Heap: 'I'm the blue person!'

We can see here the skewed interpretation that arises from an orientation to pictures rather than words, and to L-forms of verbal language rather than H-forms. The Heap, who does not speak but just roars and is violent to professors and machines, is maximally comprehensible to the visually oriented, and he also represents that tendency, as an ideal type of the non-verbal hero.

We did not give children the sound-track on its own – it was so sparse as to be incomprehensible even to us. So we supplemented the sound effects with a voice-over narration, to see how a group of children went in decoding a purely sound version of a segment of the same length. Still working with the first 5 minutes, one surprising result was that these children had a poorer grasp of the names than children who saw the full version sound plus vision. The interviewer began with a general question:

Interviewer:	Now what did you think that was all about?
Marcus:	When, um, well Fangface, oh well this Heat man's obviously *orange*, um, and he keeps on stealing the professors, 'cause . . .

Andrew: [Breaking in]: I reckon he –
Marcus: . . . someone doesn't want them, and this other person
                 probably wants to make that invention.

Marcus gets Fangface's name correct, but he mishears 'The Heap'
and then uses his mishearing to recreate a visual image. What is
significant is that he needed to project some image, even though it
was only a guess. In this interview, Sherman Fangsworth was referred
to as 'Shybro', and Pugsy as 'Gobbo, or whatever his name was'.
But this first comment contrasts markedly with those of all the other
groups in that it addresses itself directly to the plot as a whole. Verbal
language is oriented to wholes rather than parts. Andrew's
intervention, which he came out with as soon as Marcus let him, was
an accurate plot prediction, before the interviewer had asked for one:

Andrew: I reckon that that bloke, you know, the one whose
                 unauthorized [said very indistinctly] . . . He musta
                 conjured it up or something.

Again the word 'unauthorized' acts as the cue for a successful plot
prediction. The children in this group had a good grasp of the sequence
and structure of the story, but they had very idiosyncratic versions
of particular episodes. They were clearly affected by a strong need
to visualize the story, and these visualizations introduced meanings
that were not in the original. The children did drawings after the
discussion, and these dramatically showed the extent of the skew.
Marcus's Fangface, for instance, was a dog with big ears and two
teeth. His 'Heap' was indeterminate in outline and shape. Lee-Ann,
one of the girls, had a very cuddly, long-eared animal as Fangface,
under the heading 'Fangface a weir wolf'. The children depended
on visual images to concretize a narrative, but these images were
uncontrolled by verbal language. So whereas verbal language and
visual images work together to key each other so that in spite of the
amount of redundancy each limits the scope of the other, either on
its own seems to generate a chaotic plethora of meanings.

   Another modification to the cartoon that we introduced was to affix
a warning notice saying, 'ADULTS ONLY, PARENTAL GUIDANCE
RECOMMENDED', before showing the first 5 minutes to two groups,
a total of ten children aged 8–9. The notice is in fact a conflation of
two of the codes broadcast on programmes in Australia, AO or PGR.
The children's reactions while viewing were the same as those of other
groups; mainly dead-pan expressions, with some smiles at a few
incidents, and general relaxation and smiles when the film was stopped.

The global judgements also were the same: 'good' (said with smiles), and 'funny'. It was as though the notice did not exist. But when the interviewer specifically asked, both groups could recall it and both asked why it was there. In the whole series of interviews these were the only two questions that were asked of the interviewer, which is a significant comment both on the interviewing situation and on the questions. One group insisted that the words should not have been there. That group was also opposed to censorship in all forms. The other group, however, agreed that censorship was sometimes necessary. Initially four of the five children said that *Fangface* did not deserve an 'AO' (Adults Only) notice, but the interview went on as follows:

Interviewer: Why did you think they should have put 'AO' on the cartoon?
Marnie: 'Cause, um, oh, if say a 2-year-old was watching it and they, they might have got a bit scared when they were . . . when Fangface was changing.
Angela: When he swallows Pugsie. [Smiles.]
Interviewer: Mm.
Richard: Or when, when they hear the ow-oow [imitates howl], like that 'n' they go, they go out for a camp and hear it, y'know, they get a little bit scared.
Interviewer: So what were the things about that Fangface bit that you thought were really scary? That might scare somebody?
Angela: Oh, the thing when that, that, where, where that big monster [outlines shape with her hand] came in to come and get him, that was a bit scary . . .
Marnie: Yeah. [Others nod.]
Angela: In the dark, too.
Interviewer: Why was it scary, that bit?
Richard: Didn't scare me, but you know . . .

The warning notice on its own was apparently unable to affect their initial perceptions of *Fangface*, but as supplemented by the coercion of the interviewer it could begin to turn a funny cartoon into a horror movie. Even after further discussion the children had not necessarily changed what they thought of the cartoon, but they changed what they afterwards said about it in this situation, producing an alternative reading which coexisted with but did not supplant the initial reading. The progression of Angela's statements is interesting. Initially she said that Fangface should not be 'AO'. Then she gave a counter-instance of its being frightening: 'When he swallows Pugsie', said with a smile to signal that she knew that it was really funny, not scary. Finally she gave an instance that might be scary enough to justify censorship. By this stage there was a majority in favour of censorship. That became a view legitimated by verbal discourse as an official position, even though it was an unjustifiable judgement. The point is that language did not determine what they perceived initially, but cumulatively it determined what they said, and therefore what they will be judged to have thought by researchers, by teachers and parents, perhaps later even by themselves.

The 12-year-olds reflected specifically on the role of language in fixing some thoughts and perceptions and allowing others to disappear.

Interviewer: Were you thinking these things when you were watching that?

All: Yeah.

Interviewers: Were you?

Len: But you don't feel much about it when you are watching but after somebody, anybody asks us what we felt, then you say what happened.

Geoffrey: You don't really take it into consideration.

Interviewer: That's an interesting comment. You don't, you don't feel much when you're watching?

Mark: You don't really think about it if you aren't asked. If you aren't asked, you don't think about it again.

For these children it is as though their own thoughts and feelings do not really exist unless they become public and visible through language: the language of others requiring attention and consciousness, their own language reinforcing or sometimes deforming their fluid, inchoate structures of meaning.

In order to counteract the bias of the verbal, we tried another way for children to communicate their interpretations of *Fangface*. We showed the full cartoon to another group of fourteen children, seven boys and seven girls, then asked them to draw something in response to it. We related these drawings to the cartoon not as direct recall accounts, but as transformations of it: transformations that might delete aspects of it or fuse it with other meanings. Thus drawings were taken to be important clues to this set of transformational processes, rather than a record of the contents of a child's visual perception or visual memory of the cartoon.

To illustrate what we mean by this we must return to basics for a moment. A cartoon consists of moving pictures, which is to say it is primarily a structure of diachronic syntagms with auxiliary synchronic syntagms. A drawing, however, is a synchronic syntagm. Children of this age took about 5 minutes to do a single drawing. A single drawing has to transform a very complex set of diachronic syntagms into a single synchronic one. Plot disappears: it cannot easily be represented in a drawing because it is not a synchronic visual category. In practice, of seventeen drawings, nine consisted of a single character, usually facing the viewer, which we took to indicate that the preferred form in which all the actual and potential meanings of the cartoon are transformationally realized, is a single character. In four pictures the characters were shown interacting, so we can also see that a particular episode can be used as a transformational equivalent of the show, but it is not the preferred form.

The remaining five drawings showed no characters, but settings, the gang's car, or The Heap's mountain retreat being the favoured ones. The characters chosen to carry the meaning in this form were predominantly the monsters, Fangface and The Heap. In all, a total of seventeen characters were drawn, and twelve of these were monsters (eight of The Heap, and four of Fangface). By that count The Heap emerges as the most potent carrier of meaning for the cartoon, even though he was not seen very often. The pictures of The Heap were all in blue, and all children drew his trousers carefully, with all but one showing his hair long and giving him a feminine appearance.

The exception was a picture which put Professor Arnoss's bald head on a Heap body. Four of the drawings of The Heap also showed him with the ray gun in his hand. The Heap, we can see, is more frequently represented with distinctive features (blue, long hair, carrying a ray gun) than through characteristic actions. Fangface was always coloured brown and in three out of four drawings had his single tooth prominent (illustration 3). No-one drew his hat, and no-one drew him eating.

In addition to monsters the children drew pictures of settings without any characters. In the full cartoon there were three main settings: the house (inside and out), the university (laboratory and grounds), and The Heap's cave, which was a laboratory concealed by elaborate mechanical means inside a mountain. This third setting carried in most explicit form the contradiction between nature and culture. It was also the most favoured setting for children to draw (four drawings – as many as of Fangface). All the drawings of it showed both the rugged mountain, with the door, though in the cartoon the door was a concealed one. One boy glossed his drawing as follows:

That's the cave and the door's half open – there's the black, that's how dark it is, and that's the handle you pull up, and this is

Michelle. 7

Francine 5

Illustration 3

Illustration 3 (contd)

the grooves and there's the scallops [the crags on the mountain] and you sort of crawl in and have a cubby.

The gloss shows how efficiently a drawing of a setting can encode a cluster of significant features: in this case nature and culture, inner and outer, danger and security, through the darkness of the cubby.

We asked all the children to describe their drawings and we classified both the drawings and descriptions into two groups: predominantly transactive and predominantly non-transactive (see Kress and Hodge, 1979, for this distinction, which is discussed at greater length in chapter 3). In English sentences a transactive has a real object, acted on by the agent: e.g. 'he hit it'. A non-transactive has no definite object: e.g. 'he ran'. The transactive drawings were ones which showed a character doing something *to* something or someone else, like 'hitting it' or 'carrying him'; the non-transactive drawings showed a character just doing something like 'running' or 'flying'. This classification revealed one major difference: whereas most of the drawings were static, non-transactive forms, most of the descriptions emphasized action. In fact, of the seventeen pictures, fourteen were non-transactive and only three were transactive (showing characters acting on something else). Of the descriptions, there were only four non-transactives, and eleven transactives. A picture showing a single individual would be glossed as an incident:

That, um, the monster is pushing in the door. He banged the door down and he um he carried the Prof back, when he was laughing at the Prof in the cage.

Neither the actions nor the objects of the actions are shown in the drawing, so the differences between the two codes can be seen clearly from this example. The visual code filters out actions and the flow of time, preferring to focus on a collection of features outside of time. In so far as it generalizes, it does so in different ways: by showing representative features juxtaposed. In contrast the verbal code handles episodes (diachronic syntagms) far more easily, and it can reorder these with effortless facility, as, for example, in the flow of the one sentence, 'The Monster bangs the door down, carries the Prof away, and laughs at him in the cage.' Because it is ordered in time, verbal language moves effortlessly through it: visual language being ordered in space resists the flow of time. Thus visual language finds it difficult to represent episodes, while for a single picture it is impossible to represent an abstract plot.

For this section our data have been limited in quantity and depth, but with that caveat we offer some observations on some important differences that may exist between visual and verbal codes, on television and for children's responses.

1. In a cartoon the visual code seems to carry more meanings than the verbal code, for child viewers.
2. Without a verbal track the meanings in the visual track would proliferate unmanageably; without a visual track the visual images projected by child decoders would proliferate anarchically.
3. The verbal track is better at carrying certain kinds of meaning: especially abstract or large-scale diachronic structures ('understanding the myth' in Lévi-Strauss's terms).
4. Verbal language is also the main mediator of meaning. It is the form in which meanings gain public and social form, and through discussion are affected by the meanings of others.
5. Single images recorded in visual form tend to code character not plot, synchronic syntagms, not diachronic ones, representing the meanings of a show by a cluster of significant features attached to an individual, rather than by a sequence of actions or events.

Conclusion

What we have tried to do so far is to give an indication of the possibilities for understanding and research opened up by a form of semiotic theory that can work profitably alongside a number of other distinct research traditions. At this stage we have been concerned largely to produce insights not proofs, to work towards methods rather than conclusions, because any tradition that works blind or fails to address its own methodology cannot be consistently productive. But some important points have emerged already. By 9 years old, children seem to be remarkably adept at reading television programmes designed for them. They effortlessly imbibe ideological content. They also see lines of fissure in that content, contradictions which find analogous structures within their developing psyche. They try to balance these contradictions between different aspects of the total semiotic potential of the given programme, contradictions so diverse that a single coherent meaning for the programme becomes unlikely if not impossible. But for the researcher, or the parent or teacher or media manager, the complexity and invisibility of the process of reading constitutes the major problem: how to decode a response which is constantly transforming itself in the face of a multitude of forces, including the role of the interviewer and researcher; how to read children's readings. This is a methodological problem which we progressively address in the next three chapters, in which we consider the pattern of children's developing capacities to read television, their grasp of reality and their understanding of social context and norms on their viewing and interpretations.

Chapter 3

Television and the mind of the child
A developmental perspective

Behind the widespread concern with children and TV as a topic for research or action lie a set of assumptions about children and their development. Only if children are different from adults in some crucial aspects in their response to TV can we justify attention to them as a special audience. So, all work in this area assumes some developmental theory. But people interested in this topic seldom examine or set out their assumptions about development. For instance, a common position regards TV as vacuous at best, and at worst shot through with insidiously corrupting ideas and values. Children, in this view, see the same meanings as adults, but lack certain defences against them, which adults either have (how is not clear) or have the right not to have. Thus (this line of reasoning goes), because of their status as potential victims, helpless before this influence, children must be protected from themselves for the sake of their future selves. A narrative along these lines is very influential in practice, because it seems so obviously true to many people. Yet it should not be accepted without question or without reference to research findings. And since control of children's TV is a major focus of legislation and proposals for legislation, assumptions about development are a highly political issue, and they should not remain unexamined. So in this chapter we want to outline a developmental framework for our own work.

Before we can do so, however, it is necessary to indicate some ideas and issues that we believe need to be set into a developmental framework. First is the role of TV in what can be called 'the social construction of reality', to use the evocative phrase coined by Berger and Luckmann (1967). In their book of that title they described the process whereby the everyday discourse that people are immersed in creates a particular version of social reality. Because that reality is taken for granted, it assumes the status and appearance of the one and only 'objective' reality. Television is almost as pervasive as everyday language in most homes. The average child in Britain, Australia and the United States watches over 14,000 hours of television up to the age of 18. This is much the same average number of hours as is spent behind a school desk. Just as one drop of water on a stone seems to leave the stone unaffected but continual dripping in time can wear away a hole, so with television we must be careful to pick up effects that may be invisible at the level of a programme, or series, but important over a lifetime.

One influential line of argument has been called the 'cultivation hypothesis' (cf. Gerbner and Gross, 1976). Researchers such as Smythe (1953), de Fleur (1964) and Gerbner et al. (1980) have shown systematic differences between the world of television and the real world. Certain major groups in society (in America, Australia and England they are white, male, adult and middle class) are systematically over-represented, at the expense of others which are under-represented. Gerbner calls the phenomenon 'symbolic annihilation'. There is no doubt that the world of television in the English-speaking world is skewed in this way. The sex ratio of 4 males to 1 female in *Fangface*, for instance, is typical; and since the ratio of the sexes in most countries is roughly 50/50, it is not necessary to go to great lengths to demonstrate a bias here. Similarly, in *Fangface* the social class ratio is 4.5:1 in favour of the middle class: another striking distortion which is typical of American media productions. Gerbner and his associates have tried to demonstrate how such massive skewing affects the general picture of the world of television viewers. This work suggests that heavy television viewers have a vision of the world which is more like the television world than the real world on points where the television world is most skewed (see also Hawkins and Pingree, 1980). That finding is important, but there is a surprisingly weak correlation, and one which has not always been replicated (Newcomb, 1978). We are left with two important questions. What is the process of reality-construction? Why and how is it resisted, to the degree that it is? This leads us to the crunch question, for the whole area of children and TV: are children more vulnerable than adults to this whole process? To answer this we must take a developmental approach.

However, there is another apparently contrary line of criticism of how television acts as a constructor of reality. Marie Winn (1977) accused television of being the 'plug-in drug', a kind of narcotic, dangerous because it seduces its audiences away from reality. Marcuse (1966) implicated television and other mass media in America as formers of a 'one-dimensional mind', a mind that is stunned, paralysed, incapable of criticism or opposition. Instead of forming a version of reality that penetrates and determines the general sense of reality, television in this view builds up a hermetically sealed alternative world, which sucks helpless victims into its glossy irrelevance, neutralizing them as effective agents in social and political life. Again the developmental perspective is crucial: is there something about children's ways of responding to TV that will leave them zombies in adult life? Are there kinds of early experience (of TV, or excluding TV) that will equip them better to be critical effective citizens in a modern democracy?

In this chapter we want to look at these issues as they bear on children's responses to television. Our major assumptions are that television is refracted by children's minds, which develop different strategies for coping with the 'realities' on television and in the world they come to know; that the child's 'construction of reality' is a process of negotiation that unfolds in time under specific social circumstances; that both the content and the forms of thought that mediate it evolve in ways that will determine the ideological effects of television; and that the years from 0 to 12 are a crucial period for us to study if we are to understand why television has such a variable effect on the formation of ideas and world views.

Theories of development: a semiotic synthesis

The act of 'reading television' (Fiske and Hartley, 1978), decoding and interpreting its messages and relating them to the other systems of meaning in everyday life, obviously draws on general cognitive and perceptual strategies. In order to understand it we need to set it in a more general framework taking account of the development of children's perception, language and thought. Our approach will be to outline the substance and implications of what seem to us to be the development theories most relevant to semiotic research within a broad structuralist framework, moving on to consider our data on cognitive, social and ideological development in children's responses to television in terms of this general account.

There have, of course, been a large number of different lines of research which have explored the development of structures of language, thought and perception in humans. In spite of differences of approach and terminology there is a surprising degree of consensus that has emerged, a consensus that can be deployed usefully on the topic of children and television. Before we sketch out the general terms of this common view we need to restate the basic forms of the structuralist semiotics that we will use to organize our own version of the synthesis.

At the foundation of structuralist semiotics is the previously discussed distinction between the two planes in which structures exist: syntagmatic and paradigmatic. Syntagmatic structures, or syntagms, are relations among elements in real space and time, whether in material reality or in acts of perception, language or thought: the relation of unit to unit in an actual sentence, or of figure and ground in a percept, for instance. Paradigmatic structures are of their nature abstract, the pre-existing features or categories that underpin syntagms by assigning a value to component elements. Among examples of paradigmatic structures would be sets of terms like old/young, male/female, or high/low status that organize the world of social meanings.

A third fundamental category is the concept of transformations considered as a change affecting structure or parts of a structure. This concept has a long history, going back at least to the Greeks in the Western tradition of thought, used importantly though in different senses by twentieth-century theorists such as Chomsky (1957), Lévi-Strauss (1963) and Piaget (1968). We use the term to refer to structural changes in either the syntagmatic or the paradigmatic plane (cf. Hodge and Kress, 1983). A clear example of a syntagmatic transformation in language would be the change of an active sentence (e.g. 'he opened the door') to a passive ('the door was opened [by the man]'). In film, a flashback is a straightforward syntagmatic transformation. A simple paradigmatic transformation would be to replace 'door' by 'portal', or to negate the sentence. Both kinds of transformation must be perceived as actual changes, performed by someone or something. Imputed transformations assume an agent and a direction, even if agent or direction may not always be visible on the surface, or not known with certainty by an interpreter who invokes them.

Finally, a topic we will only touch on in this chapter is the relation between structures of reality and structures of interpretation, in language, perception and thought. This relationship involves more or less distortion, a better or worse 'fit'. We will call the semiotic system concerned with this relationship the modality of the structure. It is a species of transformation existing at the interface between reality and thought, so important that it warrants treatment in a separate chapter.

Here, however, let us suggest some logical relationships between these kinds of structures and processes which have important implications for a developmental theory, and which can thus guide our study of the empirical data.

1. Paradigmatic structures are prior to the syntagmatic structures that depend on them, since syntagms cannot have any meaning unless the elements have assigned values which are given in a paradigm.
2. Synchronic structures are prior to equivalent diachronic structures, since diachronic structures depend upon memory to mediate them.
3. Differentiation of structures is prior to integration since integration requires previous differentiation. (Note that integration, as an act deployed on what is differentiated, is different from the lack of differentiation that preceded the act of differentiation.)
4. Paratactic structures are prior to hypotactic structures of the same scope since hypotactic structures are inherently more powerful as principles of organization.
5. Structures are prior to their transformations, since transformations operate upon existing structures.

Since we are investigating children and their development with regard to television, we must consider at least the two basic questions regarding children's responses to television and/or to life:

1. What paradigmatic and syntagmatic structures typically are available to which children, and when?
2. Are there certain transformations which are unavailable or peculiar to children, and if so, which children and when?

The growth of children's perception and thinking

An immense amount of development has occurred before a child takes a real interest in the television set at about 2 years old. These first 2 years of life see a number of crucial developments, but because children are not very forthcoming in describing them we can only observe their behaviour and hypothesize and reconstruct the processes. The obvious starting point is perception. From the moment of birth children make distinctions, and hence develop paradigmatic structures. Children also make simple connections. They integrate elements to form simple syntagms (e.g. a breast and milk: and later, a tone of voice and Mother). Early syntagms typically consist of two terms, so they are binary paratactic structures, not hypotactic ones, and they are synchronic rather than diachronic: young children can fail to see an object as the same object if it disappears then reappears (Piaget, 1954). These early structures resist transformations: the same object from a different angle may not be recognized. Their fit with reality is poor: a round disc with a smile drawn on it will be responded to as if it were Mother.

Perhaps the major intellectual achievement of the growing child is the acquisition of verbal language. Many writers have set up an opposition between language (verbal language) and thought, asking whether one determines the other (cf. Whorf, 1956; Piaget, 1959). In terms of semiotic theory the whole issue shifts its ground. It is clear, as Piaget has shown, that children can think before they have acquired any facility in verbal language. Thought itself, however, must proceed in signs of some kind, since without a system of representations no thought is possible (Peirce, in Greenlee, 1973; Katz, 1974). The acquisition of verbal language must follow the development and deployment of other semiotic systems which together constitute the possibilities of thought in the adult human. In addition to having a place in a developmental sequence, there is another way the acquisition of verbal language illuminates fundamental processes of thought. Verbal language, like the other semiotic codes, is the product of thought, and can only be learnt and used as a result of thought. Cracking the verbal code is a major intellectual concern of infants and children, occupying large amounts of time and energy. It would be surprising if the strategies and processes involved were unrelated to other more general features of thought.

Infants observing the adults around them interpret other codes before the verbal code. They notice pitch differences very early. They can recognize their mother's pitch from that of another female by about 3 weeks old (Mills and Mellhuish, 1974). By a month they can distinguish between different sounds such as 'p' and 'b' (Eimas et al., 1971). That is, they develop the paradigmatic structures that are the basis of the full phonological system or the basic alphabet of sounds of their language. But they do not begin to crack the phonological code as a system till much later: about 12 months old. Jakobson (1968) has made an important study of the process by which the paradigmatic structures of the phonological code are acquired, seemingly in all cultures. To illustrate the process, here is a hypothetical sequence of sounds produced by a child:

Stage I: two sounds, a vowel and a consonant, b, a ('bababa . . .').

Stage II: three sounds, two consonants and a vowel, b, m, a ('baba', 'mamma').

Stage III: four sounds, two consonants, two vowels, b, m, a, oo, ('baba', 'boo boo', 'mamma', 'moo moo').

The first stage consists of an elementary paratactic structure, consisting of two terms maximally opposed. The second stage is a minimal hypotactic structure (figure 9). The third stage applies the same principle to the other category (figure 10). Here we see again that a paratactic structure precedes a hypotactic one. We also see a kind of dialectic between differentiation and integration, because the initial distinction, between vowels and consonants (or flow of sound and obstruction of sound) is modified by the new sounds; 'oo', said with lips close together, is more consonant-like than 'a'; and 'm', said with the lips closed but the sound coming unimpeded through the nose,

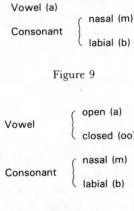

Figure 9

Figure 10

is more vowel-like than 'b'. The second two sounds are transformations of the first. In the full development of the sound system, normally acquired substantially by the age of 3, paradigmatic structures grow by transformations, differentiations followed by integrations, into ever more powerful hypotactic structures, which have an ever closer fit to the target structure, in this case the parents' dialect.

However, verbal language is more than its sounds. Children follow a regular progression in the kinds of utterances they can produce. The first stage (lasting until about 18 months) consists of one-word statements, supplemented by pointing or intonation. These are paratactic synchronic syntagms. The next stage consists of two-word utterances: diachronic paratactic syntagms. It takes about six months to go on to the next stage, three word utterances, which are hypotactic structures, which have the form shown in figure 11. However, it is important to insist that a very young child is capable of grasping

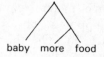

baby   more   food

Figure 11

hypotactic structures. For instance, at the two-word stage, children seem unable to produce hypotactic syntagmatic structures such as full sentences, but at a lower level of structure such as separate words, they are capable of hypotactic structures. This is true in the sound system because a word is a hypotactic syntagmatic structure of sounds: e.g. 'Mama' is as shown in figure 12.

M   a   m   a

Figure 12

Children's syntactic range increases rapidly to stabilize at an average of about four and a half words by the age of 4. By 5 years old most children have acquired the basic rules that generate the basic sentence types of the language. What they cannot easily perform is syntagmatic transformation. For instance, children before the age of 5 cannot interpret passives correctly, so they are likely to interpret 'the lion was eaten by the boy' as 'the lion ate the boy' (Chomsky, 1969).

We can expect similar difficulties in a young child's interpretation of televisual syntagms. Anecdotal evidence suggests that this is so. One instance reported to us concerned a news programme, which showed a long shot of a reporter standing alone on the steps of parliament house, facing the camera and talking into a hand-held microphone. The camera then zoomed in until the reporter's face filled the screen. A girl aged 5 was watching and asked, 'Who is he talking to?' The girl here seems to be applying a three-term syntagmatic structure, assuming the speech is directed at a specific person. Younger children would not have this problem: their overhearing it is taken for granted. This girl appears to be over-correcting against an earlier type of mistake based on a simpler syntagmatic model; but she fails to follow the conventional meaning of this syntagm ('I the reporter transport you to the scene of the action') because she is not making the conventional transformation of herself into a standard viewer (and of the standard viewer into surrogate witness and participant).

In describing cognitive development, the work of Piaget (1975) has been very influential. Piaget focused on what he called 'schemes', which are syntagmatic structures, which constitute the practical science of the infant, its theory of relations, and hence of the world. Piaget saw a general progression in the kinds of 'schemes' children have. Up till age 2 is the 'sensorimotor' period: the period is defined by the semiotic modes which he presumes are dominant. During this period the infant's scheme passes from synchronic to diachronic, and concepts such as the notion of the object are acquired. The next phase is called 'pre-operational' by Piaget. Again it is defined by the semiotic mode that distinguishes it. It is the power of representational thinking which enables the emergence of complex diachronic structures, since it allows a representation to stand for an original structure which is no longer present. This is also the precondition for a development of modality, because it is now possible to produce a range of deliberately false representations: lies, fantasies, games. This stage coincides with the acquisition of the basic forces of verbal language.

The next stage, 'concrete-operational', begins at about 5 years old. During this stage the child acquires a number of intellectual capacities that are in effect transformational operations, equivalent to such operations as the passive transformation in language. Over this period children rapidly accumulate transformational operations, some later than others. By the start of adolescence (about 12), children are ready to move on to the fourth stage, 'formal operational'. This stage allows more powerful transformations: transformations of transformations, multiple successive transformations, the abstract, hypothetical logical thought that distinguishes the scientist. This 'period' is different from the others in that it is not achieved by all normal persons, even in Western culture (cf. Watson and Johnson-Laird, 1977). It is itself a more abstract, hypothetical construct, a projection of structures and transformational capacities, irrespective of whether people normally reach this stage all or most of the time. As such it becomes normative rather than descriptive, compared to the earlier stages: and as a concept, more open to ideological influence. Piaget's 'formal-operational' man is suspiciously like a top executive in a multinational, offered as a universal human ideal (Piaget and Inhelder, 1956). So we find that in Australia, for instance, upper-class children are more likely to achieve it than others (cf. Connell, 1977). We cannot adopt a straightforward developmental approach to these accounts of conceptual growth, since the early forms are not superseded, but continue on into adult life as functional forms of thought, and some people continue to operate mainly in these earlier forms.

Piaget's major contribution has been to the study of syntagmatic structures in their evolution and transformation, with a less consistent focus on the development of paradigmatic structures. In tracing the development of children's 'ideas' or 'concepts', we need to be clear what we mean by these words. We have seen that infants from a very early stage discriminate using features, and build them into structures such as high/low, dark/light. However, these structures are not usually termed ideas. Vygotsky (1962) distinguished different stages in the development of concepts. An early stage he termed 'complexive' thinking. To illustrate what he meant by a complex we can take an experiment he described. Young children, given the task of forming blocks of different shapes and colours into groups, would group two blocks which had one element in common (e.g. both blue), then add another block with something in common with the second (e.g. both triangles), then another with the same property as the third element (e.g. both red). So the group might be built up as shown in figure 13.

Figure 13

The 'concept' that is produced would look like a heterogeneous group to a thinker at the concept stage. What the complexive thinker is doing is to link the features paratactically, not hypotactically. A concept is a hypotactic structure of features. In complexive thinking each act of judgement is isolated from the preceding acts: the child ignores or forgets that the decisive feature previously was triangularity or whatever, and adds a square on grounds of colour. Similarly, a concept like 'Mum' may consist of a set of features that distinguish a particular woman, qualities she possesses, things she does. It will be a set of typical syntagms, not necessarily ordered. Vygotsky contrasts this with scientific concepts, whose distinguishing feature is to be part of a hypotactic paradigmatic structure. A poodle, for instance, is a class of dog, which is a class of domestic animal. Vygotsky sees 'complexes' emerging spontaneously from below, kinds of ideas which are richly concrete, diverse, and unstable. 'Concepts' come to the child from above, through sources like the education system, and tend to be abstract, fixed and powerful.

Two more theories are useful to our consideration of the development of perception and thought because the basis of one's work is visual, the other social. First, Witkin et al. (1962) distinguished between what he called 'field-dependent' and 'field-independent' perception. A person with field-dependent perception is less able to decompose and rearrange a visual syntagm, to focus on particular elements or re-create new wholes from their parts. That is, such a person tends not to organize the field in such a way as to allow both integration and differentiation (lack of hypotactic structuring), and does not, therefore, have transformational facility. Witkin's later work (Witkin et al., 1977) suggests that adults who are field-dependent have many features of what Piaget called ego-centrism, and they also tend to have dogmatic, authoritarian views.

Bernstein (1971) has developed a similar case about language and perception. He distinguished between object-oriented perception and structure-oriented perception. He correlated these with two major codes of language in English, which he called restricted code and elaborated code, which correspond to L-forms and H-forms of language respectively. Restricted language codes, and object-oriented perception, involve simple, undifferentiated structures (low hypotaxis) and limited transformation. Bernstein found a correlation between this kind of code and a specific kind of family structure – a position-oriented family with fixed roles, a simple hypotactic structure, and with no scope for negotiation of roles. He also found a correlation between this kind of code and working-class speakers. Since middle-class children are socialized into elaborated code language, structure-oriented perception and negotiable role relationships, Bernstein argues they have access to sources of power that are closed to those without them. He compares these codes to forms of linguistic and intellectual capital which the material haves possess and the have-nots do not. So class inequalities are perpetuated and increased – though Bernstein notes the sense of alienation and emotional impoverishment which accompanies the more powerful middle-class codes and modes of perception and thought. (We should note that Bernstein's views have aroused some controversy; for a fuller discussion, see Hodge, 1983.)

As with language, and cognition, so with social structures: the child's growing capacities for perceiving and operating on structures are confronted with complex hypotactic structures of the adult world. Such abstract forms as class consciousness or national consciousness are only possible in terms of these broad hypotactic structures, and the child's consciousness initially cannot contain them. Since the smaller-scale structures are still highly functional – even adults are usually members of family groups – it is likely that these structures, like L-forms of language, survive strongly into adulthood, coexisting with hypotactic structures and related to these in a variety of ways, ranging from complementarity to antagonism. As a start to a consideration of the interaction of developmental theories and the emerging categories of political thinking, we have found the work of Connell (1971) useful. Connell, studying the growth of political consciousness in Australian children, saw a three-stage progression that approximates to Piaget's stages.

Stage I: The stage of dramatic contrast (up to 8). (A binary division, based on differences of wealth.)

Stage II: The stage of concrete realism (8–12). (A simple, more inclusive hypotactic scheme, with three terms: rich, poor, and a middle class.)

Stage III: The stage of true class schemes (12–16). (A fuller sense of gradations of class, and of possible movements within it – including the class alignment of the individual.) Stage III is not acquired by all teenagers.

If Connell is right, it would be premature to look for critical consciousness among the children we are looking at. Only by 12 is this capacity beginning to develop. But in any progression the existence of the early stages is essential for the later ones, and it is in childhood that this crucial progression occurs.

We can summarize some general implications from this brief and partial cross-disciplinary survey:

1. There is a progression in the structures projected by children, from paratactic to hypotactic, from synchronic to diachronic, from small-scale to large-scale, from structures to transformations, with paradigmatic forms developing ahead of syntagmatic.

2. In this progression nothing is superseded: later stages are

logically dependent on earlier ones and coexist with them.

3. Later stages cope with structures of a scale and complexity beyond those of earlier stages. They are indispensable for effective action in an adult world.

4. Earlier stages survive because they are functional. They are the site of pleasure and the play of emotional energy. If later stages are essential for power, earlier stages are essential for desire.

5. Up till the age of 5 the structures of language and thought systematically lack major dimensions of the adult's. This will affect the structures of reality children can construct or interpret.

6. Only after about age 12 are the powerful transformational possibilities available that allow for critical, abstract consciousness: though not available to everyone.

Turning now to television and children, we can see some important unanswered questions. How does the content of television interact with children's growing powers? How do they assimilate its forms and contents into their general development? How do earlier stages map on to later stages? What is a 'healthy' progression? How does this process fit into the overall process of ideological formation and socialization?

Television and mental growth

We have already made a case for viewing paradigms as the most basic of all structures, the precondition for all others. One research tradition that has developed methods of establishing paradigmatic structures operating in mental life stems from the work of George Kelly (1955) and Banister and Fransella (1971). We adapted their methods of Personal Construct Theory, as it has come to be called, in order to investigate the form and contents of paradigmatic structures as they are displayed in the attempt to make sense of the world of television and the child's everyday world. For this phase of our study we used a small sample – 17 children, aged between 6 and 12, described by their teachers as of average ability. Eight of these children were retested 3 months later, to see whether constructs remained stable over that time. We found that in general they did. In order to check the generality of our conclusions and differences between children of different social class, we then analysed two kinds of material from a sample of 400 children, from two different schools, one in a working-class district, the other in a prestigious middle-class suburb. We collected both drawings and essays from the two schools, plus taped interviews with a total of 160 children.

Kelly was interested in what he called *constructs*, that is, the operative categories used by people to organize their social experience. According to Kelly, most people use a limited number of constructs, although they may use a larger number of words to describe them. He saw development of construct structures along the same lines we outlined in a previous section: greater scope of constructs, more coherent hypotactic organization and greater transformational facility with age. His method for getting at these constructs was what he called *triadic elicitation*. Working with adults, he would get them to name 22 individuals, from different categories of relationship, such as father, or teacher. He would then take three individuals from the list, and ask the subject to devise a way of grouping them so that two would go together, and one would be excluded. The criteria for including the two, and excluding the one, would provide data for working out the features that people *actually* use in conceptually organizing their society. This approach has been used to answer other questions; for instance, Nash (1973) employed the method to determine the categories teachers used in their judgements of their pupils.

In our adaptation of this method we asked children to name people they knew who were important to them, then to select four people for the triadic task, with no restrictions on who was chosen. They did the same with characters from television, choosing five for the experiment. The experimenter then wrote the names on separate pieces of card, plus the child's own name, so that the children had ten cards before them, to use in forming groups. We were concerned that the children should have a task they could understand and perform competently: even the 6-year-olds seemed to have no difficulty with this arrangement.

Taking the characters from real life the children chose as significant, we can see one surprising difference in the older children. They tended to mention members of the family more, not less, often than the younger children (table 1). This suggests that these older children are

Table 1 *Significant others by age* (percentages)

Age (years)	Family	Pets	Friends	Others
6–8	46	13	31	9
9–12	55	14	23	8

still using their family as the significant others, in spite of the increasing importance of their peers in other respects. The category of other (usually a teacher) does not increase at all. The picture is compatible with a period of consolidation during this age, with children not attempting to make new areas of social experience meaningful.

There were a number of significant changes in the kinds of construct structures children had at different ages. Older children had a larger range of features (table 2; the criteria used to make distinctions among

Table 2   *Features of self by age*

Age	Total features	Self features
6–8	4.5	2
9–12	7.25	3

triads). The younger children tended to use the same features repeatedly to organize different groupings, and the older children used a greater number of less frequent constructs. Five of the triads included the self, and on average, the younger children used two constructs, while the older children used three constructs to differentiate self from others. So the concept of the self (and, presumably, other significant individuals) seems less richly specified for the younger children.

Along with this went a tendency to use a limited range of primary constructs. The four categories male/female, young/old, human/ animal and real/unreal accounted for 61 per cent of the younger children's constructs, as against 39 per cent of the older one's constructs (table 3). It is unlikely that the older children have forgotten

Table 3   *Primary constructs by age* (percentages)

Age (years)	Primary constructs	Others
6–8	61	39
9–12	39	61

these construct primes. More probably they have elaborated them, and are now able to operate with more flexible and differentiated hypotactic structures.

There is one interesting type of construct present for all ages of children. Some constructs are oriented to paradigmatic structures. They treat the elements to be grouped as needing to be assigned to an abstract paradigmatic schema (for example 'both boys', 'both animals'). Other constructs organize syntagmatic relationships within the group, looking for what goes with what in the real world (for example 'both live together', 'play together'). We will call the first kind paradigmatic constructs, and the second, syntagmatic constructs. Syntagmatic constructs are less abstract than paradigmatic ones, so they seemed a lower form of thought for many thinkers such as Bernstein (1971), who saw concrete thinking to be part of a cognitively inferior restricted code. However, we have suggested that developmentally speaking they are more, not less difficult. Table 4 shows the balance from our triadic groups.

Table 4   Paradigmatic vs. syntagmatic construct by age (percentages)

Age (years)	Paradigmatic	Syntagmatic
6–8	73	27
9–12	69	31

Although there was not a significant increase in the number of syntagmatic constructs, there was no sign of a decrease over the age group. If we add to this the slightly greater tendency to include members of the family among older children (see table 1), we can see signs of an important shift of interest from classification (paradigmatic) to interaction (syntagmatic) schemata, which can also be seen in the larger sample of the essays.

In order to see what syntagmatic forms children use at different ages in order to describe their experience of television, we asked 157 children, aged from 8 to 12, to write an essay entitled 'If I could be on television I would be . . .'. Children younger than 9, we felt, had insufficient mastery of writing for analysis to show anything other than their difficulties with writing. First we considered their use of basic syntagmatic forms, non-transactive, transactive and relational (see Kress and Hodge, 1979). Non-transactive forms have a surface form of a subject and a verb, but no object (for example 'he stands'). As a syntagmatic form they are less differentiated, a hypotactically less developed form than transactives, which have a subject plus verb plus object (for example, 'he bites apples'). The third type, relational, links things with other classes of things, ('X is a Y') or things with attributes ('X is red, blue', etc.). The figures for the extreme age groups are as shown in table 5. The proportion of non-transactives remains fairly constant and high – another reminder that more primitive forms

Table 5   *Types of syntagmatic construct by age* (percentages)

	8–9-year-old	12-year-old
Non-transactive	67	65
Transactive	11	23
Relational	22	12

do not simply disappear with age. A typical essay characterized by non-transactive forms is the following, which began:

> If I could be a television star I would be the girl with curly hair on Johnny Young. I would like to *sing* and *dance* with other people. It would change my life by [= because] I would be *practising* all the time. I'd where jassey closes [= clothes]. (Girl, aged 8.)

Where non-transactives predominate, as here, the subject and the action form isolated units, coexisting with other events and objects, not interacting with them, not integrated with them in a chain of causes and effects.

Of the other two categories of syntagmatic form, there seems to be an increase in transactives with age, and a decrease in relationals. Relationals show the exercise of judgement, developing paradigmatic facility, linking nouns to other nouns, or nouns and adjectives. A typical relational-dominated essay began:

> If I could be on television I'd be Dorothy on the Wizard of Oz her *real* name is Judy Garland. I'd like to be her because she does *scary* parts and *beautiful* parts and most of all she is *pretty*. She wears a *blue* dress with a *white* apron, she has *brown curly* hair in *pigtails* with *blue* ribbons, and *brown* eyes. (Girl, aged 8.)

Unlike the previous child, this girl is concerned to itemize and classify and describe. The activity that predominates, in the essay, is not her imagined actions, but her present acts of perception and judgement. This activity goes along with the concern with paradigmatic development at this early stage. However, the older children are developing more complex, hypotactic paradigmatic structures. One indication of hypotactic structures is a mention of two-subclasses of a larger category: e.g. 'I have met nearly all of the pop groups, members, and leaders' (boy, aged 12). Here pop groups are seen as consisting of two classes, members and leaders, which is a hypotactic structure. Another indication of hypotactic paradigmatic structures is the presence of classifier-adjectives (see Kress and Hodge, 1979). An example is:

I'd like my very own studio with everything I'd need from apples to zebras. I'd have a special *dressing* room and *costume* room and a kitchen for my special needs. (Boy, aged 12.)

'Dressing' and 'costume' classify two different categories of room, which are part of the hypotactically organized world of this young would-be superstar. Clearly this is a higher level of paradigmatic activity, and the older children do it more frequently, as we can see from table 6. However, it is in transformational facility that children

Table 6   *Hypotactic structures by age*

Age (years)	Percentage >2 hypotactic paradigmatic features
8–9	30
12	65

show most development over this time. One measure of this is use of passives, again taking >2 as an indication of the presence of this form. No children aged 8–9 used >2 passives. By aged 12, 15 per cent of the children did. These children would be considering what could be done to them in their role as stars, as well as what they would do. It is interesting that in this fantasy task at least, no younger children, and only a small proportion of older children, took up this option. They are still largely egocentric.

Another indicator of transformational facility is rank-shifting (Halliday, 1976). Rank-shifts turn basic sentence forms into

Table 7   *Rank shifts by use* (percentages)

Age (years)	>2 Passives	>2 Rank-shifts
8–9	0	4
12	12	58

subordinate clauses, phrases, or words. Rank-shifting has the effect of assimilating a number of individual sentences into a single syntagmatic frame. It is an indicator of hypotactic syntagmatic forms, as well as of transformational facility, marking a new development in the potential scope of syntagms. Table 7 shows the comparison between younger and older children. To illustrate the kind of syntagmatic structure that rank-shifting enables, consider the two extracts that follow:

If I could be on television I would be Godzilla. I like to fight and help the people on board the Galico. I would like to be Godzilla because I can breathe fire. (Boy, aged 8.)

If I could be on television I would be bionic woman because she can run fast and anything to do with sport she can do. The bionic woman helps the police in getting the bad people and helping the good. (Girl, aged 12.)

The younger boy integrates two clauses – he fights, and he helps the people on the Galico – but these are presented as two otherwise unrelated things he likes doing. The older girl represents a more complex hypotactic relationship, between the bionic woman helping the police, combining to get the bad people, and helping further people who are good. Although the paradigmatic categories of this girl are simple ('bad' and 'good'), the syntagmatic relationships she is attempting to handle are complex in their scope. A typical non-rank-shifted structure with a similar pro-social content is the following by an 8-year-old girl:

I would like to be Wonder Woman on channel 9. I like Wonder Woman because she is strong and helps people.

In this girl's thinking, the separate thoughts are contained in separate sentences that are on the same level, and she joins them together. The older girl is perceiving stronger relations between different thoughts, and integrating them into a larger scheme.

Another set of data supports a developmental schema of this kind. Ratings surveys and studies of children's programme preferences in Australia (cf. Edgar and Callus, 1979) show a consistent increase in the syntagmatic scope of the shows that children most prefer. Very short forms (cartoons, magazines) decline in prominence by the age of about 10, when children begin to show increasing preference for adult programmes – feature films, which last 2 or 3 hours, or series (like *Dallas* or *Sons and Daughters*) which weave different plots over episode after episode. Shows like this, which are especially criticized by lobby groups as unsuitable for children, often have a moral ambiguity which may generate more complex paradigmatic structures for children, especially young adolescents (cf. McLeod and Chafee in Wartella, 1979; and Palmer, 1980). A study of one such 'adult' (and a much-criticized) show in Australia, *Prisoner*, showed that it was much richer transformationally, as measured by number of cuts per minute, than the programmes made specifically for children and given a 'C' certificate (see Fisher, 1982).

It is ironic that it is precisely the kind of programming that children have the greatest cognitive need for, as they are approaching adolescence, that is most commonly subjected to criticism by lobbyists: cartoons and magazine programmes (studded with cartoons) for younger children, and 'adult' prime-time series for older ones. The persistent popularity of such programme types with children, we would suggest, is a healthy sign, and not a danger signal, though that does not mean we believe that there could be no better programmes for children, or adults for that matter.

From different kinds of data a consistent picture emerges of how children's abilities develop, a picture which confirms the general account we sketched in the previous section. What we have shown is that these developing powers operate on the world of television as well as on other aspects of the child's experience. Television is not time-out from thinking, as so many fear: it provides grist for the mills of thought, innumerable opportunities for normal cognitive growth. Without television, of course, children's minds would be exercised on other things, but that does not alter the fact that today's children use television to think with, that thinking being limited by, and adapted to, their general powers at each stage. Younger children have paradigmatic facility, they comment and judge freely, but their paradigmatic structures tend to be loosely organized, paratactic. Similarly, they tend to work with small-scale syntagms paratactically organized, their units of significance strung together like beads.

Their most marked difference from older children, however, is their lack of transformational facility. Transformations are the precondition for complex syntagmatic and paradigmatic structures, for abstraction, extrapolation, criticism, and intervention, or for recognition and grasp of these operations. From 9 to 12 is a crucial stage for these powers to develop. The type of television programming that would seem most conducive to such development would have the editing techniques pejoratively labelled 'hype' by Anderson et al. (1977), as exemplified by video-clips, currently so popular among the young (see Fiske et al., 1984) or by films such as the Star Wars trilogy, whose virtuosity appeals to young as well as old. However, for transformations to become power for the viewer there must also be time and scope for them to develop – opportunities in school or at home for various operations to be tried out. As we will suggest in chapters 5 and 6, these opportunities are not always provided as richly as they might be, especially in schools.

Gender and constructions of reality

The media's construction of reality is skewed in a number of specific ways, amongst which the dimensions of gender and class are particularly obvious. What we need to know is how this skewed world is mediated by the constructs of different kinds of child viewers, boys and girls, middle-class and working-class. We will begin with gender, because it is a more overt category. Boys and girls are taught early to know what sex they are, and gender is easy to count in the media world. The male:female ratio on *Fangface* is approximately 4:1, a ratio that is typical enough of television and the media generally (cf. Durkin, 1985). The ratio in the populace is a convenient 1:1, so we have a ready touchstone of 'reality', a reality which is well known even by children. But what do children of different sexes do with these competing visions of reality?

In the triadic experiments, boys and girls tended to adopt people of the same sex as significant others in their lives (excluding animals). The breakdown is as shown in table 8. There is almost an exact

Table 8   *Interviews: Sex of significant others by sex of respondent* (percentages)

Sex	Male figures	Female figures
Boys	63	37
Girls	36	64

symmetry here, with boys using about twice as many males as females, and girls vice-versa. It becomes interesting to ask, then, how this symmetrical pattern of preferences works with significant others from the sex-biased world of television. From the triadic group we got the breakdown shown in table 9. Assuming a sex ratio of about 4:1 on television we see that boys magnify this ratio by 8, to 32:1, and girls resist it, by halving it to 2:1. The girls' world of significant television characters is skewed, to much the same degree as their world of significant others in their real world, but with males now in the

Table 9   *Interviews: Sex of significant TV characters by sex of respondent* (percentages)

Sex	Male figures	Female figures
Boys	97	3
Girls	64	36

majority. For boys, skew multiplies skew to leave the impression of a world even more emptied of females than television studios would dare to present at their most sexist. The same tendency of boys to magnify and girls to resist media gender bias can be seen in the larger samples. In the drawings the breakdown is as follows: boys 12.7:1, girls 1.7:1.

Table 10   *Drawings: Sex of significant TV characters by sex* (percentages)

Sex	Male figures	Female figures	Indeterminate
Boys	88	7	4
Girls	58	34	8

In the essays the breakdown again illustrates the same tendency: boys, 14.5:1; girls (massively in the opposite direction) 1:4.4. Here the nature of the task, describing a character they would like to be, accounts for the stronger allegiance to sex roles by both girls and boys (table 11). We can see from these figures one effect of the massive gender bias in television and other media as it interacts with other ideological structures. Children do not simply reflect the bias. It seems rather to establish a baseline which some children resist and others exaggerate. The triadic task brings out one important consequence of this bias. It introduces a distortion in the significant characters that

Table 11   *Essays: Sex of significant TV characters by sex* (percentages)

Sex	Male figures	Female figures	Indeterminate
Boys	87	6	7
Girls	17	75	8

people use to *think with*, to organize their conception of the world. Girls suffer some deprivation from this, a degree of symbolic reduction, or reduced significance, in spite of the counter-bias they employ to resist. However, for girls the biases of the two worlds, television and reality, tend to cancel each other out, giving them a more gender-balanced world picture. From this it would seem that the gender bias of television does not drastically diminish the significance of being female, for girls; rather, it enhances the importance of being male, for boys. In one sense it is the boys who are deprived: deprived of females among their significant others. Their total world view reflected in all the figures is so distorted that it is more than 80 per cent male.

How can they understand females, if only 20 per cent of their constructs are deployed on women? In this analysis, television contributes more to girls' understanding of males than it does to boys' of females. If the gender imbalance on television signifies male power, its necessary price is male ignorance of the female other. This would mean male weakness, if knowledge is power. But knowledge is not always the basis of power, and power exercised without knowledge and understanding is not always nullified: more often, it is simply expressed more crudely and brutally, without recognition of the independent capacity for thought and feeling of the non-powerful. We suggest that the incredible bias of the boys must, at these ages, contribute to a chauvinistic view of girls and women.

Social class and structures of thought

Gender bias on television seems to be concerned with the content rather than forms of thought. We found no marked differences between boys and girls in the development of various cognitive structures and powers. With class, however, there were signs of differences in both forms and content. In the essays, we compared the powers of language for the two samples (table 12). The difference in the basic syntagmatic

Table 12

	Working class (%)	Upper class (%)
Basic forms		
Non-transactives	65	71
Transactives	22	11
Relational	14	17
≥2 Hypotactic paradigms	44	69
Transforms		
≥2 passives	2	11
≥2 rank-shift	23	47

forms is not large. We note a higher proportion of transactives among the working-class sample, which signals a stronger sense of interrelationships in the physical world, a better grasp of concrete reality, but none of these differences is marked. The development of hypotactic paradigmatic structures, however, is much less great among the working-class children. These children show a lack of complexity and coherence in their paradigmatic structures. This should lead to less complex and nuanced judgements, more black-and-white thinking. The same picture emerges with transformations. They use passives less often. They use rank-shifts much less often. They are likely, therefore, to show more of what Witkin called field-dependent thinking, or what Bernstein called object-oriented perception and a restricted language code.

Normally both essays and drawings had a central figure – in the essays, the person they would like to be; in the drawings, something from television. We attempted to classify the main figure in each case in terms of status, as high, medium, and low: and in terms of sex (male, female, and indeterminate). We also attempted to classify actions described or depicted as pro-social, anti-social, or neutral. The results are summarized in table 13. With the essays the subject was

Table 13

Feature	Working class		Upper class	
	Essay (%)	Drawings (%)	Essay (%)	Drawings (%)
Status of ideal				
high	11	8	20	16
medium	34	40	54	48
low	55	52	26	36
Sex of subject				
male	52	74	57	72
female	43	22	30	20
ambiguous	5	5	13	8
Quality of action				
pro-social	44	9	27	2
anti-social	6	29	7	39
neutral	43	62	49	59

an ideal, whereas with the drawings it was usually a favourite character, and this might have contributed to the differences between the two media. However, in both media the working-class children systematically preferred low-status characters. The upper-class children chose high-status people more often, but their preferred category was middle, not high. The working-class children's preferences polarize, whereas the upper class children bunched in the middle.

With sex the drawings show the same bias towards male characters for both working-class and upper-class children. The essays show a different pattern, especially with the working-class children, who were almost equally divided between male and female. Behind these figures is a very strong tendency for boys to choose male figures (90 per cent) and for girls to choose female figures (98 per cent). Among the upper-class girls there was a much greater tendency to aspire to be a figure of the opposite sex. Although no boys wished to be a female, 35 per cent of the girls opted to be a male character. Again we see a greater tendency to polarize among the working-class children, which leads them to identify more strongly with the social categories of class and gender that have been assigned to them. This is consistent with Bernstein's (1971) views, that working-class children are socialized into relatively fixed, non-negotiable roles. It gives them both a potentially strong sense of class consciousness and a more rigid attitude to sex roles. It seems more plausible to suggest that this cultural feature interacts with television to make them less able to construct alternative possibilities from it, rather than to see television as the cause.

A final aspect to look at briefly, concerns the valency of the actions depicted or described. The working-class children in their essays much more frequently mentioned pro-social reasons for their choice of a character, 44 per cent as against 27 per cent for the upper-class children. In the essays (written for teacher consumption) there was only a low level of anti-social motive expressed by both groups, but in the pictures (which the children gave a commentary on) there was far more anti-social or violent action. Again, it was the working-class children who expressed less of this (29 per cent as against 39 per cent of upper-class children). Drawing is a 'low' code compared to writing, so it is unsurprising to find the more subversive meanings represented more strongly in that code. However, in both codes the working-class children represent themselves as more law-abiding and more virtuous, and it is the upper-class children who are more likely to express subversive judgements.

One response to this might be to take it at its face value, and argue that these working-class children support a pro-social viewpoint, that they are more 'moral' in the judgements that they make on television – a comforting conclusion for those who worry about the effects of heavy television viewing, especially on children from the lower classes. Another possibility, however, is that both these codes are seen by these children as alien, controlled by the values of school, so they are more inhibited in saying what they think than upper-class children, more anxious to provide the teacher with the views they believe will be approved. Even if the difference only concerns the meanings they can produce in such circumstances, however, and not necessarily the thoughts they think, such a difference is still important, and has important consequences for how far their individual thoughts can become socially effective.

Conclusion

A developmental perspective does not come up with a simple value-judgement on whether television is good or bad for children. Some extreme positions emerge as untenable. Television is not simply a 'plug-in drug', as Winn feared. It is a staple object of thought for children, on which they display and exercise their growing capacities of mind to a degree that their parents and teachers appear to barely suspect. These capacities unfold according to their own logic; syntagmatic and paradigmatic structures developing in scope and complexity, and transformational facility increasing. Children in general prefer programme types that are the best available for their cognitive development: cartoons for younger children, prime-time serials for older ones, in spite of often-expressed disapproval by parents and educators.

However, television does not automatically produce these qualities of mind, any more than a pencil and paper irresistibly makes people write. The progression we have sketched out has its inner logic, but it is not inevitable; nor are its earlier stages superseded or intrinsically less valuable. Children are socialized into certain ways of thinking, through institutions such as the family and education. Working-class children are socialized into different ways of thinking about TV as about other things; or more precisely, there are certain powerful and highly valued ways of thinking into which they are not so strongly socialized as are children of high socioeconomic status. In so far as these ways of thinking are powerful and desirable, we have here what can be called 'cognitive deprivation', an exclusion from 'cultural capital'. The major difference that we could detect concerns transformational facility. The relative lack of transformational facility could be seen as central to what Marcuse called a 'one-dimensional mind'. However, the more paratactic, transformationally simpler modes of thought that working-class children deployed have their own strengths and functions. These modes of thought produce simpler, more fixed and polarized structures. They tend to represent issues in terms of black and white, not in shifting shades of grey. This may lead to more sexist thinking, in a gendered social group; but it may also lead to effective resistance to shades of grey, so that complex structures of mystification are less easy to impose. Whatever judgement we make on these modes of thought, the role and responsibility of television in all this is ambiguous. It is not television (or any of the other media) which thinks, but people who think; and they do so largely as a result of how and what they see and believe and want already. Television programmes constrain or enable some kinds of thinking, and specific programmes can be judged as better or worse for these purposes, but to see television as an autonomous cause of a mode of thought (or its suppression) is, on the basis of our findings, seriously in error.

Neither is television just a set of barbells for the growing mind to exercise itself on. It has an ideological content, presenting a version of the world that is sytematically and sometimes drastically skewed. Something like Gerbner's 'symbolic annihilation' does occur to devastating effect, so certain classes of person almost disappear, while others loom much larger than they do in ordinary social life. But this effect does not seem to work evenly or consistently. Strategies of resistance are deployed by those who are 'annihilated'. It may be possible for a disadvantaged group to put their invisibility to tactical use; or conversely, there can be disadvantages (such as under-estimating the oppressed) for a dominant group which is consistently presented with a world overly made in their own image. Though there are possible strategies of resistance, and complications do arise when an ideological form is refracted through a social formation constituted by inequality and struggle, that is not to say that the distortions are ever benign or can be so offset that they have no effect. It means that ideological effects cannot simply be read off from ideological forms analysed in isolation from the cognitive and social processes that constitute them. Essential to understanding the dynamic nature of those processes is a developmental perspective, one that recognizes that people are not born preformed into an ideological role, but have their developing potentialities shaped and formed and constrained in specific ways by experiences and institutions such as television.

Chapter 4

'God didn't make Yogi Bear'
The modality of children's television

The fantasy-effect – problem or solution?

The relation of fantasy to reality in children's television is a highly emotive and controversial topic. What is that relationship, and what ought it to be? Researchers, teachers, parents and children disagree widely in the answers they give, but all display a similar concern. We saw that Winn (1977) labelled television the 'plug-in drug', claiming that television is a kind of narcotic which seduces children into an unreal world. Her concerns are shared by many people who made submissions to an enquiry into children and television commissioned by an Australian Senate Committee, in 1978:

> 5.64 The committee received many complaints, stemming mainly from the observations and experiences of teachers and parents, that television is adversely affecting the learning behaviour of children.
>
> 5.65 It was claimed that the escapist material mainly watched by children is stifling children's imaginations and the development of their creative instincts. The committee was given numerous examples of how television characters and plots permeate through the daily lives of children. Their school compositions are based on television plots, their play is a re-enactment of television action scenes and their conversation centres on the programmes they watch.

Interestingly, people today tend to think that the issue is one peculiarly important to our society, but it is not: educators and moralists have worried for thousands of years about the effects of fantasy on children. Here, to give a broader perspective on these issues, is the classic statement by Plato in his famous work *The Republic*, explaining why (in his fantasy republic) he will ban the works of Homer and Hesiod, greatest of the early Greek poets, for telling stories which are 'false' and 'untrue' to impressionable children.

> If by any means we can make them [future guardians of the state] believe that no one has ever had a quarrel with a fellow citizen and it is a sin to have one, that is the sort of thing our old men and women should tell children from the first; and as they grow older, we must make the poets write for them in the same strain. Stories like that of Hera being bound by her son, or of Hephaestus flung from heaven by his father for taking his mother's part when she was beaten, and all those battles of the gods in Homer, must not be admitted into our state, whether they be allegorical or not. A child cannot distinguish the allegorical sense from the literal, and the ideas he takes in at that age are likely to become indelibly fixed; hence the great importance of seeing that the first stories he hears shall be designed to produce the best possible effect on his character.

Plato lived over 2000 years before television was invented, yet the concerns he articulated have a very familiar ring. 'Reality' and 'truth' have become counters in a battle for control over minds and behaviour. 'Reality' in this view is what children *ought* to think, now how things are, because they will act on the basis of what they believe things to be. Plato spells out the belief of Winn and the Senate inquiry, that children are passive and helpless, unable to tell truth from fiction, but he is frank in simply trying to exploit that helplessness – for the worthiest motives, of course. That exploitation raises wider problems, however, for as Plato himself recognized, if the guardians have such power, who is to guard the guardians? We realize, therefore, that the problem of reality and its definition has within it a continuing political dimension, which underlies both Plato's and the Senate Committee's position.

Interestingly, Plato also links the problem of unreality to another controversial topic, violence. It is worth noticing a contradiction in his argument here, because it runs through so many of the modern studies as well: he disapproves of violence in fictional works not because it does not really happen but because it does. Furthermore, the depiction of violence has dangerous effects not because the audience sees it as fiction, but for precisely the opposite reason, because they cannot tell the difference between fact and fiction. In this view fictionality, if the audience is aware of it, diminishes the effects of violent content. In that respect fictionality (or fantasy) and violent content, far from being faults which exacerbate each other, would seem to cancel each other out, if the key condition is met: that the audience is aware of the fiction.

Contemporary research confirms this view. Studies in the 1960s and 1970s were especially concerned with the effects of television violence (see Comstock et al., 1978, for a comprehensive review). Himmelweit et al. (1958) found that the more real a television stimulus is perceived to be, the greater the involvement and fright it engenders. McLeod et al. (1972) found that perceived reality was clearly related to higher levels of subsequent aggression after violence viewing. Hawkins (1977) reviewed the history of such viewing studies, and concluded that they repeatedly indicate that the child's perception of television reality is a mediator of all 'behavioural effects' in responses to television.

These findings should come as no surprise. Common sense would say that children will not be so strongly affected by what they do not believe in, though this common-sense view has not found favour amongst the many industrious researchers who have counted up 'violent incidents' on television without any account of whether the violence is realistic or not. As a result of these horrific figures, cartoon violence, in which characters like Tom and Jerry suffer violent death and deformity at an alarming rate per programme, has become a favourite target of lobbyists on children's television.

However, some researchers make rather different claims about the effects of the perceived reality of television content on how people will respond. Aristotle talked of the effect of the horrific incidents in Greek tragedy as a 'catharsis', a purification or purging of emotions like pity and fear. Modern researchers talk of the 'catharsis theory' of media violence, the theory that watching media violence can reduce aggression, not increase it. The so-called catharsis theory, and its major proponent, Feshbach (1961), typically get unsympathetic treatment from the dominant tradition (see, for example, Eysenck and Nias, 1978). It is easy to understand why. The catharsis theory complicates a neat account of cause-and-effect linking violent television content to violence by viewers in real life. The catharsis theory proposed that sometimes exactly the opposite happens. The crucial factor turned out to be what Feshbach described as the perceived reality of the content, or its modality, to use the linguistic term.

A number of researchers have designed experiments that explore this theory (see especially Feshbach, 1976; Noble, 1970, 1973). In one important experiment Feshbach (1976) made up a film-clip which combined news footage plus scenes from a drama, both concerned

with campus violence. One group of subjects were told that the clip
was all news material (i.e. it was real). Another group were told that
it was all drama (i.e. non-real). A third group, the control group,
were not shown the film at all. All three groups were then put in one
of the typical test situations for this class of experiment: all subjects
observed a person whom they believed they were able to hurt by
pressing a 'hurt' button which caused painful noise. The tendency
to be aggressive was measured by the intensity and duration of their
pressing on the hurt button. What Feshbach found was that the group
who believed the film clip was totally real had aggression scores twice
as high as those who believed it was drama, with the control group
midway between. All these differences were statistically significant.
In this experiment Feshbach demonstrated that television violence
does increase the tendency to be aggressive, just as the majority of
researchers think – but only if the violence is believed to be real. When
it is believed to be unreal, even when this is indicated only verbally,
this reduces aggression. The fantasy effect can, it seems, actually
reverse the effect of a specific media content.

The work of Feshbach and Noble points clearly to the need for
a comprehensive theory of modality, a theory which explains how
we judge whether something is or is not actually real. On what
basis do people make judgements about the reality of television?
How does that capacity develop? How does it vary in different
categories of viewer? And how do judgements about reality
interact with other aspects of responses to television and the
world?

It is obvious that this capacity takes time to develop, so there will
be a period when children can be expected to make different modality
judgements from adults, and be affected differently by the same
content. Research supports this view (see, for example, Morrison and
Gardner, 1978; Hawkins, 1977; Noble, 1975). However, though
young children may have difficulty making modality judgements, that
is not to say that adults make them with effortless certainty; they may,
on occasion, not even want to. Coleridge, the Romantic poet and
literary theorist, talked of the 'willing suspension of disbelief' as
essential to the proper response to literary works. That is, the belief
that a work is literary leads you to cancel out your dominant modality
system – in the interests of a higher level of response, not a lower one.
The dramatist Brecht (1964), in contrast, criticized the illusionism
of conventional theatre, because it ensnared its adult audiences. His
own theatre tried to distance his audience by means of what he called
the 'alienation effect', which drew attention to the processes by which

illusions were created, and thereby raised the audience's level of consciousness and powers of critical thought.

So reality is not an absolute, a once-for-all fact about a medium like television. It always involves processes of discrimination and judgement, operating on all classes of message on all media: television, film, radio, speech and writing. It is these continuous processes of discrimination and judgement which enable us to distinguish between different kinds of programme and even between different moments of a single programme.

The many markers of modality

In order to illuminate this set of issues from a semiotic perspective we must add 'modality' to our lengthening list of terms. 'Modality' concerns the reality attributed to a message. The term comes from linguistics, and modality has been studied more extensively in verbal language than in any other semiotic medium (cf. Halliday, 1976; Kress and Hodge, 1979) so we will illustrate our account initially from speech. In a language such as English there are a number of words whose function is to convey modality – that is, to indicate degrees of certainty of a sentence. If we start with a simple sentence, like 'It's a monster', we have a statement that seems to claim total certainty. Thus we can say it has a strong modality. We can weaken that modality status by adding modal auxiliaries, like 'may', 'might', etc.: 'It may be a monster.' We can further weaken the claim by adding a modal adverb like 'possibly' or 'perhaps': 'It may possibly be a monster.' Or we could try to strengthen it: 'It's absolutely certainly a monster.'

If we confine ourselves to these specialized modality markers in verbal language, it may seem to be a straightforward matter. However, there are a number of other things to say about how modality judgements work.

1. Modality is intrinsically related to negation

The close relation between negation and modality can be seen if we look at a statement like 'It may possibly be a monster.' This is only just short of saying 'It's not a monster.' Weak modality taken to the limit is negative modality. Doubt is a kind of negation. So is fantasy; and though the degree of uncertainty is a continuum, there is a modality flip-over effect whereby the weight of modalities of uncertainty suddenly switch over from overall positive to overall negative. So far from being surprised at the 'catharsis effect', we should have expected it. Fantasy is weak modality: it is a kind of negative. To call something 'fantastic' is to recognize that it is probably untrue, that the world really is not like that.

2. Underlying every modalized statement is an unmodalized positive

This principle counteracts the force of the first principle. We can see it at its clearest with negatives. If someone says 'There isn't a monster in that room', in order to interpret that statement we have to imagine the possibility of there being a monster in the room, and then negate that thought. Yet the positive possibility hangs over the negative like an after-image, as the key to its interpretation. Practically speaking, the use of a negative is a well-known way of sowing doubts. The statement 'Of course you're not going to fail', draws attention to the possibility of failure, which may increase the level of anxiety sufficiently to cause failure. In the same way as a negative, a statement with weak modality conveys its opposite at some level. So one can expect every fantasy image to contain a contradiction: it will have both a negative, at one level, and, at a deeper level, a positive. We can thus begin to see why effects of strongly modalized texts can be such complex things.

3. All signifiers of the relation between message and reality can become markers of modality

In addition to the explicit markers of modality that we have mentioned, other parts of speech can have a modal function. For instance, to add 'I think, typically weakens modality: 'I think it's a monster.' Even 'I know it's a monster' is weaker than the straightforward statement: 'It's a monster.' Paradoxically, the accumulation of indicators of certainty still weakens the modality of a statement: 'I know absolutely and for sure that it's definitely a monster' suggests an uneasy assertiveness, striving to counteract an underlying doubt. A general rule of modality judgements is that anything which indicates distance, in space or time, between the speaker and the reality invoked, or between speaker and message, can weaken its modality. So another way modality is carried is though tense: 'I used to be afraid of monsters' half implies that that is no longer the case. A more general principle, which subsumes that one, is that the awareness of any transformational process acting between speaker and reality or speaker

and message can weaken its modality. Distance is one transformation.
So is the process of judgement. So is negation.

4. Modality is multi-semiotic

Human communication is typically multi-semiotic, deploying a variety
of codes, so that mesages in one channel can be modalized in another.
Laughter is an important indicator of modality in speech. The
statement 'It's a monster' is modally weakened by laughter,
strengthened by a scream. Non-verbal and paralingual cues such as
a shrug of the shoulders or tone of voice also affect modality, which
is why the sound track of a film can subtly affect the modality of the
image.

5. Modal judgements draw on independent knowledge of reality

People do not rely solely on modality markers in messages. They
continuously compare messages with reality itself, or more exactly,
with what they believe about reality. If a cuddly little dog came into
a room, and someone called out, 'It's a monster', others might
conclude that this was just a joke; or they might think the person was
mad; or that the person knew something that they did not. This
possibility leads on to a final proposition about modality, which, so
far as children are concerned, is perhaps the most important.

6. Modality is not a fixed property of a message:
it is a subjective, variable, relative and negotiable judgement

The modality of a statement is not its actual relation to reality, its
truth, falsity or whatever: it is a product of the judgement about that
relationship which the speaker makes, wants or enables the hearer
to make, and the judgement that hearers do actually make by drawing
on their selective reading of the variety of cues that are available as
potential bases for modal judgements. Thus it cannot be assumed that
modality according to the speaker is the same as for a hearer: nor
for different hearers. It is not merely reproduced, it is individually
constructed; and since there is so much to learn about so many
modality cues, about communication and the world, it is very likely
that the modality judgements of children will be systematically different
from those of adults, leading to very different responses to the same
message compared to what adults assume is necessarily and objectively
'there'.

Because television is a visual as well as a verbal medium, we need to continue our exploration by considering how modality operates with visual media. For convenience we will use the following picture from a *Marvel* comic for purposes of illustration, but our assumption is that essentially the simple principles apply to the full range of television fare – cartoons, drama, news and documentaries. Our procedure will be to give an idealized account of the full modality system available to adults, before considering the basis of modality judgements of children as they emerge.

We will take internal indicators of modality first, starting with the richly generative general principle that transformation signifies weak modality, i.e. a distancing from reality. Illustration 4 (page 108) is a two-dimensional form, as is the image on a television screen. However, the picture itself codes a three-dimensional reality, though less fully so than a photographic or filmic image. The picture is static, but movement is signified. Colours in comics and television cartoons are flat, unshaded primary colours, whereas the colours in 'real-life' television drama can be either 'natural', or heightened by some means. The picture in this case shows part of the scene, with a sharp frame. The less of a scene that is shown, the weaker the modality, because the portrayal of only a small part of the whole indicates a transformational deletion of it. Close-ups, in film as in comic strips, signify subjective perception (equivalent to the verbal 'I think', or 'It seems to me'). Details, such as the studs in the metal door, carry strong positive modality. Overall, though, this comic is inconsistent in its use of detail; as are most cartoons. For example, the Batman shadow is just sketched in outline, on a flat background, without any other details. The picture has words attached, some of them in unusual type. A television show has a soundtrack, which will have either natural voices or unusual ones, plus a music score and sound effects.

Summarizing the features that individually and together assign a modality value to an image such as this one by their presence or absence to a greater or lesser degree, we have the features shown in figure 14. Clearly these features are mostly not either–or (absent or present), but have many grades in between. Applying them to the illustration, we get a complex picture of its modality. It is a two-dimensional medium for instance (weak modality) but it signifies a three-dimensional image (strong modality). It is static (weak modality) but signifies movement (strong modality). This picture was in black and white, with limited shading (weak modality). Although the general impression would be weak modality, we see some features claiming strong modality (e.g. three-dimensionality of image, signified

Printed by Eastern Suburbs Newspapers, 140 Joynton Avenue, Rosebery 2018.
Published by Murray Publishers Pty Ltd, 154 Clarence Street, Sydney, 2000.
Sequences in this issue c D.C. COMICS INC. 1980
*Recommended price
DISTRIBUTORS: GORDON & GOTCH (A/SIA) LTD, MELBOURNE;
MURRAY PUBLISHERS PTY LTD, SYDNEY.

Illustration 4

± Three-dimensional medium
± Three-dimensional representation
± Movement in medium
± Movement in image
± Whole visual field
± Detail

± Colour $\left\{ \begin{array}{l} \pm \text{ Primary colours} \\ \pm \text{ Shading} \end{array} \right.$

± Speech
± Music
± Sound effects

Figure 14

movement, detail). We can also note inconsistencies between different parts of the picture.

For example, the detail and foreshadowing (three-dimensionality) on Batman is greater than that of his enemy, Metallo. Batman, it seems, is slightly the more real of the two. Similarly the metal door is slightly more real than the rest of the apartment building.

With a picture like this, it is clear that modality judgements are also made in terms of external criteria. Metallo's clothing and appearance (especially the head and riveted upper body) would be categorized as unreal by most people's normative version of reality. So would Batman's ability to descend on an apartment building from a great height, as well as some of his other feats. The background, in contrast, with its skyscape of office buildings, is sufficiently like a typical urban skyscape for it to have reasonably strong modality, especially for city-dwellers, though all such judgements are culture-specific, based ultimately on an individual's normative model of the world. Any departure from that normative model will signify unreality. The conventional use of slow motion in some television shows (e.g. *Six Million Dollar Man, Incredible Hulk*) to signify incredible feats of strength is an interesting case in point. Audiences accept it as a modality indicator (normal rules of physics are about to be suspended) rather than as an indication that the character is now moving very slowly.

A further indication of modality is the box containing the names of the writer, artist, etc. All these indicate the status of the comic as an artefact. They are like an alienation effect, to use Brecht's term. Some comics have constant intrusions from the writer or editor. Cartoons vary in the extent to which they present the production team. Credits for films and drama can be short or long: and they can emphasize characters' names or actors', and production or cast. All these choices can affect the potential modality of a television programme, though they will only do so if the viewer already has a model of the production process. Without that, the names will be ignored.

In order to see how many of these features form part of the modality structures of children, we asked the 9-year-old children who watched *Fangface* some questions about reality and cartoons. All of them answered this kind of question easily, with multiple specifications of the unreality of cartoons, and no doubts about their modality. One group responded as follows:

Interviewer: Er, how did we know that that was a cartoon?
Adrian: Oh, you can tell by the . . . picture and . . .
Craig: Pictures.
Christie: It's coloured in. Not like real people.
Adrian: And they weren't well drawn.
Stephen: [to Adrian] Were!
Christie: And you can't go out and see a cartoon walking across the road or something. It's just . . . [others laugh] piece of paper.
Adrian: You can tell, say, if a cartoon character went into a movie, a, a different thing, it wouldn't fit in exactly . . . wouldn't fit together properly.
Christie: Be the wrong colouring and he wouldn't . . . he wouldn't look real.

These children are articulating most of the internal modality features we presented above. One child has pointed out the two-dimensional status of the cartoon ('a piece of paper'), contrasting it with three-dimensional figures on a real road. They noted the different quality of the colours, in contrast to a movie. One makes the subtle observation that a cartoon character does not fit in to a movie background. The quality of the drawing is another signifier of cartoon status, and unreality.

This group did not mention sound, but a group that had only the sound track, without vision, still judged it was a cartoon from that alone:

Interviewer: Was this show real?
Paul: No.
Andrew: Cartoon.
Interviewer: Who thought it was a cartoon?
Marcus: Me. [Others raise hand.]
Interviewer: Everyone. How do you know things are cartoons?

Marcus:	Because they usually have . . . [Pause.]
Paul:	Sound effects.
Andrew:	You can kind of tell, because if a movie's on and you hear a – you know? It's different.

These children were not able to articulate the difference precisely, but they were able to tell, with certainty, purely from the sound, that the show was not real, and that it was a cartoon.

We can say definitely, then, that children by the age of 9 use a large number of formal features as the basis for their modality judgements, distinguishing cartoons from films, and films from real life. There is considerable redundancy here. They have many more modal features than is necessary to make a discrimination, so the judgement is made with effortless certainty. However, they also made a large number of observations on the unreality of the action. These comments by one group were typical:

Adrian:	And I don't think that cartoon was really true. [Other boys laugh.]
Interviewer:	Don't you? Why not?
Adrian:	Oh, you wouldn't see The Heap runnin' about in the streets and Fangface changing and changing back again.
Christie:	You don't, you don't have those sorts of things like people changing into things, really.
Interviewer:	Mm. And what other things about the cartoon extract you saw you felt weren't possible – not real?
Christie:	Oh, him eating up Pugsie . . .
Adrian:	Yeah . . .
Christie:	and then spitting him out again. He'd be all chewed up. He wouldn't be alive.
Adrian:	Yeah, and his mouth's about here [spreads arms to indicate size of Fangface's mouth]. When he got out he was about that big [indicates Pugsie's height].

As with the formal features, children in all groups were quick to list a large number of impossible incidents or attributes, with evident enjoyment. Some of their comments revealed sharp observation, as with the last boy's comment. Each of the two systems of indicators of modality, internal and external, show considerable redundancy. Taking them together, the degree of redundancy of modality markers is massive, for children aged 9. It is clear that by this stage, in spite of the fears of Plato and his successors, children can make very definite modality judgements about fantasy programmes.

In the course of the triadic interviews we asked children some questions about television and reality. One 6-year-old answered as follows:

Interviewer:　What sort of things happen on television?

George:　Like space adventures and cartoons.

Interviewer:　Yeah. What kinds of things happen to people on television?

George:　Um. Zoltare gets in G. Force and then his robot, he's got that, and then he gets 'em and they grow small, and they lie down, then they just jump down their heap again.

Interviewer:　So does that sort of thing happen in life? Does the same sort of thing happen everyday around you?

George:　[Shakes head.]

Interviewer:　What about if somebody gets killed on television?

George:　Um. . . . They're not really killed.

Interviewer:　They're not really killed on television?

George:　They're just pretend bullets and they just pretend they're killed and they get all dead on purposely.

Interviewer:　I see . . . and what happens in life when somebody gets killed?

George:　Um . . . they die.

All nine children we put this question to responded in the same way, even the youngest, aged 6. All distinguished between violence and its consequences on television, and what happens in real life. The basis in every case was some recognition of the processes of media production – acting, pretending, use of tomato sauce, or some reference to the illusionism of actors and directors. A version of Brecht's alienation effect is, it seems, part of the normal development of modality structures in quite young children.

Children were normally quite clear about the effect of weak modality: it turned something that would otherwise have been frightening into the opposite, something funny and/or exciting. One group pushed this kind of discussion into interesting areas.

Marnie:　When I was two, um, I washed my hair and I got away with watching 'Cop Shop', and that night I stabbed my Teddy! [Laughs. Two other children laugh.]

Interviewer:　Did you really?

Marnie:　Mm.

Interviewer:	Why did you do that?
Marnie:	I don't know, I think there was, there was pretty scary things on for a 2-year-old, and . . .
Interviewer:	Mm.
Marnie:	. . . so I went and got a knife and stabbed my Teddy. [Laughs. All the other children laugh or smile.]
Interviewer:	How did you feel when you did that?
Marnie:	Um . . . [pauses] . . . it's pretty hard to explain really.
Interviewer:	Try. Think about it and we'll come back.
Angela:	I watched, I watched a television programme and . . . it was a movie, and they chopped somebody's head off, it was this old, um, 'slike people at Armadale and things, and I went in there one night and I was in bed, and I just got my doll, and I just pulled the head straight off. [Demonstrates. Marnie and Steven smile.]
Interviewer:	Did you? And how did you feel when you did that?
Angela:	I felt pretty good when I did it! [Laughs. Other children laugh.]
Interviewer:	Mm. And why do you think you did that?
Angela:	[Pause.] Most probably just to feel what it was like . . .
Marnie:	Yeah.
Angela:	To actually do it yourself, you wanted to know how, how it was done, and how you would feel, if you did it.

A little later, the interviewer asked children about what they called 'rude' things on television.

Interviewer:	But you said you have to learn sometime, Marnie?
Marnie:	Yes.
Interviewer:	Can you go on about that a bit?
Marnie:	Well, if you are only very young, and you see . . . and your mother and father are only young, and you see them doing it, and things . . .
Interviewer:	Mm.
Marnie:	It's real . . .
Angela:	[To Danielle.] Experimenting. [Both girls have hand over their mouths. The boys are looking at the ground.]
Marnie:	You really want to know what they're . . .
Interviewer:	Yes.
Marnie:	. . . up to and all this.

Interviewer: Yes, and you think that you can increase your understanding by seeing similar things on television?
Marnie: Yes.
Angela: Plus experimenting with it yourselves. [Marnie laughs.] You try it out with your Teddy or something. [Everyone laughs.] Like Marnie stabbed her Teddy.
Interviewer: Mm.
Richard: If you stab your Teddy, your Teddy isn't going to do anything.
Interviewer: What do the rest of you think about what Marnie just said, because it's an interesting point.
Angela: Oh . . . there was . . . I used to live in the Eastern States and, oh, my friend's mother and father were having a kiss on the front verandah, so I go and kiss my Teddy on the front verandah. [Laughs.]
Interviewer: [Laughs.] Is there anything wrong with that?
Marnie: No.

This discussion is worth quoting and discussing at length because of the issues it raises so clearly. At first glance these two girls seem like monsters triggered off into exactly the horrific violence that television lobbyists fear as a result of television. The concept of modality can help us bring these fears into perspective. At the outset it should be said that these two girls are not regarded as violent or delinquent by their teachers. They are confident, well-dressed, popular 9-year-olds. Looking at some modality indicators in their utterance, we note that both girls laugh in reporting these incidents, and the other children laugh, also. The laughter suggests that these statements are not to be taken at face value, but are distanced in some way. In general, the incidents are also distanced by being put into the past. Marnie claims she was 2 when she watched *Cop Shop* with such drastic consequences. The child who could understand enough verbal language to know that it was *Cop Shop* she was watching, and then remember the incident 7 years later, would be a remarkable child. It is likely that Marnie is putting the incident further back in time than it had actually occurred.

Angela's story of kissing her Teddy, interestingly, starts in a different time and place ('I used to live in the Eastern States') but significantly shifts to the present tense ('I go and kiss my Teddy'): kissing Teddy is a less serious crime than stabbing him. With Angela's Teddy we begin to have a credibility problem. Did she, too, have a Teddy she kissed, or is she just re-using Marnie's Teddy motif?

Even with Marnie we can ask whether the story is just a good story, or an actual incident, given her laughter and the laughter of her friends.

Even assuming that it is true, we need to take account of the modality of the action: stabbing, kissing or beheading Teddy or dolls, rather than people. These children are quite clear about the difference between cruelty to people, and cruelty to dolls, which is essentially a modality difference, since the dolls, although made of real materials, also are three-dimensional messages, signifying people. Their modality, then, is stronger than that of a cartoon, but still far removed from that of real people.

This difference tends to be discounted by researchers into television violence and children. One classic type of experimental study that has 'proved' a relation between television and aggression uses a kind of doll called a Bobo-doll, which when hit bounces back up again (Bandura et al., 1963). Children who watch a film of an adult bashing a Bobo-doll, and who are then put in a room which contains, among other things, a Bobo-doll and Bobo-bashing equipment, are likely to imitate the film (especially if they are boys). But in this experiment not only does the film have a high modality status (it is a realistic depiction of Bobo-bashing), but the test-action has a lower modality status than aggression directed against people. The same problem arises with another common type of experiment, which uses children's expression of attitudes in spoken or written form as the dependent variable. Experiments like the Bobo experiment, which ignore both the modality of the television stimulus and the modality of the response, are simply not valid demonstrations of the general effects of television violence on children.

With all these words of caution, what these children have to say throws light on the modality of television for children. The two girls claim that watching television and playing with dolls are both important learning experiences for them, specifically in their attempts to understand and come to terms with the dangerous feelings and actions associated with violence and adult sexuality. Though we would be unwise to judge these two girls as potential homicidal maniacs, we would be equally unwise to suppose they had no interest in violence or sexuality. For these girls some television simply had too strong an emotional charge when they were younger. Earlier in the interview they all said that they now preferred 'exciting' or 'scary' movies. They enjoyed the 'scary' bits of *Fangface* and laughed at its improbable violence. What happens, according to these children, is that the emotional charge reduces in intensity with age, as they become more aware of the unreality of various programmes. As a result, what we can call the valency of the emotion changes from negative (painful, distressing) to positive (pleasant, exciting or amusing): the modality flip-over effect. Modality does not create the emotional response, but it determines the valency and force of that response, and hence contributes decisively to whatever effects may come from watching television.

We will summarize some provisional conclusions about modality and children's television, with a number of propositions. First we will take the primary relationships involved in the model (figure 15).

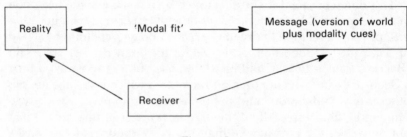

Figure 15

1. Modal fit is a process of judgement on the part of the receiver of the message. The closer the message is judged to be to reality by the receiver (i.e. the better the modal fit), the more it will be responded to both emotionally and cognitively as though it were reality. When taken to be real it will, therefore, affect behaviour and learning in the same way as would the relevant aspect of reality itself.

2. The greater the transformational distance between message and reality (i.e. the weaker its modality), the weaker will be the relation between receiver and message, both cognitively and emotionally. A less strong response, and less learning, will take place. For example, cartoons are massively transformed in comparison to, say, the news.

3. As well as weakening the perceived relation between message and reality (i.e. a poor modal fit), modality changes can invert it, so that the receiver will interpret the message as signifying its opposite. Its emotional charge can also reverse valency, from negative to positive (pain to pleasure), or positive to negative (pleasure to pain). Thus the modality of cartoons can shift the giving of pain (Jerry running Tom over with

a steam roller) to an enjoyable event – drawings do not feel pain, even drawings of cats.

4. Even with an inverse modality, however, the surface content of the image coexists as part of the content. An image of violence is still an image of violence, and viewers who enjoy it are still endorsing those impulses in themselves.

5. A response to television (or any other message) is a function of both its content and its modality. So with other things constant, one could intensify the response by intensifying the emotional charge, or by strengthening its modality; similarly one could decrease the intensity of the response by weakening modality, or by decreasing the emotional charge. The point is that the same media product might be responded to as unbearably intense, or very boring, depending on the modality system brought to bear on it.

6. Responses to television are themselves messages, with their own modality value, ranging from concrete actions to various dramatizations or expressions by words or other means. Again, the weaker the modality of the response, the weaker the connection to the reality of the responder, and the weaker the emotional charge they express. So responses with many indicators of weak modality cannot be taken for real actions, although they are at the same time an expression of the basic content of the message, and show the existence of that content for the person concerned.

Since modality so powerfully affects how television content will be responded to, we need to consider some of the factors that can affect it. We have seen that modality judgements are highly complex, many-layered and variable, but we can isolate some dimensions of them in the fuller version of the modality model shown in figure 16. This

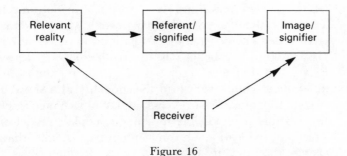

Figure 16

model shows the distinction between different parts of the visual message, the image or signifier, and the signified or referent, in order to allow us to consider both how the image relates to what it is an image of, and how that relates to our version of reality. In this design the primary modality judgement is concerned with the presumed relationship between the referent and reality as these are understood by the receiver, but the relationship between image and referent, or signifier and signified, can come to act as an indicator of the primary modality relationship. Thus it comes to acquire an aspect of modality itself, which we call 'secondary modal fit'. The model allows us to suggest further propositions about modality:

7. Whatever increases the transformational distance between an image and its referent weakens the modality of the message. So all markers of the conventions of visual media that we noted earlier indicate weakened modality for those who recognize them. These are what we have called the internal markers of modality. They are features of the message itself, yet their modal significance still has to be learnt. Another way of increasing the distance is by a recognition of the processes of media production; that, too, has to be learnt, and children have not normally been exposed to that kind of learning. In these terms different semiotic codes are assigned a general modality value. For example, a moving picture has a high value, drawings less; and words less still. So some people believe that 'the camera can never lie', assigning it a very strong modality. It is essential for everyone to understand that cameras can and frequently do lie, and that television pictures do not have absolute modal status.

8. External modality criteria can act on any part of the model. Feshbach showed that modality can be affected simply by telling viewers that a film was either real or not, and there are many other ways of influencing people's judgements. But other criteria come from the X-relationship: what individual viewers know or believe is the truth about their world. Extreme differences here, based on cultural or even age differences, could transform the modality of a show, from realism to fantasy or vice-versa, and totally change its effect. In principle it is possible to change people's model of the world, by education or some other means, and that will change the modality of certain kinds of content.

The development of children's reality constructs

First we should consider the evidence about the nature of modality systems from a developmental perspective. A basic assumption is that children's modality systems evolve over time, and that this development is very important in understanding their responses to television. However, as we saw in the previous chapter, they may also have a different *kind* of system of modality, suited to the development of their general cognitive powers and strategies. In this section we will look at some indications that this is indeed the case. Jaglom and Gardner (1981), studying younger children (aged 2–5) than our sample, looked at the way these young children calibrate the world of television against the world of reality. They hypothesized three stages: Stage I, when children make virtually no distinction; Stage II, when there is an absolute distinction made between the two (here they use the metaphor of a 'membrane' between television and reality which is impermeable); and finally Stage III, when this 'membrane' becomes semi-permeable, so that children are able to make some connections and some distinctions. This pattern corresponds to the general pattern we have noted for the development of paradigmatic structures: from non-differentiation to sharp differentiation (a binary paratactic structure) and then to re-integration in a complex hypotactic structure.

In the older children we studied the same dialectic continues. This can be seen in children's choice of television characters, in our triadic elicitation described in the previous chapter (table 14). Young children's liking for cartoons is as well known as it is lamented.

Table 14   *Children's choice of television characters* (percentages)

Age (years)	Cartoon	Drama	Star	Real life
6–8	76	13	11	0
9–12	28	58	9	5

Cartoons above all other forms are the target of criticisms about the unreality and mindless violence on television. The popularity of programmes for these young children is directly the opposite of the order of reality, going from most unrealistic (cartoons) to most realistic (real-life characters). There is a clear shift between younger and older children, who use many more characters from drama, and fewer cartoon characters, and more real-life characters, though the bulk of the characters are still fictional. Overall we can see a definite preference shift towards stronger modality in their favourite characters as the children get older.

In these experiments, some of the triadic groupings of characters we offered them included both television and non-television characters. With these triads, younger children had ' ± television' (e.g. 'on television/not on television'; 'on television, not in real life') as their construct 46 per cent of the time, suggesting that it was a very salient construct for them. For the older children ± television was mentioned on only 20 per cent of the occasions. In view of other evidence we cannot conclude from this that older children somehow cease to notice the difference between television and reality. It is more likely that such an obvious difference is taken for granted, and so other more interesting possible groupings are sought. In Jaglom and Gardner's terms the boundary had become more permeable. With these cross-boundary triads the older children formed 53 per cent of their groups containing both a television and a non-television character. This occurred with only 31 per cent of the groups of the younger children.

It is clear that the process of assimilating the two worlds has progressed a long way with the older children: they operate on a more complex structure, one that includes both television and reality as an increasingly seamless whole. Their constructs have greater scope, and link television to reality. Their preferred programmes, so much more realistic on the surface, pose for them new problems of discrimination. As their powers of discriminating between reality and television, and the power of their modal structures, increase with age, so too do the demands that they place on those powers. Eventually, if they are to be effective citizens and competent viewers of television, the real test will be whether they can perceive the modal status of news and documentary programmes. Young children do not watch the news much, so unless they develop modal strategies on other programmes during earlier stages, they will not be able to cope with such subtle modalities when they are adults.

It was this problem that made us use the triadic elicitation method to explore one particular set of constructs, those used to discriminate between television and reality, with nine of the children, aged between 6 and 12. We asked them to place the characters into the two categories, more real and less real. We then asked them to give their reasons for making that judgement. These reasons we took to indicate criteria of reality, that is, the components of their modality structure.

The first set of discriminations we asked them to make went across the reality/television boundary (90 characters altogether). They could put the characters either into different boxes – real and unreal – or into

the same box – equally real or unreal. There are three possible
relationships: they could distinguish television from reality, and see
reality as more real: they could see television and reality as equally
real: or they could see television as more real than reality (table 15).
The younger children mainly called the television characters less real.
As the age goes up the number of judgements of the equal reality
of television and real-life characters also rises. Of course, as we have

Table 15   *Reality inter-television/life by age* (percentages)

	6-year-olds	9-year-olds	12-year-olds
Life more real than television	80	70	56
Television and life equally real	20	30	40
Television more real than life	0	0	4

seen, the realism of preferred characters also rises with age; but that
does not explain the phenomenon of reversed modality, whereby some
12-year-olds regarded a small minority of television characters as *more*
real than real-life characters.

This was part of a pattern that emerged (table 16) when we asked
the children to say whether some characters on television were more
real than others on television, or whether they were equally real. That
suggests that older children are marginally more likely to discriminate
between the reality of different television characters though the

Table 16   *Reality intra-television by age* (percentages)

	6-year-olds	9-year-olds	12-year-olds
Some more real	33	44	44
Equally real	67	56	56

difference is not striking. For the sake of thoroughness, we also asked
them to distinguish between the real-life characters on grounds of
reality, and the results we got were somewhat surprising (table 17).
The total number of characters involved in these is only 36, so the
exact numbers are unreliable, but the striking thing to emerge is the
strong tendency of the three 12-year-olds to identify some real-life
people as more 'real' than others. Unsurprisingly it seems that their
understanding of the notion 'reality' is rather different from that of
adults.

Table 17 *Reality: intra-real-life by age* (percentages)

	6-year-olds	9-year-olds	12-year-olds
Some more real	17	0	67
Equally real	83	100	33

Although these figures might give the impression that 12-year-olds' minds have been so addled by television that they cannot tell truth from fiction any more, a close look at the reasons they provide shows just the opposite. One girl, Darlene, for instance, could discriminate between Doreen (a character in a drama) and Jonathon Coleman (a presenter) as follows:

Darlene: They seem just as real, the same. . . . Oh, I suppose, Jon seems more, than Doreen, 'cos sometimes he says his own words, like on the, makes up his own question and that.
Interviewer: And Doreen doesn't?
Darlene: Yeah, she has to go by the script.

And a little later:

Darlene: Jon, he makes up his own questions and that, um, on *Wonder World*, and he acts natural, and Doreen, well when she acts, you can tell that she's acting out a role.

For Darlene, 'reality' includes a concept of authenticity. It also leads to sharp attention to forms of speech and action, the greater naturalness of spontaneous discourse as against the performance style of even realistic drama.

But Darlene also makes some judgements that are different from adults ones: For instance she regards Max, her dog, as more real than Nicole, her friend.

Max seems more real to me than Nicole because I see Max everyday and 'cos Nicole doesn't go to this school and, um, I'm more close to Max.

Lisa even discriminated between her mother and father on the same grounds:

Um, my Mum seems more real than my Dad because, my Mum's a lady as well, and my Dad's a boy. And my Mum, she's always, we always go out together and my Dad, I always see him too but my Mum she always picks out my clothes and she just seems more real than my Dad.

Younger children make judgements which are perceptive but different. George, aged 6, comparing his friend Shaun and Yogi Bear, found Shaun more real for the following reasons:

George:	This one, Shaun's most real and Yogi Bear is less real.
Interviewer:	Okay, and why is that?
George:	Because Yogi's a film and Shaun was born.
Interviewer:	Can you give me another reason why Shaun is more real?
George:	Because God made him.
Interviewer:	I see. Didn't God make Yogi Bear?
George:	No.
Interviewer:	How did Yogi Bear get created?
George:	Um he . . . um a man or boy . . .
Interviewer:	Who made Yogi Bear?
George:	He was just a film by a camera and they're moving him but you can't see the hands. I don't know how they make cartoons.

George's concern with the mechanics of media illusions is typical of children at this stage. In the triadic experiments and the interviews we found almost an obsession with these mechanics. It seemed that children needed to have *some* account of how the message was produced, as the basis for judgements on its modality. If they lack a factual account of the process, as George does, they will invent one. This need is so urgent that it provides strong motivation for a media education course which could provide them with a more solid basis than the myths and folklore that circulate among children. It is interesting that George is juxtaposing two mysteries created by adult society: the mystery of media production and the mystery of procreation. At this point in his life, he is closer to demystifying the media than he is to demystifying sexuality.

To illustrate the point that some degree of contradictoriness in modality judgements is a sign of development, we can compare Kym, the youngest girl in the sample (aged 5) with Natalie, just a year older. Kym showed no confusion in her judgements. The whole interview took 25 minutes, compared to 36 minutes for Natalie. Kym's judgements were made primarily on the basis of ± television. She refused to see any within-category distinctions. Everything on television, for her, was equally unreal. Everything in real life was equally real: in Jaglom and Gardner's terms, an example of an impermeable 'membrane'.

Natalie's responses were less certain, and showed some contradictions. For instance, she put both Kym, her friend, and Tom and Jerry in the real box.

Natalie: Both just as real as each other.
Interviewer: Why is that?
Natalie: Well, Kym's here and she's real and, Tom and Jerry,
                Oh, Tom's a cat and we've got cats here, and Jerry's
                mouse and we've got lots of rats here.

In this judgement, Tom and Jerry's status as cartoon characters does not enter in. A totally permeable 'membrane'. But on a later occasion she compares Mr Ed the talking horse, with Monkey, whom she puts in the unreal box.

Natalie: Mr Ed.
Interviewer: Is what?
Natalie: Realler. Like Monkey's just in Japan. They've just
                made him. Someone's dressed up as him and Mr Ed's
                a horse.

For the next test she put Monkey into the 'real' box, Tom and Jerry into the unreal box.

Natalie: Um . . . Monkey's more real.
Interviewer: Why is that?
Natalie: Like Monkey's dressed up and Tom and Jerry are
                just a photo of people dressed up.

In this discussion we see her now making a nuanced judgement about Monkey compared to other media characters, where before she seemed unable to tell the difference between Tom and Jerry and her friend. She mentions a two-stage production process with Tom and Jerry, through 'photo of' and 'people dressed up'. Like George, whom we looked at before, she has a mistaken idea of how a cartoon is made, but she is trying to build up a theory of media production as the basis for a theory of media modality. In fact, what accounts for the apparent vagaries of her responses is her employment of modality judgements without an overall modality schema. She does the right kind of thing on each occasion, but she does not link the different occasions. Her judgements thus produce a haphazard rather than a systematic pattern, as when she put Monkey into the Real box along with herself:

Natalie:	Just as real.
Interviewer:	Monkey's just as real as you?
Natalie:	Yeah, like Monkey's in Japan and I'm here.
Interviewer:	Why are you real, how do you know you're real?
Natalie:	Like, I was born in Mum's tummy and I'm here. I was a baby and now I came here.
Interviewer:	And how do you know Monkey is real?
Natalie:	Like he came out of an egg, like what chickens do.
Interviewer:	Really?
Natalie:	Yeah, that came out of this mud and went right on top of the mountain and then became a monkey.

If we apply logic to these judgements, we find that Mr Ed is more real than Monkey, who is as real as Natalie's self, so Mr Ed is more real than Natalie. Are we then to conclude that television has produced an identity crisis? Not from this evidence. A more plausible explanation is that Natalie is deploying a wider range of features that specify reality than she can yet integrate. One of them is 'here/not here', which she mentions almost every time, but does not always incorporate into a reality judgement. Another is 'born/made', with a further refinement of 'dressed up', which is a more sophisticated form of Kym's 'on television' (or 'a cartoon character'). Natalie uses the simple distinction, + television, only intermittently. The 'errors' she makes, the self-contradictions or absurd judgements (by adult standards) that she sometimes makes are the visible signs of important cognitive growth: eventually her currently separate judgements will become integrated in a complex but coherent system.

The criteria offered by these children mainly fell into a few general categories: 77 per cent (97 out of 126) were as in table 18. Our sample is too small to justify firm conclusions on the basis of these figures,

Table 18   *Reality criteria by age* (percentages)

	Age 6	Age 9	Age 12
± on TV programme	20	28	5
± made	23	52	22
± acting	14	0	16
Total media-related	57	80	43
± known, close	29	16	35
± unusual acts	14	4	22
Total ± familiar	43	20	57
N (Responses)	45	45	45

but some patterns do emerge which confirm the general developmental framework we have sketched out.

1. Calibrating television against reality is a major concern for children throughout this age group.
2. The simple binary paratactic opposition between television and reality drops in importance as more complex bases of judgement evolve.
3. Methods of media production (actual or hypothetical) emerge as the most salient criterion of reality for 8–9-year-olds. This is also the period of greatest preoccupation with media-internal criteria.
4. Older children use more features to specify reality than do younger children, including a range of transforms of the basic categories (see also chapter 3).
5. Media-external criteria have become more important to older children. That is, they are using (testing) their developing knowledge of reality generally as the basis for modality judgements.
6. Development is accompanied by a greater tendency to make 'errors' (by adult standards) in judgements of reality. This is because during this period judgements are made in terms of a complexive concept, i.e. a paratactic set of features, not totally integrated and stabilized into a single, coherent hypotactic structure.
7. This greater capacity for errors is, however, indispensable for adequate cognitive growth in this dimension. The process of development of this concept involves important general learning of:
   (a) the nature and role of media processes as constructors of reality;
   (b) the development of differentiated spheres of knowledge (first-hand/second-hand, and mediated knowledge);
   (c) modality cues in speech and action.

Modality, age and class

In order to widen the basis of our investigation of children's modality systems, we used drawings and essays done by children, aged from 5 to 12 (drawings) and from 8 to 12 (essays), from two schools that draw on two different socioeconomic classes (see previous chapter).

In the essays the task was to name the person on television the child wanted to be. There is the same shift in modality we saw from the other experiments, as can be seen from table 19. In the essays the older children used hypothetical modality markers in their language more often: 15 per cent had two or more examples of this linguistic form (e.g. 'if I could . . . I would be/do . . .). Only 4 per cent of the younger children used this form. This is hardly unexpected.

Table 19 *Children's choice of person to be* (percentages)

| | | Ideal characters | | | |
	Real life	Star	Total + real	Drama	Fantasy	Total − real
Aged 8–9	11	9	20	40	35	80
Aged 12	25	19	44	33	29	56

However, what was more surprising was the modality of the actions these children offered as what they would do as their favourite character. We classed as 'everyday' those actions which average children could already perform (e.g. being popular, helping their friends, etc.); 'extrapolations' those actions which can be performed by human beings, if they are sufficiently rich or famous (e.g. meeting presidents or famous sportsmen); and 'fantasy' those actions which are beyond human capacity (e.g. flying faster than a speeding bullet, like Superman) – see table 20. There is very little change over these

Table 20 *Characteristics of children's choices of person to be by age* (percentages)

	Everyday	*Extrapolated*	*Fantasy*
Aged 8–9	24	45	31
Aged 12	23	40	37

3 years. The older children if anything are slightly more likely to envisage fantasy actions, but the bulk of the actions described, for both age groups, are rational and possible. In their idealizations, it seems, these children predominantly link fictional characters with real or possible actions, and not with fantastic ones.

In the drawings, which were simply images drawn from television, there was one phenomenon which intrigued us. Surprisingly often, children when asked to draw something from television also drew the television set, or a channel logo, alongside or around it. More young children (aged 5–6) did this than any other age group: nearly a quarter of them. This is consistent with what we have seen elsewhere: that these younger children need to make the distinction ± television strongly. This marking, surprisingly, re-emerges at about 12, with a trough of disinterest in between (table 21). We also wanted to compare children of different social classes. There was very little difference in the modality of the characters they said they wanted to

Table 21 *Depiction of television set or logo by age* (percentages)

	Age (years)		
5–6	*8*	*10*	*12*
24	2	6	15

be in their essays. The only difference worthy of comment, here, is the greater wish of upper-class children to be a star of some show, and to reap the rewards of wealth and fame accordingly. But there was more difference in the modality of the actions they envisaged performing (table 23). The number of fantasy responses remains fairly constant, but the lower-class children are more likely to envisage performing everyday actions in their imagined roles. That is, the response they envisaged was more real, even though the characters they wanted to be were more unreal.

In the drawings there was one interesting difference between upper-class and lower-class children. In both real-life (real plus star) and

Table 22 *Choice of character-type by class* (percentages)

	Real	*Star*	*Total + Real*	*Drama*	*Fantasy*	*Total − Real*
Lower class	27	4	41	34	25	59
Upper class	23	24	47	29	24	53

Table 23 *Choice of anticipated action by class* (percentages)

	Everyday	*Extrapolated*	*Fantasy*
Lower class	35	40	25
Upper class	26	48	26

non-real (drama and fantasy) categories, upper-class children had a significantly greater interest in non-human inanimate things (table 24). The lower-class children have a greater interest in super-heroes, which is consistent with the other evidence. The upper-class children's much greater interest in the products of technology is not simply a question of modality, but it is significant that machines (robots, cars, spaceships, etc.) which are more remote from their own mode of existence, and hence have a weaker modality, figure more prominently in the world they construct from television experience.

Table 24   *Choice of subject by class* (percentages)

(a) *Real life*

	Human	Animal	Machine
Lower class	38	20	42
Upper class	26	10	65

(b) *Fantasy*

	Human	Super-human	Totally human	Animal	Machine/robot
Lower class	29	17	46	34	14
Upper class	28	5	33	31	33

It must be said that whilst we can launch a series of hypotheses, we are not in a position to come to any definite conclusions about social class and modality from our data. Patterns of programme preferences along class lines, if they emerged clearly from a larger sample, would be interesting but not decisive. What matters is the nature, scope, precision and power of modality structures and modality judgements of different groups in society. Do working-class children make different modal judgements, especially at the high-modality end of the programme spectrum: news, documentaries and the like? In the next chapter we report on an attempt to probe more deeply into this area with a particular disadvantaged group in Australia, but that too is inconclusive. It is commonplace in social research for data to raise more questions than they answer, and here more than anywhere else in the book we wish to stress the importance of the gaps in knowledge that we have opened up, rather than to suggest that we have achieved closure by proof.

Conclusion

The main point we have made in this chapter is that judgements about 'reality' are complex, fluid and subjective. Modality decisively affects interpretations and responses, so it cannot be ignored in any account of the media. However, it is itself so strongly affected by innumerable forces that it cannot be treated as a simple variable. No television product has a fixed modality value which will apply for all classes of viewer. Television products range between two extremes, but none is totally real (for most viewers) and none is totally unreal (again, for most viewers). The definition of reality is so important ideologically that it becomes the site of ideological struggles rather than an automatic yardstick that can be simply applied in any instance. Modality has an almost magical power: able to transform a message or an experience into its opposite, truth to fiction, fiction to truth, pain to pleasure, enjoyment to distress. All these considerations make modality a crucial factor in the study of television and its effects.

Children's modality systems are similar in principle, but there are some differences that are important for understanding their responses to television. Young children do distinguish between fantasy and reality, but they do not know what is needed to distinguish with the precision and subtlety assumed for adult television. So their response to adult programming is typically skewed, and they have distinct needs of their own. Their modality judgements tend to be polarized, contradictory and unstable. They are likely to under-read modality cues, and respond with an intensity that seems inappropriate or disturbing to adults, especially if the modality of the programme is ambiguous or disguised. Paradoxically, it follows that children do in fact need a diet rich in explicit fantasy – including cartoons – in order to develop a confident and discriminating modality system. They also need, and crave, an understanding of the processes of media production.

In sum, children's modality systems are developing throughout childhood: their grasp of reality, the idea of reality, or the reality of television is not a simple matter. During this process of growth, children will often make modality 'mistakes', but it seems that their concepts of reality must sometimes be put at risk if they are to develop a complex and fruitful modality system, an elaborate hypotactic structure of the requisite scope, coherence, and flexibility (Tripp et al., 1984). Much is at stake with modality and its development: the capacity to cope not just with television but with the full range of messages, on all media in all semiotic forms, to respond with intensity where intensity is appropriate, and warily where scepticism seems required. Catchcries of 'escapism' and 'illusionism', or 'creativity' and 'imagination' over-simplify the difficult and important issues that surround the question of reality in children's television.

Chapter 5

Society and the viewer
The construction of meaning

Social context and modality

In discussions of the effects of television it has long been recognized
that some children are especially vulnerable to excessive influence.
These are the children who provide horrific headlines, and create such
anxiety in concerned parents and public bodies. 'New York, Sat. –
A lonely, overweight schoolboy shot himself dead after his father
banned him from watching television' (*Sunday Times*, 20 February ✗
1983). Young Genaro Garcia, 225 lb. at the age of 13, felt totally
rejected by his peers, and unable to cope with the demands of a new
school. His suicide note is reported to have ended 'In my heart I will
take my television set with me. I love you.'

As in the case of Garcia, there are typically many influences at work
in these unfortunate cases. Apparently television became excessively
important for him because the rest of his world was so distressingly
unsatisfying; but no-one could claim that television was responsible
for that world. Television is always but part of an overall structure
of relationships, and its effects can be determined by them in ways
that can have damaging consequences. Although public opinion is
probably unduly worried by isolated incidents involving television and
some act of violence (usually reported with only a brief account of
the full situation) that does not mean we can ignore this kind of
phenomenon in our account of the normal processes of interpretation
of the media. We must take it into account, not only because it is
so serious, but also because such extreme cases help our understanding
of the problem.

Aberrations, pathologies, behaviours which break the accepted rules,
are often illuminating about the basic structures and tendencies of
the overall system. For instance, young children first imitate adult

speech correctly, saying such things as 'I ran'. Later they begin to make mistakes, saying 'I runned' instead. This kind of mistake is termed a 'virtuous error' by linguists, because the child is doing the right thing (applying the general rule for forming past tenses), but doing it in the wrong circumstances (an exception). The error or deviance from the norm of adult speech is one way by which we can gain access to and understand the normal development of speech.

The kind of viewer who is likely to be most strongly influenced by television is the child who, like Garcia, is a heavy viewer and socially isolated. Social isolation, poor adjustment to peers and family, and low self-esteem are associated with high viewing (cf. Edgar, 1977). Edgar and Callus (1979) also found evidence suggesting that a different modality structure may operate with such children. Low-esteem children were more likely to respond intensely to television shows (finding horror shows scary, having nightmares, etc.). They were more likely to identify with a television character.

The Australian Senate Inquiry of 1978 expressed a representative concern about low-esteem viewers, and about the problem of 'latch-key children': children who had both parents working and who therefore watched television without parental supervision until one or both returned. In such circumstances the opportunities for shared and mediated experiences are severely curtailed, and whether this constitutes damaging parental neglect or not is a controversial issue. The role of parents in the viewing process is a major problem; it is another focus for concern by the Australian Senate Committee, who again voice a widespread public anxiety. They note that parents do not control their children's viewing in Australia. They quote a survey by Canavan which found that 41 per cent of children's viewing time is controlled by them, and only 30 per cent by the parents, the remaining 29 per cent being a joint family decision. A similar picture emerges from USA in the Surgeon-General's Report (1972). These figures, however, are open to a range of reactions, since the question of control is quintessentially a political one. How much power should parents have to determine their children's viewing? Should children have more or less self-determination in their own viewing patterns? These same questions should also be asked of the State. They are questions of power, and so they will never have a neutral, non-ideological resolution; but it is clear that the greater the sense of conflict between parents and children, or family and society, the more acute these issues will be.

In order to investigate the basis for these fears and concerns we need to fit them into a larger explanatory framework. Our starting point will be the theories of Bateson and his associates. Bateson's (1973) focus of concern was schizophrenia, which as a pathology of modality systems is of obvious relevance for an understanding of how people's interpretations of television can go wrong. Bateson began from observation of importance of 'play' in the social life of human beings and other higher animals. In play, otherwise dangerous or disruptive actions and attitudes may be harmlessly tried out. 'Play' turns out to be a serious and important accompaniment of the learning process in both animals and people, and is essential to higher thought processes.

Encoded into much children's television is a set of signals indicating that the product is *merely* play. To understand problems such as those of Garcia we need an explanatory account both of these signals and how children acquire the ability to read them. It is clear from the previous chapter that in our terms these signals are the markers of modality, and these need to be attached to the actions and communications of others and of the self. Bateson's work is relevant here because he showed how schizophrenics systematically lack or misuse these signals. They suffer from defective modality, so they conflate real and unreal in a variety of ways, or they distinguish too sharply between the two. Bateson argues that the source of this defective modality system is a particular kind of social situation, one consisting of both hostility and antagonism and also dependence: what he has labelled 'double-bind'. What he is claiming is that the two problems of schizophrenics (reality aberrations and sense of conflict) are not unrelated conditions, but that one is the cause of the other. Schizophrenics do not change the material social and perceived relational circumstances which create the double-bind which entraps them; instead they escape from their impossible situation by reinterpreting or adjusting their sense of reality so that they no longer perceive their circumstances to be those of unbearable unreconciled conflict. If we apply this account to television 'addiction', it would suggest that not only the quantity but the quality of television watching is affected, even determined, by the child's dominant social relationships. Though mutually determining in some ways, television viewing may well be a symptom rather than a cause of the child's social relationships.

A similarly intrinsic connection between modality and social relationships emerges independently from a study of the normal systems of modality in verbal language (see Halliday, 1976; Kress and Hodge, 1979). Modal auxiliaries in English, like 'may', 'can', and 'must', are systematically ambiguous. Sometimes they have purely a modality value (indicating whether the statement is certain or uncertain in differing degrees). They also have an interpersonal value, coming from the relationship between the persons involved. For instance, 'may' can be used in a sentence like 'It may rain tomorrow' or in a sentence like 'You may go swimming, Smith', where the speaker has power to give permission. Although the context often removes the ambiguity, there are many occasions where ambiguity remains, and is functional. If a parent says to a child, for instance, 'You can watch television after you've finished your homework', the 'can' is ambiguously permission and a statement of potential fact: 'I allow you to watch television', or 'You will be able to watch television.' The parent is both asserting and masking authority, in a weak but very widespread and 'normal' example of what Bateson called double-bind. We can represent the general communication situation schematically as shown in figure 17.

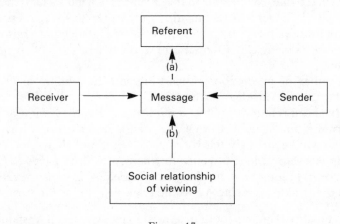

Figure 17

What we have said so far suggests that signals of modality can express *either* modality proper (a), which is a referent–message relationship *or* social relations of the message (b), which is a sender–receiver relationship. Another way of putting it is to say that social relationships can be transformationally expressed as modality relationships. This is precisely what happens with schizophrenics in Bateson's account. They express the conflicts in their social relationships through disorders of modality. It is also what happens in everyday conversation, for everyone who expresses social insecurity unintentionally for tactical reasons by seeming to doubt their own opinions (e.g. 'Excuse me, sir, I wondered if this little memo I've written might possibly throw some, er, light on the matter', said to his boss by a man who believes he has the definitive solution to the problem). In the case of television, the sender is absent, and has to be projected by the viewer. It is likely that the process of reconstruction will be affected by the viewer's primary social relations. In the case of Genaro Garcia television became the loving person his parents and peers, in his eyes sadly were not. In so far as this process is widespread, we have a transformational sequence as follows:

General social relations → context of viewing → TV relations → modality

This formula sets out an expressive relationship in which each successive stage is potentially reinterpreted in the light of meanings made from the previous stage and transformed accordingly. The transformation may be direct, as when the context of viewing is 'rewritten' so that it conforms to the existing external social relations. It may also be inverse, in a negation of the previous stage, creating a compensation for it by reversal, as when a viewing context is reperceived as being closer than it is in response to a sense of alienation elsewhere.

A number of predictions concerning modality follow from this formula. Let us consider viewers who are socially isolated, or whose primary social relations involve a painful sense of alienation or gap. We assume that it is likely that the inadequacies of these primary relations will be strongly felt by such viewers, and that if television viewing is a desirable experience for them, it will be partly because it transforms in some way the distressing inadequacies of their everyday life, as they did for Garcia. We would expect the following to be true:

1. Modality relations (both in television content and in response to television) will often serve to express something about the social relations of the viewer. Over-emphasis on the reality of television content expresses a sense of social isolation, a rejection of general social relations in the lived world in favour of those experienced via television. Over-emphasis on the unreality expresses the opposite: a rejection of the world as mediated by television in favour of lived experience.

2. Isolated alienated viewers will tend to close the modality gap in television content. They will either prefer highly realistic shows or they will treat non-realistic shows as highly real. Viewers who find social isolation painful are likely to want to express its opposite. Modality transformations are one way of doing this

because they enable viewers to narrow the gap by asserting the reality of the shows they watch.

3. This will lead to intense responses and high involvement, a close identification with the characters and events of television, which will be responded to as though a part of the real world (with all the ambivalent and sometimes negative feelings aroused by the real world for such a viewer).

4. If programme-makers have aimed at a total effect, relying on the modality systems of normal viewers to achieve a balance between emotional intensity and imputed reality, this balance will be upset by viewers who systematically transform modality structures in atypical ways.

5. In some respects their modality judgements will be like young children's in the way they depart from adult norms, but with children this is due to what they have not yet experienced or learnt, and will pass with time. With these viewers, however, the modality judgements come from what they have experienced only too strongly, and as long as they are involved in those social relations, they will continue to misread modality in the same way.

6. The context of viewing relationships (whether the person is viewing alone or in company) is an intermediate variable. It makes a difference whether people view on their own or in company. The closer the social involvement in the viewing situation, the greater the modality gap that is tolerable. This fact is recognized by programme-makers who include audience responses on sound tracks, especially laughter, which helps to create the modality gap that is essential to make something funny. It is also recognized by parents who watch scary shows with their young children on their knees or cuddling up to them, and by children such as one of our researchers', who watched 'Dr Who' from behind the sofa. In general it can be said that shows with high emotional charge and high modality reinforce bonds among viewers watching in company (if there is company to be had) as a natural strategy to weaken the modality of the show and hence weaken its emotional force. But company on its own is not enough. Garcia watched television alone in his room, with the door locked against his family. He tried to choose cohesion with television rather than the reality of living with his family.

7. The same formula also applies to the normal viewer. However sophisticated the modality structures children or adults may have developed, they can still operate with a collapsed modality structure. Coleridge called the process a 'willing suspension of

disbelief'. It is a kind of double-think experienced by everyone who enjoys television. It is a recognition simultaneously that the show is unreal, a mere fiction, and also that it engages with the feelings as though it were real. It involves an intellectual knowledge of the isolation of the viewing experience, yet also a warm feeling of social oneness generated by the box. The social context of viewing is both an important element in the viewing experience, and also a construct of that experience. This contradictory process is only more starkly present in what are classified as problem-viewers. For good or ill, it is part of the make-up of the vast mass of television watchers, of all ages and all classes, who constitute the audience in any television community.

Black viewers and reality

In terms of this account we predicted that children who are high-viewing social isolates will have a distinctively skewed modality system for television and other media. We decided to explore this hypothesis with a series of interviews of a group of children who seemed to be in this category: 10 children aged from 9 to 12, Aboriginal or part Aboriginal, who had been separated from their families and were boarded out in a number of homes, organized by a single institution. Each home consisted of two foster-parent figures, usually white, with about four or five Aboriginal children who boarded there, but attended ordinary predominantly white schools. Three of the children, however, – Kristie, Charlotte and Lisa – boarded with a white foster-mother who had two of her own children living in the house. Two other children (Jill and Shawn) had a foster-mother who was herself part Aboriginal, and was regarded as 'kin' to them, though this kinship may not have been biological. All these children lacked the support of a stable home background. All were Aboriginal, which carries a heavy stigma in white Australian society. All were keen watchers of television.

We were interested both in the modality judgements these children made, and in the basis for those judgements. The pattern of judgements seemed, to our surprise, to be not markedly different from those of other Australian children of their age. Most liked cartoons and comedies (low-modality shows), which they responded to with the relaxed enjoyment that indicates that they attached low modality to them. Most of them found the news boring, in common with other children of their age. Only two of the older children professed to like news programmes, and one was very keen on weather reports. All these responses could be easily matched in larger samples of white children. There were, however, some differences in the bases of their modality judgements. Almost all of these were media-related. In 85 pages of transcript there were only two instances where a child invoked non-media criteria of reality. James, aged 10, criticized a prison show (see chapter 6) for unreality for depicting inmates going to the toilet unsupervised at night. From his knowledge of institutions he felt that that was unlikely. The Flintstones, for Kristie aged 9, were unreal because they wore 'funny clothes', and lived in 'rock houses'. James briefly invoked a normative view of reality to judge that James Bond's feats might be unreal, even in America (where he believed James Bond came from), but fell back on a media-related criterion:

Interviewer:	And do you think that would happen in America?
James:	No.
Interviewer:	No. Why? Why not?
James:	'Cos you wouldn't be able to do that, what he does.
Interviewer:	No. Why don't you think you would?
James:	Well, you would be able to but it's just trick control.

Like other children of their age, these children attempted to build up a theory of media production as a basis for modality judgements; but typically it was either vague, like James's 'trick control', or ingenious but inaccurate, as with Connie, aged 10, who thought that The Incredible Hulk built up his muscles with green playdough; or wrongly premised, like Shawn, aged 12, who believed that talking monkeys on an advertisement must have been carefully trained. Two of the children – Paul, aged 11, and Raelene, aged 10 – gave an account of one media illusion:

Interviewer:	What would you think of say blowing up a house or anything like that [on television]?
Raelene:	Oh actually they pretend. They . . . but when they're making it, they don't blow up the house.
Interviewer:	Oh?
Raelene:	It ma-, it ma-, it makes the film, the people who're filming makes it blow up.
Paul:	And they take a photo of something.
Raelene:	Yeah, yeah.
Paul:	And take something else.
Raelene:	Yeah.
Paul:	And they must join it up together.
Raelene:	Yeah.

On only one matter did the children have any consensus view about media unreality. Almost all the children liked *Diff'rent Strokes*, the main reason being because it showed blacks. Three commented particularly on the age of Arnold, the diminutive star of that show, estimating it at 15, 20 and 24. These guesses acknowledge a difference between the age of the actor and the age of the character, but they exaggerate it, overcompensating for it. This illustrates what seemed to be happening generally with these children. They suffered from information-deprivation about the media, but they overcompensated by making what little they knew do more work.

These children also suffered from information-deprivation about the world outside their immediate experience. Their notions of geography were haphazard. For instance, one child listed New South Wales as a foreign country, along with India and Pakistan, but this kind of inaccuracy could be found among many of his white contemporaries (cf. Connell, 1971; Hawkins and Pingree, 1980). More revealing was their specification of Aboriginality. Eight of the children did not distinguish between Aborigines and American blacks. Arnold and Willis, the two blacks from *Diff'rent Strokes*, were typically given as examples of Aboriginals on television. One boy called Arnold a Negro, but went on to describe his own cousin as a Negro too. The same boy included Indians from Westerns as Aboriginals. The only child who did not assimilate Aborigines to other blacks was Paul, aged 11, who used the local Aboriginal term 'noongah', and included only local Aboriginals in it. The others seemed to operate with a strong binary paratactic structure, dividing the world into black and white. In one interview this exchange took place:

Interviewer: Do you see a lot of fights and that sort of stuff on television?
Lisa: Yeah, not lots of them.
Charlotte: Not lots of them.
Interviewer: Yeah. Do you like it? or –
Lisa: Yeah, sometimes. If there's a black and a white I say 'come on Blackie'. [Laughs.]

The modality operations at work here are worth following in some detail. By applying a simple inclusive paratactic structure, black–white, Lisa has assimilated the action into her schema of reality, and she claims that she has the greater involvement that follows from that ('come on Blackie'). But her comment has a relatively low modality, signalled by her laughter. So it seems that once the initial simplifying modality judgement has brought it closer to her world of experience, other modality judgements then come into play to give it distance again. The result is that she enjoys this violence. This does not mean that she endorses it in real life, though such a show provides an outlet for expressions of hostility and aggression that all these children feel towards whites.

In general, these children preferred paratactic structures, neat divisions into good and bad, black and white, men and women, which lead to definite judgements that may not always coincide with the nuanced judgements of respectable adults. For instance, Paul and Raelene liked *The Dukes of Hazzard*, and saw the sheriff in that show as unequivocally the baddie:

Interviewer: The sheriff's the baddie, is he? Or is he the goodie?
Raelene: [Laughs.] He's the baddie.
Paul: He's the bad one.
Interviewer: He's the baddie. [Laughs.] And what does he do, then? What sorts of thing does he do that makes him a baddie?
Paul: He's, he's a policeman.
Raelene: Yeah.

These children clearly do interpret some aspects of their television experience differently from non-disadvantaged whites, and they do have some different bases to their modality judgements; but as far as we could see, the significant differences came from the different models of reality these children have managed to build up: different models of media production and of the world outside their own experience. They suffer from information-deprivation, which they try to make up for; not always successfully in individual instances, perhaps, but with overall a close enough approximation to white child norms. All of these children had problems at school, and school potentially would be a main source of the knowledge they lack. Clearly it would be desirable on many counts if they understood more about the media and the outside world. However, their lacks are not sufficient to put them in the category of those who are especially at risk from the influence of television. In none of them did we find the tendency to a collapsed modality that we have argued is the essential condition for dangerous effects from television. So their limited experience, with the fact that society has classified them all as socially disadvantaged, seemed not to have produced the effects we had expected. We had to ask the question: why not?

Looking at the children more closely, we were struck by indications that these children, in spite of their backgrounds, were not socially isolated in either their general experience or their experience of television. All of them watched television in the company of other Aboriginal children of their own age, and there was a close bond between the children living in the one house. They reported that usually there was considerable interaction between the children watching any one show and they would talk about shows afterwards, or act them out. Television-watching for these children was almost always a social and bonding activity. Where that was not so (some children reported watching shows at another house belonging to a relation or a friend) shows would be more likely to be reported as 'scary' and disturbing. These children may have lacked the support of a white nuclear family, but to differing degrees they were all integrating strongly into a community. Aboriginal society emphasizes diffuse kinship relationships rather than the exclusive parent–child bond, and most of the children had access to these. And Aboriginals in a predominantly white society experience hostility from outside, rather than discohesion from within. Their position as a minority group is likely to intensify the power of their modality structures, not weaken them. We came to see that our expectations had been based on ignorance and prejudice. Worries about the effects of television on children of this kind seem to be misplaced. If a high proportion of these children is likely to go to prison at some time in their life, as statistics suggest will be the case, the probable cause will not be the unreality of television, but the harsh realities of their own lives, struggling against the odds in a white world.

Sex, power and the negotiation of meanings

Most current research assumes that meaning, perception and thought occur essentially within individuals. Society only comes in at a secondary stage, as an influence or a control. However, if, as we have argued, society affects even the modality of a television message, the reality it is assigned and the nature and intensity of the emotional response, we cannot defer consideration of society and the social context of viewing. It is too much bound up with the television experience for us to artificially separate it out. Many researchers acknowledge this intermixing of individual and social factors, but see the social dimension as 'contamination of the real meaning' that television has for the child. So they try to control these contaminating extraneous meanings, implicitly supposing that the communication of a randomly selected child with a standardized questionnaire is as close to pure meaning as is possible in this world.

Our own interview material, by these criteria, seems sadly impure and contaminated. It has grown mainly from a situation where a small number of children talk to an unfamiliar adult female, in unfamiliar surroundings, with a video camera recording the exchanges. Clearly these are not typical conditions for viewing or talking about television. We would be unwise to assume that what children say, under these conditions, is either what they 'really' think or everything they think, without suppressions and distortions. It is, in the first place, simply what they say. But what children say when in a situation like this is by no means uninteresting or unimportant for an understanding of television and its role in the social process. Discourse about television is itself a social force. It is a major site of the mediation of television meanings, a site where television meanings fuse with other meanings into a new text to form a major interface with the world of action and belief. In chapter 2 we saw one revealing instance of this process, when members of one group moved from an anti-censorship to a pro-censorship position in the course of a discussion, and in the process totally revised their judgement of the programme they had just seen. What is established by discussion as a consensual set of meanings (even if that consensus includes tolerated differences and contradictions)

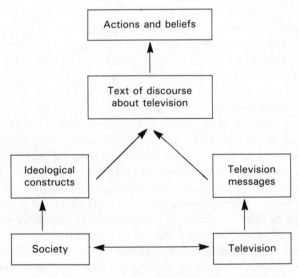

Figure 18

acquires a public force and status. It is likely to feed back into social life, and the choice and interpretation of television programmes. We can represent this set of relationships in figure 18.

Texts of discussions about television are not simply more or less imperfect guides to a set of all-important internal mental units, 'what children think'; they are direct examples of an important social fact, the social process of the construction of meanings. This process necessarily involves the insertion of television meanings into general ideological constructs which are not specific to television or to discussions about television. Much to the regret of those who wish to deal with television meanings as if they were pure and uncontaminated, we must be prepared to find that non-television meanings are powerful enough to swamp television meanings. If that is how television works in practice, then it is that process that we must study, and which is important for us to understand. Once again, therefore, readers must bear with us as we employ a fairly detailed linguistic approach to our data.

Our *Fangface* interviews, although typical in some respects, were systematically skewed in one direction. They represent discourse marked by an asymmetry of power. They thus have things in common with other kinds of discourse with the same asymmetry, such as teacher–student or parent–child exchange. In such exchanges, struggles for control and strategies of resistance can be studied as they affect the form and possibilities of communication, contributing substantially to the meanings that the participants will take away from the occasion, whether or not those meanings have much to do with television or any other ostensible topic of discussion. However, in order to focus on features of the exchange that come from the relatively formal, power-laden situation, we compared the discourse of our *Fangface* groups (children aged 8–9) with a wider range of children, seven groups of four or five children aged from 5 to 12. These children were asked to talk about television in any way they wished. The conversations still took place in the school context, and the interviewer remained in the room, at some distance from the children, because the schools were unhappy about a total lack of supervision. However, she was not part of the discussion, and the conversations were much closer to normal peer group discussions. We then compared some of the features of the language of these conversations with those of the more formal interviews as a way into reconstructing the dynamics of the two kinds of situations and their effects on discourse about television. The results are presented in table 25. These figures have many implications about how the two kinds of situation work to

Table 25   *Features of language by situation* (percentages)

	Simple sentences			Compound sentences				Negatives		
	One phrase	One clause	Total	Para- tactic	Hypo- tactic (ext.)	Hypo- tactic (int.)	Total	Ext.	Int.	Total
Peer discussions	14	61	75	17	2	6	25	4	6	10
Interviews	20	37	57	18	14	11	43	26	20	46

mediate television. In the peer discussion there are many more simple sentences (one phrase, or one clause). Such sentences typically form self-contained meanings which relate paratactically to the sentences of others. In such a discussion there is less subordination of meanings, or of participants. Each coexists with all the others, relatively unmodified, relatively without influence on others. There is less pressure towards a consensual meaning of television: or more precisely, the consensus is a looser one. Within the category of simple sentences, children in the interview groups used a higher proportion of single phrase sentences (e.g. 'yes', 'no', or 'Fangface' or 'The Heap'). Forty-four per cent of their simple sentences were single-phrase, compared to only 18 per cent of the peer discussions. A single word or phrase indicates a deletion of meaning, usually the meaning of someone else: (e.g. 'Who's your favourite character?' 'The Heap' [is my favourite character]). The higher rate of single-phrase sentences in the interview groups, then, signals a double suppression of the meanings of the self. First of all, the form of the sentence comes from outside; second, most of it is then removed from the surface of the utterance.

With compound sentences the proportion of paratactic forms is much the same in the two kinds of situation, but the interviewer-led group has many more hypotactic forms than the peer-group interaction: 25 per cent as against 8 per cent. The strongest contributor to these figures is external hypotaxis; that is, where a person completes a hypotactic form initiated by someone else. This is a strong form of the subordination of individuals and their meanings, as against the looser, more egalitarian parataxis of the peer group. As well as external parataxis, however, the children in the interview groups produced more hypotactic structures of their own. These imitate the adult structures produced by the interviewer, setting up self-contained structures of power as a way of coping with the power-laden situation of the interview. That is not to suggest that these children do not mean what they say in hypotactic structures in interviews. If they produce those meanings they demonstrate that they have internalized them, and that they give them a social value, in interactions with adult authority figures. Conversely, this kind of meaning about television is relatively unavailable in peer-group discussion. It is neither encouraged nor reinforced.

A final difference between the interview group and the peer group is the much higher level of negation in the interview group (46 to 10 per cent). In the peer group, consistently with the loose relationship indicated by parataxis, the children much less often directly disagree with the meanings of others, though that does not mean that they agree strongly, either. What goes on in the peer group discussions is akin to what Piaget called 'collective monologue', in which children communicate their own meanings but do not react to what others say, or expect others to react to what they say. In the interview the group is held together in a hypotactic structure dominated by the interviewer, but this imposed cohesion goes along with a much greater tendency to notice conflict and disagreement. As with hypotactic structures of speech, so also with negatives, children in interview situations are likely to internalize this form in their own speech, stating both sides of an issue. The interview is characterized by overt conflict, internal and external, compared to the tolerance and consensus of peer group discussion. In this struggle for meanings there are two main options: either silence and self-suppression, or hypotaxis, the creation of powerful, adult-oriented meanings which exist contradictorily, alongside other kinds of meaning.

We can generalize a little further in expanding the two discussion types. In peer group discussions the ideological messages of television will take a predominantly paratactic form. Only in discourse involving authoritative adults – such as parent–child or teacher–student discussions – will individuation and explicit development of powerful hypotactic forms be marked. It is in these conditions that television meanings are most strongly reinforced or contested. Many concerned parents and teachers hear child views of television only in these situations, and are appalled at what they hear. What they do not notice is their own replies, and the dynamics of the discourse as a whole, in which their contribution has great if not irresistible force.

Up to this point we have looked only at markers within verbal language, comparing two types of discussion in these terms. We now turn to dynamics within groups, drawing on non-verbal as well as verbal markers. As we argued in chapter 2, if we want to catch the multiplicity of messages passing at different levels in different semiotic systems, it is necessary to record more than a verbal text. Birdwhistell (1972) has estimated that 65 per cent of the messages conveyed in normal face-to-face interaction come via non-verbal channels. Most of these messages concern interpersonal meanings which communicate attitudes to the self and others, and situate verbal meanings in relation to people and people in relation to meanings. They are the major carrier of the meanings which control the group's social interaction. In a group of six people, like our interview groups, Birdwhistell's estimate of 65 per cent will be on the low side, since while one person is speaking the rest will still be communicating non-verbally. A transcript of the words alone, then, will give a very impoverished record of the dynamics of an exchange, and its social meanings.

Our interview groups all consisted of a mixed group of boys and girls, with the interviewer, representing authority, making up the third element. Our interest focused on the dynamics of the interaction between boys and girls in this situation (the same methods could have been used for relations between any other class of interactant). Firstly we looked at the verbal language, to see what differences there were between the girls and the boys. The figures are as in table 26. Here

Table 26   *Features of language by sex (average per interview)*

	Simple sentences			Compound sentences			Negatives			
	One phrase	*One clause*	*Total*	*Para- tactic*	*Hypo- tactic*	*Grand total*	*Ext.*	*Int.*	*Total*	*Mimetic gestures*
Girls	5.4	15	20.4	9.6	3.9	33.9	3.5	5.4	8.9	0.5
Boys	12.7	32.8	45.5	13.9	7	66.2	5.5	6.0	11.8	4.9

the over-riding fact that emerges is the boys' dominance of the verbal channel. Each boy talks twice as much as each girl, on average, though they certainly do not watch twice as much television, and it can be doubted that they think twice as much. This greater verbal dominance spreads over all kinds of speech, though it is greater with simple sentences than with compound sentences. The negatives repeat the same dominance, but less strongly; that is largely because girls' rate of internal negation is nearly the same as that of boys, from less than half the average number of utterances. In fact, girls have internal negations in 16 per cent of their utterances, as against 9 per cent for boys. That is, they incorporate negation, opposition, into their own speech much more than the boys do.

This verbal dominance by boys is not counterbalanced by non-verbal dominance by girls in the gestural code. In fact, boys used mimetic gestures much more often than girls did. Girls used an average of 0.5 gestures per interview, whereas boys averaged 4.9 per interview. Girls are even more strongly suppressed in the non-verbal channel than in the verbal, which is especially significant given the normal tendency to express intimate, 'low' meanings in this channel. Girls' ideas may be suppressed, but their feelings are suppressed even more, in the dynamics of a group like this. The gestural code has a stronger modality than the verbal code, so the girls' virtual exclusion from it is a suppression of this stronger modality. This is in line with findings from the Bobo-doll experiments of Bandura (1965), when girls were found to be less likely to imitate television violence in an experimental situation.

Another important indicator of group dynamics and modality is laughter. We have already discussed the modality value of laughter. Typically it weakens the modality of an utterance, sometimes even inverting it. As Freud (1960) has pointed out, this weakening or inversion of modality normally goes along with another quality, the presence of a subversive counter-meaning, some meaning which is disapproved of or forbidden by an authoritative figure. So a discussion where there is no laughter is likely to be one where counter-meanings are totally suppressed, as in many formal situations. Laughter indicates both awareness of authority meanings, and a subversion of them. It is a function of both the pressure of the authority figure, and the degree of the subversion. With the small group discussion there seemed to be almost continuous laughter, though we were unable to tell who was laughing or what they were laughing at. There was considerably less laughter in the interviews. This gives a rough indication of the degree of formality of the two situations, and likelihood of counter-meanings being expressed.

We then tried to investigate the patterns of laughter within the group, especially comparing boys with girls: who was laughing at what, and what social relations were expressed by it (table 27). From this

Table 27 *Frequency of laughter by sex*

	Average per session	Percentage at interviewer	Percentage same sex	Percentage other sex	Percentage self
Girls	7	2	22	76	3
Boys	10	2	74	24	24

we can see that girls laugh less than boys during discourse about television, though for neither sex is the interviewer funny. Girls' words were not usually explored for counter-meanings or for inverted modalities; but there was something of a consensus between boys and girls that boys were 'funnier': more likely to express subversive or counter-meanings. They were much more likely to indicate, by laughing at themselves, that they felt they had produced such a meaning. They provided the group humorists, the licensed fools. Laughter is a double-edged weapon, depriving words of official sanction as well as carrying subversive content. To laugh at someone is to deprive their words of official status, and impose on them some counter-meaning (even a non-meaning) that they had not intended; but that does not seem to be happening here. In general the boys seem deliberately to set out to be funny, and their efforts are acknowledged. As with the comparison of mimetic gestures, we see a far greater suppression of counter-meanings in girls than in boys, compared to the relative suppression in the verbal channel. The fact that girls laugh in essentially the same proportion as boys suggests that these meanings exist for them with equal force. They have simply been trained more effectively not to express them, or not in a situation like this, mixed company with an authoritative adult present. Because the girls are not rewarded as much as boys for producing subversive child-meanings about television, they are in effect being socialized into not recognizing or acknowledging them, and thereby into a more serious, adult stance in relation to television and enjoyment.

As well as talking or not, laughing or not, children in any group must always look somewhere, and this is a continuous signal of their relationship to others and to the flow of meanings. Children normally look at the person they are talking to. If they look away, that break in eye contact is itself significant. Similarly, children listening to someone scan the face of the speaker to pick up non-verbal responses. If they look elsewhere it usually has a reason: either someone else's reactions are more important or the topic is uninteresting. We investigated the patterns in the interviews, and table 28 contains the results. This table seems to clarify a number of things. Both girls and boys direct most of their speech at the interviewer. It is primarily speech for her: views about *Fangface* packaged for adult consumption. Boys look away more than girls when talking, and they break contact even more often when others are talking. Although both boys and girls are strongly controlled by the adult figure, boys opt out more, so they are freer of that control, less consistently aware of the interviewer's attitudes. However, even when others in the group are

Table 28 *Direction of gaze by sex* (percentages)

	Boys	Girls
1. While talking:		
at interviewer	73	79
at peers	13	15
away	15	6
2. When others talking:		
at interviewer	33.6	45.5
at peers	33.7	35.4
away	32.6	18.9
3. Orientation to peers (others talking):		
to boys	51	84
to girls	49	16
4. Orientation to peers (self speaking):		
to boys	53	83
to girls	47	17

talking (not the interviewer), both girls and boys are likely to be
scanning the interviewer to gauge her reactions: again, girls more
so than boys. When a child talks, and directs his or her attention to
peers, however, a surprising tendency emerges: boys address their
remarks almost equally to girls and boys, whereas the girls' remarks
are addressed much more strongly to boys than to girls. The boys
are the more significant others for them, after the interviewer – not
the other girls. When others are talking the pattern is the same. The
boys divide their attention evenly between girls and boys. Girls are
an important part of their audience, though not more so than boys.
However, girls pay closer attention to boys, five times as much as
to girls, though boys speak only twice as much. So not only are the
boys granted twice the verbal space in the discussion, as well as much
more access to non-verbal channels, they are also given much more
importance: especially by girls. Girls in fact are only given equal
weighting by boys, not by other girls.

What this kind of analysis gives us is a class of message that is
repeated a large number of times in every such situation. The message
at issue includes not simply a kind of content, but also rules as to
who has access to it and who has not. It is an ideological message,
specifying classes of social agent (in this case males versus females,
adults versus children) and the status of their meanings. The analysis
partly confirms the existence of this content, and partly explicates a
number of instances in which it is learnt and reinforced. The fact that

all the children we studied reacted in sufficiently similar ways to the slightly novel situation we placed them in showed the capacity of the ideological schema to generalize to new situations. It also no doubt confirmed, for the children, the applicability of the schema, thereby reinforcing its taken-for-granted status.

This set of messages, which amounts to an ideology of sex roles, is omnipresent, a major meaning carried by the substantive discourse about television. Arguably it is actually more pervasive and powerful in shaping behaviour and attitudes than anything that was thought or said about *Fangface* as such. The accumulated burden of such messages, carried in innumerable other discussions, would seem to be overwhelming.

However, there is another level of analysis which throws further light on the ideological processes at issue: how does this set of messages about sex roles interact with other messages in the course of a group discussion? In *Fangface*, the cartoon we used to explore this question, the content had a sexist bias that is fairly typical for the media: one female out of five main characters, playing a minor, largely passive role. The interviewer set the discussion at some points to examine sex roles. Figure 19, and the following interview, show one exchange – complete with non-verbal annotations:

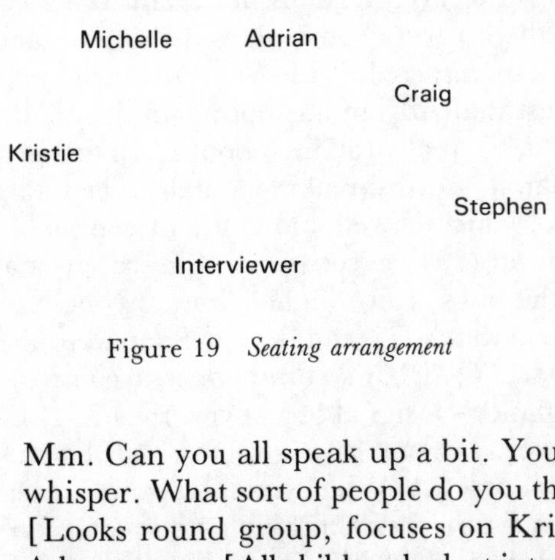

Michelle   Adrian

Craig

Kristie

Stephen

Interviewer

Figure 19   *Seating arrangement*

Interviewer: Mm. Can you all speak up a bit. You don't need to whisper. What sort of people do you think they were? [Looks round group, focuses on Kristie.]

Kristie: Adventurous. [All children look at interviewer. Kristie leans back slightly.]

Interviewer: Mm. Can, let's take say, the girl, Kim. [Stephen looks across to Kristie. Adrian and Craig exchange glances, and smile.] What sort of person do you think she was?

Adrian: Hmm. A smart person. [Grins.] She thinks she . . .
                 she thought she knew all the answers, nearly. [Adrian
                 looks at interviewer, smiling. Craig also smiles, looks
                 at interviewer. Stephen looks ahead, then at Adrian
                 and smiles. Kristie looks at Adrian. Michelle smiles
                 and looks at interviewer.]
Interviewer: Mm. Anything else?
Adrian: 'Cos she thought she was . . . they would have another
                 adventure. [Adrian looks at interviewer. Stephen and
                 Craig look down. Michelle looks at interviewer.
                 Kristie looks at Adrian.]
Interviewer: Mm.
Kristie: Um, she was always ready to have an adventure. She
                 already thought of the not obvious clues. [Kristie looks
                 at interviewer. Michelle looks at interviewer. Adrian
                 and Craig look at interviewer. Stephen looks at
                 Kristie, then down.]
Interviewer: Mm. [Pause.]

If we attended only to the verbal content of this exchange we would
probably have to interpret Adrian's comment as a wrong judgement.
Kim, the girl in the cartoon, does not seem to be a 'smart person'
who 'knew all the answers'. She plays as humble and deferential a
role as a male chauvinist could wish. Some of the non-verbal indicators,
however, suggest that Adrian has not misunderstood the cartoon; it
is more that he is not really talking about it. In this group of children
Kristie is a talkative, norm-breaking female. The total number of her
utterances is 98, which is well above the masculine average. In this
group only Adrian (131) exceeds her. She receives a high number
of gazes from the boys (105), higher than anyone else in the group.
It is not untypical that she is the first to respond to the interviewer's
question. However, Adrian's comment is accompanied by a smile
plus sideways glance – a signal of a covert meaning. Craig also looks
at the interviewer, but smiles, signifying that he shares the covert
meaning and endorses it. When the interviewer asked the question
they looked at each other, establishing a male common meaning. The
other boy, Stephen, looked at Kristie when the interviewer asked the
question. Later on he also looks at Kristie. It seems likely that the
three boys are establishing a connection between Kim (the cartoon
character) and Kristie. The comment 'A smart person' then would
be directed at Kristie rather than Kim. The grin is not the only signal
of the presence of a counter-meaning. Adrian's sentences show a

fracture: 'she thinks she . . .' (present tense as though about someone who is present) 'she thought she . . .' (past tense, i.e. a different modality). At the beginning of his sentence Adrian looks at the interviewer but signals, through his smile, a challenge to authority meanings. However, half-way through he opts out of the challenge, and reverts to a safer (but silly) observation, and gives it a rising pitch, indicating its lower modal status. Pressed to continue his line of argument, he starts as he ended the previous statement, breaks off and completes his statement with an innocuous but irrelevant statement, no longer about Kim. This sentence, too, ends with a rising tone. Adrian now looks at the interviewer, his brief challenge over. That challenge was a sexist put-down of Kristie. Once the challenge was over the other two boys looked down, withdrawing. When Kristie resumed, most of the group looked not at her but at the interviewer. Only Stephen, who was not included in the original male consensus, divided his gaze between Kristie and the floor in front of him.

We can see in microcosm from this exchange one rather surprising way in which media content can have social effects. On the one hand the cartoon shows people who strongly conform to the ideological stereotype. Adrian gives a counter-reading, which ostensibly claims that the cartoon breaks the stereotype, but his real target is Kristie and her aberrant behaviour, which he can then describe with a negative judgement ('smart person'). His attempt to control her behaviour is itself controlled, however, by this situational context, which enforces a sexist ideology in different ways. The primary effect of the television show, here, is not as a direct influence – a version of the world which is uncritically repeated by its passive victims. What it does is to provide the pretext for a struggle in which Kristie is briefly and lightly punished for breaking sexist ideological norms. We can see that this is not merely a direct reflection of the content of the show from the fact that Adrian can administer his put-down more effectively by a desexist *misreading* of the show than by a correct reading of its actual sexist content. This is not to say, however, that the sexist content was irrelevant. Adrian needs it to establish the covert meaning of his comment and its application to Kristie.

An exchange like this shows how the dynamics of interaction in a group, far from being a distraction from the real meanings at issue, can be important meanings in their own right, as well as a key to how the surface verbal meanings are to be understood at a deeper level. The following exchange illustrates some further possibilities that a close analysis of non-verbal as well as verbal language can reveal.

Interviewer:	Can you tell us who you'd like to be? [To Catherine.]
Catherine:	[Leaning forward and whispering.] Miss Piggy. [Others laugh. One child looks briefly at C, others look at interviewer.]
Interviewer:	Miss Piggy. Why would you like to be Miss Piggy?
Catherine:	[Whispers inaudibly.]
Interviewer:	[After pause.] Do you know why?
Catherine:	No.
Interviewer:	What sort of an animal is Miss Piggy? [All children look at interviewer: two with hands in air.]
Catherine:	[Whispering.] She's a pig. [All children look at her briefly; then three turn back to the interviewer.]
Interviewer:	She's a pig, um. Is she a nice pig? [Catherine nods. Boys exchange glances, and laugh together. Girls look at interviewer.]
Julian:	She's not a nice pig. [Moves closer to other boys. Two other boys whisper to each other and laugh. One girl looks at boys: others at interviewer.]
Interviewer:	You don't think she's nice?
Julian:	She hits Kermit. [Emma mimes a karate chop in the air, and looks at Sharon who is looking at a boy. Boys continue to look at each other, then turn to interviewer.]
Interviewer:	She hits Kermit. [Pause.] Let's go round the girls, because the girls haven't really told us much yet. [To Emma.] Who would you like to be?
Emma:	Miss Piggy. [Emma looks at interviewer. Rest look at Emma.]
Interviewer:	You'd like to be Miss Piggy. Why?
Emma:	She crashes Kermit the Frog into pieces. [Karate chops the air, looking at interviewer. Others laugh, looking at Emma.]
Interviewer:	Why do you want to crash Kermit into pieces?
Emma:	[Pause.] Well . . . he is silly sometimes. [Looks away before speaking, then looks at interviewer. Girls look at each other then interviewer; as do boys.]

These children are talking about another show which has a strong male bias. Of the six most important regular characters in *The Muppets*, five are male, ranging from the physical Animal to the smooth-talking entrepreneur, Kermit. Miss Piggy is the only female in this group. She is vain, capricious, violent and ridiculous, sometimes adopting a pose of simpering femininity, at other times revealing a physical savagery that leaves Kermit, her reluctant paramour, in fear of his life. The stereotypes of femininity sit uneasily on her gross shoulders, and her real nature is their opposite, though she is still a kind of image of the female: not a passive, helpless flower for men to protect, but a rapacious, castrating female who would overwhelm the unfortunate objects of her love.

Analysing *The Muppets* using content-analysis of the traditional kind, we would have to see it as a strongly sexist show, which provides a limited range of negative stereotypes of women, in contrast to a much fuller range for boys including more positive models. Turning just to the surface content of the girls' responses to this show, we see them filtering out the male options in favour of the female role. However, if we stayed with the words alone, we would have to conclude that Catherine does not understand Miss Piggy's nature (she thinks that she is a 'nice' pig) and that Emma is another potential victim of video-violence, roused to fierce aggression against frogs and males for the most trivial of reasons.

The non-verbal dimensions fill out a picture with different implications. The interviewer has created space for the girls to speak (and she has to keep that space open or the boys will fill it again). Within this exchange boys and girls are polarized, but the boys formed the more cohesive group, whispering to each other and looking at each other more often, offering a continuous commentary on the girls' speech, though both sexes defer to the interviewer. The boys laugh more than the girls, sometimes with them [in response to Emma] but sometimes at them [Catherine did not laugh].

The two girls, Catherine and Emma, make the same identification with Miss Piggy, but its social dimension and function is clearly different. Catherine is socially isolated. She typically looks at the interviewer or away rather than at her peers, and they look less often at her even when she is speaking than they do at Emma. Her two statements here (her only words in the whole interview) are clearly offered only because the interviewer requires them. She says them in the direction of the authority figure, and then she leans forward; but she speaks so quietly that the interviewer can hardly hear her, and her peers also are partly excluded. It is her quietness that alters the modality of her statement, allowing her peers to invert her meaning (from 'nice' to 'not nice'). Their laughter serves to re-interpret her utterance. The group assumes that she really knows that Miss Piggy could not be called 'nice', and restores her real meaning, though she does not smile or acknowledge that assistance. There is total opposition between her fantasy figure, Miss Piggy, boisterous and outgoing, and her social self, which is painfully shy and withdrawn. Miss Piggy seems to be a compensation representing what she is not, rather than a likely influence on her behaviour. We see two aspects of her self which are not integrated, and this lack of integration is related to her uneasy position in the group, isolated both from peers and authority figures, with just sufficient support from each to encourage her to collapse into silence and self-contradiction. The group is not totally negative towards her. Not only does their laughter make her briefly one of them, but Emma picks up her line and develops it. This one moment in the limelight did not encourage her to participate again in the discussion.

Emma is as self-confidently part of the group as Catherine is isolated. Emma sits next to Beth, and has a close relationship with her, and she also interacts with the boys, who look at her more often than any other girl in the group. Along with her social integration goes a greater integration of the fantasy figure and her social self. As well as her definite tone of voice, she uses gestural language, mimicking Miss Piggy, which is high-modality communication. However, she laughs as she does so, and the laughter of the group is mutual, unlike the laughter at Catherine. There is less distance between Miss Piggy and Emma, but her laughter signals her awareness of such distance as there is. Her relationships with her peers are strong and positive, but there is one fissure in her speech. When the interviewer asks her why she would like to be Miss Piggy she pauses, and when she answers her voice quality changes, from energetic confidence to a more sing-song, didactic tone. It is as though at this point, pushed by the interviewer, she opts out of a peer-oriented childlike sentiment to an imitation or parody of adult values. The two kinds of statement do not mesh together, either in tone or sense. Elsewhere in the interview Emma made the same kind of abrupt switch, from child-oriented utterances to stiff repetitions of an adult opinion, usually her mother's, as in the following exchange:

Emma:	Mum, Mum wouldn't let me watch anything like The Incredible Hulk or King Kong or Carry on Camping, nothing.
Interviewer:	Why not?
Emma:	Mum just doesn't like them.
Interviewer:	Do you agree with Mum?
Emma:	[Nods.]
Interviewer:	You do? Why don't you want to watch them? Why do you think it's best not to watch them?

Emma:	Well, um, in a way TV is not very good for you.
Interviewer:	Why isn't it good for you?
Emma:	[Pause.] Because it's bad for your eyes.

The girl who indulged in karate chops as Miss Piggy now says, in a quiet voice, that she does not like The Incredible Hulk. She agrees with her mother, without good reasons, where before she was prepared to smash Kermit, without good reasons. Both Catherine and Emma say contradictory things, which are a function of social conflict. The interview contains both power relations and solidarity relations, though the two children have quite different orientations to this common set of relationships. The interview allows glimpses of how these children – Adrian and Kristie as well as Emma and Catherine – interact with their peers as well as their interaction with an adult. Their child-oriented meanings may be very different from their adult-oriented meanings, so the impression we get of what they 'really think' may be different from adult–child or child–child interaction. Neither set of meanings, on its own, is 'what the child really thinks'. Our analysis suggests that the child really thinks both, and their struggle within its mind, reflecting tensions in the social relations of the child, is what determines the structure of the psyche and the possible thoughts and acts that will result.

Conclusion

In this chapter we have seen how social contexts of different kinds affect the construction of television meanings in a number of ways. We can now tentatively set out the chain of effects with figure 20. The relations in this diagram in turn suggest some further observations:

1. The experience of television must include both the context of viewing and the context of discussion of that experience. Each of these, along with media content, contributes to the meaning of the television experience.
2. These contexts are interpreted through, and hence determined by, general social relationships. They carry meanings about social relationships – relationships of power and solidarity, attitudes to authority and to peers, sex roles – which are endlessly repeated and renegotiated and reinforced in a variety of situations. These meanings are heavily ideological, and the ideology carried by the contexts of viewing and discussion is likely to be common to many other contexts.

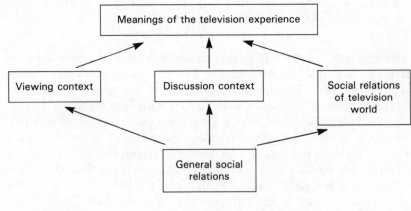

Figure 20

3. Social relationships carry immediate rewards and sanctions. The social context has a very high modality. Television is passive, and the world of television has a malleable but generally low modality.

Overall, these points constitute a compelling argument for the primacy of general social relations in developing a reading of television, rather than the other way about. It seems likely that the ideological meanings inscribed in general social relationships will have a powerful effect on the total meanings of the television experience. That is because the television content itself is but one integral part of the whole television experience, and so the ideology of that content will be heavily mediated by the child's social understanding. Research into television must therefore treat it as an integral part of a viewer's normal experience, as but one of a large number of complexly interacting aspects of our culture which both defines and is defined by other parts within the whole.

Chapter 6

Television and schooling
The hidden curriculum

> All television is educational television, the only question is, What
> is it teaching?

This question, posed by a United States Federal Communications
Commissioner (Williams, 1981) is another important one which
researchers have singularly failed to answer with regard to the
relationship between television viewing at home and formal schooling.
This failure was most clearly expressed in a recent review of the
research literature (Hornik, 1981) where the author concluded:

> Clearly enough our answers to almost all the research questions
> posed . . . are inadequate. I do not know much about television's
> impact on schooling, and we know almost nothing about the
> processes through which current effects might occur.

Apart from the lack of definite answers, relatively little research has
in fact been done on this important question. It may be that the reason
for the dearth of studies is the lack of significant results. In this chapter
we propose to summarize some of the concerns held by different
authors in the field of children and television, and to comment upon
the main findings of the existing research, suggesting why results have
at best been ambivalent.

Essentially we argue that television and schooling are not two
separate variables, such that we could regress one against the other
to show that television is bad or good for schooling. In the rest of
this book we have indicated that television watching is not necessarily
a passive, mindless activity for children, but reading it is an important
aspect of general cognitive and social development. School formally
and intentionally exists to foster such growth, so we might expect a
positive relationship between the two domains. In practice, however,

the situation is more complex. Some kinds of responses to some kinds of television could have very beneficial educational consequences, in some ways of organizing the curriculum. Conversely, some widespread educational assumptions and practices set up an opposition between television and school learning, so that each detracts from the other. It is the contradiction between these two possibilities that leads to the present ambiguous and unclear research findings, some of which we examine below. However, in this chapter we also want to explore the basis for a far more positive relationship between television and the classroom; a fuller recognition of the educational role television could and should play in the school system in contemporary society.

Television and scholastic performance: the evidence from research

There are many diverse and variously interested groups who are influential in the topic of the interaction of schooling and television. Writers such as Winn (1977), Schulman (1973), Fineberg (1977) and Postman (1979) have written about their fears that children's learning is adversely affected by television in ways such as loss of attention span, hyperactivity, lack of verbal ability and poor reading performance. It has proved to be very difficult to verify such concerns, however (Hornik, 1981; Holz, 1981), so in this chapter we will, as we have throughout this book, concentrate upon issues of meaning, drawing on what teachers and pupils think and say about television, in order to illuminate the often problematic 'effects'.

In our contact with teachers we have found that they are, as a group, very concerned about a number of problems they believe to be the result of television viewing. These concerns are well shown by a recent survey of more than 800 kindergarten to early secondary teachers in South Australia (Australian Council for Children's Film and Television, Biggins, 1981) which produced the following conclusion:

> In summary: 46.2% were concerned about physical effects, 98.7% about mental effects, 62.4% about social and personal effects and 90.7% about attitudinal and behavioural effects.

> The chief area of concern was lack of imagination and creativity (mentioned by 55% of teachers). This category included inability to make own play activities or organise time or motivate themselves; passivity, reliance on television for stimulation, lack of initiative, watching rather than doing.

The next most commonly mentioned areas were fatigue (including irritability, crankiness, tardy school performance, lack of energy), lack of physical fitness (including obesity, poor physical development), lack of communication skills (poor vocabulary, lack of language development), copying of undesirable behaviour (use of violence and bad language), loss of personal experience (not participating in active sports, hobbies or clubs, less time to learn home and family responsibilities).

The areas perceived by teachers are thus physical, social, attitudinal (or ideological) and cognitive. Dealing with them in that order one must agree that a child who has been up till 10.30 at night, and who gets up again at 5.30 in the morning for the early cartoons, is bound to be tired, listless or cranky. Similarly, children who watch television to the exclusion of all sports and other physical exercise are not going to be fit. There can be little argument about such propositions. It is important to note, however, that they are results of the way in which television is used, not effects of the nature of the medium as such.

The same is true of the social effects perceived by teachers. Both areas of concern fit the 'displacement hypothesis': there comes a point when so much time is spent in viewing that it not only takes up all the 'free time' available, but it also prevents the child engaging in the range of activities normal in a child's life. What is particularly pertinent to teachers about the extent to which television displaces other activities, is that the activities displaced tend to be those which have the same kind of function as television. Obviously reading, solitary and group imaginative play are most liable to be displaced by television viewing, and just doing nothing (Winn, 1977) most of all. So also, television can displace family conversation and other interactions, especially when the television is on for the majority of the family's waking day (Medrich, 1979). Other social effects such as isolation are likely to occur when children have their own television sets in their own rooms. The impact of such usages has been relatively well established by existing research (Comstock et al., 1978; Surgeon General's Report, 1972). The conclusion to be drawn, however, is not that television as a medium has intrinsically good or bad effects in these respects, but that it is a resource which, like any other, may be used or abused.

A few researchers have been less negative about potential effects of television on children. It has been shown in general that children learn such things as how to interpret filming techniques and syntagms (Collins, 1979; Salomon, 1979), but not that high-viewing children's attention spans are shorter for that reason, nor that intelligence is depressed (Hornik, 1978), nor that they are necessarily poorer at reading and mathematics (Morgan and Gross, 1980).

In summary the views outlined show one kind of concern: a general feeling that all is not well, that things have changed for the worse, and the television is a principal contributing factor, if not the sole culprit. As we shall see, research evidence is very ambivalent in its support for this position. But there is another kind of concern, one which is to do with the nature of the medium itself. The most recent example of that tradition is a book by Postman (1979) in which he sees problems because

> Every society is held together by certain modes and patterns of communication which control the kind of society it is . . . they set and maintain the parameters of thought and learning within a culture.

Postman's argument is essentially a semiotic one: that the electronic media dominate our communication systems, and that, because they are quite different from our old essentially digital print media, they are actively changing our society. For instance, he makes the point that because television is a more natural means of communicating than print (using pictures rather than words), it is cognitively processed in a different way: pictures are perceived rather than conceived or comprehended as words are. In this way Postman contrasts viewing television with reading television. On this basis he suggests that the most important role of schools is to check and balance, if not to reverse the effects of the electronic media. Like the other educational research, however, support for the concern is very ambivalent. An informed and closely argued review (Holz, 1981) concludes:

> his analysis . . . presents a rather selective and idiosyncratic view of the nature of television and mass communication which many readers may find stimulating and intriguing but which does not hold up well under careful scrutiny. . . . The important educational implications of the new 'information environment' have yet to be given the systematic and informed examination they deserve.

Thus the concern, though legitimate, is still essentially the statement of a point of view, not the verified outcome of a research programme. In fact, as Holz points out, much relevant research available tends to counter rather than support his argument.

Because of the demand for quantitative proof, the majority of

Table 29   *Simple and partial correlations of TV with achievement scores*
(n = 614)

Achievement score	Simple[1]	Controlling for IQ
Reading		
Comprehension	– 0.23	– 0.14**
Vocabulary	– 0.18	– 0.05
Total	– 0.23	– 0.13**
Math		
Concepts and problems	– 0.22	– 0.06
Computation	– 0.16	– 0.01
Total	– 0.20	– 0.04
Language		
Usage and structure	– 0.20	– 0.12**
Mechanics	– 0.15	– 0.05
Spelling	– 0.14	– 0.04
Total	– 0.18	– 0.07
Battery total	– 0.22	– 0.08*

[1]All simple correlations significant at 0.001.
*$p < 0.05$ **$p < 0.01$

researchers in this area have sought to correlate the amount of time spent viewing with school performance, controlling for factors such as age, sex, socioeconomic status and IQ. Although this is by far the most scientific commentary upon the problem, it has not yet produced many useful results. By way of example, we will here illustrate the results produced by just one typical study.

As expected from the teachers' survey reported at the beginning of this chapter (Morgan and Gross, 1981), table 29 clearly shows that all the measured aspects of reading, mathematics and language covary with the amount of television watched. In other words, the longer the children habitually spent viewing television at home, the worse their performance on the scholastic achievement tests. But notice how, of the separate measures, only reading comprehension and language use and structure remain statistically significant when IQ is also taken into account. This clearly shows the much more powerful relationship between the amount of television viewed and intellectual ability. As shown elsewhere (Hornik, 1978; Morgan and Gross, 1980) the lower a child's IQ the more television he or she is likely to watch. This does not prove, of course, that television is the cause of the measured differences: it may be that children of lower IQ, or those who are not so good at reading, like to watch television more.

Another interesting point about this study is that these negative effects were still present when socioeconomic status (SES) was held constant. This may seem at first to be counter-intuitive in that there is a very well known relationship between SES and language scores in particular, and between SES and achievement in general. On further consideration, however, it is apparent that the effect of holding SES constant is to single out the two groups who are least representative of the norm: namely, a low-SES/low-viewing group, and a high-SES/high-viewing group. The problem then is that it is probable that SES is not a useful indicator, as there are differences of culture and aspiration in all SES groups which would outweigh any effects due to television as such. For instance, low-SES, low-viewing children may well watch little television because their parents insist that they do extra school work in the evenings so that they will achieve highly. Similarly, some very high-SES children may watch excessive amounts of television because both their parents are committed to the pursuit of their own professional careers, leaving their children for long periods of unsupervised viewing.

● Neither is it sensible to conclude from these figures that SES does not interact with the television–school-achievement relationship. A more likely hypothesis is that there is a 'ceiling effect': television will enrich an otherwise deprived intellectual environment, but limit an intellectually rich environment. However, one suspects that all the statistically significant relationships would disappear were SES to be held constant with IQ because that has been the case elsewhere (Sharman, 1980).

Apart from such equivocations, however, the most pertinent point about this table is the minute size of the actual differences being reported. A simple correlation of 0.23, the highest measured, actually accounts for less than 5 per cent of the total variance. This means that other factors accounted for more than 95 per cent of the differences in the children's scores. Although $r = 0.23$ is statistically 'significant', in educational terms it is minuscule. Something of the order of a 300 per cent increase in the amount of television viewed decreases reading scores by 10–15 per cent. The statistical relationship could mean, in effect, one of a number of things: that for the whole group, differences were so small as to be barely measurable; that a sizeable minority of children performed no worse or even better if they watched more television; or any combination of the two extremes. In this study there is some evidence for the second possibility: the authors found that low-IQ girls statistically actually performed significantly better in reading comprehension if they were heavy television viewers.

Incidentally, they also found that reading comprehension was not improved either by the amount of time spent doing homework, or by the amount of out-of-school time spent reading.

Although this study is technically one of the best of its kind, it does not reveal the clear picture that one might have expected. All that one can say is that heavy television viewing appears to affect most children's scholastic performance adversely, though some are more affected than others and some are affected beneficially. However, such effects, when they do exist, are minimal. Furthermore, the contrary finding that there may be beneficial effects for some children has been reported elsewhere. In Australia, for instance, Sharman conducted a study for the ACER. In his summary report (1980) he wrote the following:

> In this study of 271 children (Melbourne: Grade 7) significant simple negative correlations were found between time spent watching television and (a) school performance measured as overall school achievement and (b) achievement on a test of comprehension in social studies. Therefore one might be tempted to conclude that television viewing impairs school performance. However, when other variables known to affect school performance were taken into account, principally intelligence, self esteem and association with peers, it was found that the negative association disappeared and a positive relationship was generated between comprehension in social studies and watching television.

So, although the overall picture we have is that excessive amounts of television viewing tend in general to go with slightly poorer scholastic performance, it does not help us pinpoint whether the cause is necessarily television as such. No doubt the same relationship could be observed for sport, music, and anything else which causes imbalance in the range of activities engaged in at home. Any single activity which displaces school learning by occupying virtually all out-of-school time would have the same effect. On the basis of this evidence one must reach the conclusion that the nature of television as a medium is not a major factor in scholastic performance.

On the other hand, not having found a causal relationship by this means does not prove that there is none, nor that all the concerns of the variously interested and very different groups are mistaken. If one is going to maintain the commonsensically obvious position that viewing counts for a great deal in a child's development in our culture, then we should expect it to interact with how a child performs at school. We are therefore left with the proposition that we should look for other things, or look in different ways, or look in different places. Although we were certain that there were more obvious things to be looked at in other places, we were less certain just how to look for them. What we do in the remainder of the chapter, therefore, is to work at a more analytic level, on our data, rather than attempting to prove a position by the empirical results of what is as yet limited research.

Television and the teachers' curriculum

There are two primary questions about the television–school relationship to examine: what does the school tell the child about television, and what does television tell the child about school? We deal with the first question in this section; its effects in the next section, and the second question in the subsequent section.

To begin from first principles in answering both questions, we have to pose the prior question: what aspects of the two realms of the child's experience overlap; when; and in what ways? The results of research of the kind we have already discussed indicate that there is very little overlap of television and school behaviour in terms of the skills and understandings that are necessary to basic scholastic performances as measured by achievement tests. We have also seen that paradoxically teachers believe television to have a number of severely adverse effects upon children's school behaviour. Our empirical work on this problem thus began with two hypotheses: that although (a) television does not have a consistent, strong and direct effect upon the formal school curriculum, (b) television might have more of an effect upon the pupils' cultural attitudes and understanding of schooling.

It was not easy to formulate these hypotheses in such a way that they would be amenable to traditional research procedures, for it was not clear at the outset just how the effects of such interactions would be manifest in the classroom or the home. But as it is easier to gain access to classrooms in order to monitor behaviour we employed ten teachers (junior primary to senior high school) to observe their classes and to report any indications of the intrusion of any aspect of their pupils' home television experience.

In more detail, the group consisted of five secondary teachers: one in each of the four core areas of English, mathematics, science and social studies, and one manual arts teacher. There were three primary teachers in grades 2, 5 and 7 (the kindergarten teacher had to drop out), and there was one teacher of a split grade 4/5 remedial withdrawal group. The period of observation covered 10 weeks in the middle of the third term of the school year so that the teachers had well-established relationships with their pupils.

There were three phases of observation. First, a non-reactive phase of 4 weeks when the teachers simply tried to document any indications of television viewing occurring in their classes. During this period they did nothing to indicate to the pupils that they were investigating the topic. There followed a second phase of 3 weeks when the teachers began to probe what they thought were examples of the intrusion of television into school work. During this phase they asked pupils what they meant by things they said that appeared to be about television, and what had been their source of information, ideas, words and such-like. In the third and final phase the teachers explained to their pupils what they were looking for, and asked them to help by trying to make use of what they watched on television in their classes, reporting it back to the teacher. The explanatory session for this phase included a discussion and survey of the pupils' viewing habits and favourite shows.

The teachers met with the researchers each week for a report-back and discussion session, and recorded events and ideas in research journals. Also, over the whole year we observed classrooms, interviewed teachers and pupils, and recorded feedback from the various groups of in-service teachers we met in lecturing engagements. The data thus accumulated are mainly of the 'critical incident' variety, and have been used for illustration and hypothesis-generation, not for proof or theory verification. Overall, what we found was that out-of-school television was largely excluded from lessons: there appeared to be a general understanding from the children that television was not part of school, and that it should be kept quite separate. Thus we found that the first 4 weeks produced only 11 incidents which could be classed as evidence of television experience being applied in the classroom. As one teacher said:

> I've listened all week, and I've got nothing. The kids are getting sick of hearing me say, 'Where'd you hear that?' If you'd asked me how much kids talk about television before we started, I'd have said about 50% of the time. But it's next to nothing. Even doing drastic things like giving them half an hour to talk about anything, very, very little comes out about television at all. (11–12-year-old pupils.)

The following is typical of the kind of incident teachers reported where television was mentioned:

Teacher: We were doing 'The Ancients', which I don't really see a great deal of point in doing anyway, and the nearest you got was talking about 'Up Pompei', which a lot of the kids did watch, I know that much.
Tripp: Do you remember what they learned from that?
Teacher: They got as far as the clothing and the crude jokes, I think that's about as far as it went.

Clearly television was not totally absent: it seemed more likely that the pupils were simply disguising it because they knew that to bring it in as such would not meet with their teachers' approval. The kind of evidence for this was one teacher's experience when she asked them to talk about something that they had seen on a space-adventure show the previous evening:

> The students became very disruptive, and rather than concentrate upon the discussion were telling stories like, 'Did you see that three-eyed monster on . . .?' It seemed to me that they thought that because I was condoning television it was no longer classtime.

In other words, this teacher found that her pupils equated school work with not-television so television was not-schoolwork. It seemed likely that this expectation of the pupils was one which had been engendered earlier in their schooling. So we looked for examples of when and how teachers might be developing this attitude. What we found was a number of instances of teachers excluding televisual experience either consciously and actively, or passively and unconsciously. Generally they did not seem to realize what they were doing.

An example of passive exclusion came from a secondary social studies teacher during an interview. He was talking about the more general problem of how pupils became so alienated from schooling:

Teacher: Alienation is caused by the general irrelevance of what they are taught. A lot of it I can see is not relevant anyway, but at the same time some of the useful ideas you do try to get across to them, such as that their world is not just their suburb, that there is more than that in it, other people's lifestyles, other countries that would interest them, they just won't take that either. There's no background for it because kids don't read at school or at home.

Tripp: But don't they get a lot of the necessary background
                from television? Even if they just watch 'Kojak' or
                'Charlie's Angels' they must still learn a lot about
                America. Or 'Prisoner', 'Cop Shop' or 'The
                Sullivans' must teach them a lot about other aspects
                of Australian society.

Teacher: They don't see it as such. It's just the violent and
                exciting bits that they seem to see. It never enters their
                heads that 'Kojak' is about New York or telling them
                something about America. It's just not directed, their
                television viewing, they watch at home but not to any
                purpose.

Clearly this kind of attitude is an occupational hazard: this teacher
had never tried to use his pupils' television experience in that way,
he just assumed it would not work because he regarded that experience
as fundamentally bad.

There were several other examples of active exclusion of television
by teachers. The most graphic incident occurred in a grade one class:

When a boy stood up to give his news to the rest, he began,
'On Sunday there was this film on the telly, and it was all
about . . .', but the teacher interrupted with, 'Now come on,
Johnny, you know the rules. "News" is things that really
happened to us, not things we saw on the telly. You sit down
for now, and do remember our rule next time.'

When Johnny was in school on Monday, television was said to be
something which did not really happen to him on Sunday; it was rather
something which the teacher would punish him for mentioning in class
newstime.

On the other hand, some of the active exclusions we observed were
not so overtly intentional. The following exchange took place in a
year 8 English lesson:

[The teacher was orally collecting from a class objects which could
be used as metaphors for 'voice'.]

Pupil 1:   Horn.
Pupil 2:   Trumpet.
Pupil 3:   Radio.
Pupil 4:   Communicator.
Teacher: No! not communicator. Do you see what you're
                doing? You're saying how you use your voice, not
                something else like it. I want things, like 'horn'.

Clearly this teacher did not watch 'Space 1999' or, if she did, left that experience behind her when she entered the classroom.

It is that kind of misunderstanding which so clearly indicates the kind of reasons that teachers would have for wishing to exclude the child's television experience from their classrooms. Not only are they untrained to deal with it, but it so often challenges their own knowledge and experience of life and understanding in general. In comparison with most teachers, the average pupil watches a great deal more television and quite different television programmes. Whereas 20 years ago teachers could, in a very real way, safely assume that their pupils knew a great deal less about everything than they did, today the children often know a great deal more than their teachers, albeit about things such as Batman, Spiderman, Superheroes and Dr Who, quite apart from police-violence shows, westerns and the serials.

One important result of this diversity of experience is an effective barrier between teachers and pupils, so that the teachers cannot use what the children know ('start from where they are'), nor can the children use what they know because their knowledge has no place in the classroom. There is no longer either a shared understanding, or an unquestioned supremacy of teacher knowledge: pupils and teacher tend to know different things, and will often fail to understand and communicate with each other as a result.

The extent of differences in viewing became clear in the South Australian survey of teachers which found that they objected most to the kind of programmes habitually watched by those of lower SES. Table 30 illustrates this values clash. It had to be compiled from an industry source, our study teachers and Biggins, 1981, as published figures were not available. The majority of pupils do not watch what the majority of teachers think they should watch, and they do watch what teachers think they should not. Another interesting statistic from the same report was that 30 per cent of the teachers reported children initiating talk with them about the news, weather and documentary-type programmes, and 19.2 per cent reported the same for soap operas and serials. However, 33 per cent of teachers reported that children talked to one another about soap operas and serials, whilst only 9 per cent reported children talking about the news, weather or documentary-type programmes amongst themselves. One conclusion to be drawn from such figures is that children recognize what is valued and disvalued by their teachers, and act accordingly. Thus we had some evidence to support our hypothesis in that teachers appeared to be excluding television from schooling and that this exclusion of television from the classroom was affecting the pupils' cultural attitudes

Table 30   *Viewing figures for 5–14-year-old children* (percentages)

Programme type	Police/ violence	Soap operas/ serials	Quiz shows	News/ documen- taries	'C' class programmes
Programmes teachers say children should not watch	74	55	0	0	0
Programmes teachers say children should watch	0	0	7	65	53
Actual viewing figures	64	60	45	28	37

and understanding of schooling. In fact, what we were observing through our teachers was the operation of an important but neglected part of what is termed the 'hidden curriculum', and it is this hidden curriculum which enables us to relate the idea of a child's culture to schooling in the next section.

Television and the hidden curriculum

There are two obvious questions to ask about the hidden curriculum and the television–school relationship: what does the school tell the child about television, and what does television tell the child about school? We deal with the first question in this section, and the second question in the last section.

The curriculum is usually defined as 'the planned course of instruction', which is often erroneously equated with the syllabus, which is actually only one aspect of the curriculum, namely, the 'formal curriculum'. There are at least two other aspects to any curriculum: the 'informal curriculum' and the 'hidden curriculum'. School knowledge is distinguished from general knowledge and common sense because it is essentially knowledge about the school subjects, and these could be said to approximate the 'formal' curriculum. It consists of knowing such things as literature, capitals, dates, equations, formulae, theorems, and being able to write essays and poems. But there are also many things learned in school which cannot be said to be part of the formal curriculum in the sense that they are not part of the 'planned course of instruction', but which constitute an informal curriculum which is largely unplanned. When learning about a battle, for instance, a child asks how they transported or made the guns, or fed the army, and the teacher 'digresses' to deal with the question. Such diversions are sanctioned if not actually encouraged in most classrooms. Teachers recognize the value of such questions, and allow them to arise spontaneously in the context of more formal learning, although they cannot be planned into the formal curriculum. If television is allowed to intrude overtly into a lesson it is almost always as a part of this informal curriculum.

However, something pupils soon learn about the formal and informal curricula is that teachers are generally better at answering their own questions than their pupils' questions. That kind of learning is neither overt nor consciously planned, so it constitutes a 'hidden curriculum', which is very powerful, and has a wide sphere of operation. The term was coined by Jackson (1968), and developed by others such as Snyder (1971), who realized that his college students actually learned all sorts of things from their roles and the nature of the institution which were neither intended nor sanctioned. For instance, the imposition of rules made many students conform much of the time, but it also taught them how to break the rules without being caught, or if caught without being punished. They learned how to evade, as well as to abide by the rules.

Since Jackson's original work there have been great advances in our understanding of the hidden curriculum. Writers such as Apple (1979) and Giroux (1981a) have shown us that schools are essentially sites of enculturation rather than of formal instruction. That is an idea which needs some expansion and illustration before we can go on to consider it fully, but by way of example we will look at one relevant aspect of the hidden curriculum dealt with in the current literature.

Willis (1977) made an ethnographic study of some working-class boys in a secondary school. What he documented was essentially a manifestation of the class struggle, and how that leads to the reproduction in the younger generation of existing differences between the classes in selection for and attitudes to work. Very briefly, a cycle he saw was this: most lower-class children are poorly equipped to succeed in school because their values and culture are inappropriate to the essentially middle-class way in which academic learning takes place, and so they are likely to come into conflict with it. Those who actively and overtly resist the school's priorities and values (such as Willis's group, 'the lads') tend to be seen as deviant. They are labelled by the school authorities as no good, as stirrers, and their behaviour is punished. They are also judged to be of 'low ability'. The lads resisted this labelling and treatment by denying the importance and value of school learning of which the teachers were clearly masters. They promoted instead the value of the physical, particularly manual labour, at which they could out-perform (and often out-earn) the teachers; but that very denial of the intellectual exacerbated their under-achievement, which in turn led to their leaving school at the minimum age, unqualified for anything but manual labour.

In such ways the formal curriculum of the school, although intended to enable all pupils to fulfil their academic potential, has an outcome different from what teachers consciously planned for their lessons; nevertheless, the learning encounter is managed in such a way that that is the major outcome of those pupils' experience of school. That learning is thus termed part of the 'hidden curriculum', which can thus be seen as more essentially a form of enculturation than scholastic learning.

Enculturation does not take place in a cultural or social vacuum, however: each child brings to school his or her own set of cultural and social experiences, norms and values. There are, of course, many aspects to 'the culture' of a pluralistic society, of which school is but one; television another. Just how much of what aspects of the available culture a child takes up is largely determined by this environment. High-viewing children tend to acquire a greater proportion of their culture from television than they do from other sources. There are a number of reasons for this, some of which account for the high viewing itself, but most obviously time spent viewing television displaces time spent in other ways. Because the school has its own culture, which is quite different from that of many pupils, there is an inevitable cultural clash in which pupils have to modify their existing values in order to fit into and succeed at school.

The impact of such dynamism in cultural relationships means that the interactions are generally more complex than our empirical research procedures at present allow for. For instance, here one must never lose sight of the fact that all television viewing is mediated to a greater or lesser extent by the family, the school and other factors, so that time accorded to viewing in the home is itself an aspect of culture. As we show in the last section of this chapter, the reciprocal is also true: television itself mediates culture, including the family, the school, and itself. The ways in which, and extent to which, it does so will depend amongst other things upon the amount of time devoted to what kinds of television viewing.

How does the hidden curriculum relate to cultural acquisition from the television? This is best illustrated by another example of the way in which hidden social forces are at work in schools: pupils are required to possess certain abilities before school learning can effectively take place. These abilities themselves have to be learned. Children from different backgrounds learn them in different ways and with different facility. Lundgren (1981) terms the more psychological aspects of this learning to learn, 'meta-learning'; Bourdieu and Passeron (1977) term the more sociological aspects 'cultural capital'. Perhaps the best way to deal here with what are complex notions with many ramifications in the literature, is to recount an example of the process of acquisition of cultural capital:

> One day Katya, aged 2½ years, dropped the xylophone she was playing with and all the bars dropped out onto the floor. Her father acted in the following way: first he said, 'Never mind, let's put it all back together.' Then, as Katya began to try the different bars at random, he said, 'Hold on, let's see what we've got. Look, this is a black one and that's a white one. You know the black ones go on top, so let's put them altogether over here.' Having watched as Katya did that, he again stopped her after she had again tried to put them back in the box at random. 'Look,' he said, 'can you see that this one's longer than that? See if you can find the longest first. That's good. Now find the next longest and put it down next to the longest one. Now the next. Good, now we can put them into the box in the right places, can't we?' She did.

What was happening there was much more than the simple cleaning up of an accident. Katya was learning some important things which would help her learn at school. Some of them were:

1. Adults won't do things for me when they think I can do them for myself, but they will help me to do them.
2. They help me by telling me what to do, so I have to listen to what they say.
3. I must first think about how I'm going to do something before I actually try to do it; I must work with my head before I work with my hands.
4. The process of doing something is more important than the outcome of it having been done; adults will ask me to do things which they could do more quickly themselves.

What she was learning were not absolutes in the sense that there is only one right way of learning, but essentially highly culturally specific attitudes towards a learning task. There was some less culturally situated cognitive learning taking place too. Katya was being introduced to sorting behaviour according to qualities such as size, colour, and position; she was learning the meaning of relational terms such as first, longest, above, and next. Thus she was being introduced to observational strategies and classification systems associated with Bernstein's notion of 'elaborated code'.

However, the point to draw out of this example is that the outcome of such interactions in the home is that when Katya goes to school she will find school learning very easy. Teachers like children to sit still and listen until they have been told what to do. They do instruct primarily through language, and most tasks are to be performed in a stepwise fashion. Katya will go to school with the disposition to such behaviour already firmly established. She will find that the teacher will treat her in the same kind of way that her parents do, with the same expectations, negotiations, sanctions and rewards. So there will be continuity between the home and the school. School will be congenial, and the process of school learning already familiar.

There is no need to contrast her experience with that of another child where parents would have punished the child and put the xylophone away by themselves, if indeed they had any musical instrument in the house at all. The point is that the culture a child acquires in the home constitutes a kind of capital resource in the school. Because Katya will enter school equipped to learn in the way demanded, she will learn fast and easily. That learning will itself be assimilated into her stock of cultural understandings and expertise. That is why Bourdieu uses the term 'cultural capital': it is an asset which increases in proportion to the amount already held.

If we now return to the question of the relation between a child's home television viewing and school performance, we have the proposition that there is a two-way interaction between the culture of the school and the culture of television: the child will bring television to school as a varying proportion of the cultural capital, and the school will offer its culture to the child. What interests us is this interaction between how the child perceives school as a result of what is learned from television at home, and how the school perceives the child as a result of how it perceives what the child has learned from television.

The analysis thus far suggests that children who are heavy viewers are more likely to come to school with a large investment in television culture. This becomes a feature of social consequence when one takes into account the high correlation between a child's social class, and the quantity and quality of the television he or she views. Although it seems that there are few teachers who actively punish pupils for using their television experience in class, the overall effect is to delegitimate it in school, and thus put at a disadvantage the pupil whose chief environmental enrichment has been the television. The students who suffer most in this regard are those who are the heaviest television viewers, whose television viewing in terms of content is most different from that of the teacher, and whose viewing is least controlled or mediated in the home (Medrich, 1979). One may not agree that they have less cultural capital than other children, but in scholastic performance terms they do have the least appropriate cultural capital, because much of what they do and what they have learned already cannot be used in school.

Teachers claim to watch quite different things on television from their pupils, which is clearly likely to be so even if only in view of age differences. However, although we suspect that they also watch a great deal more commercial television, particularly soap operas and serials, than they admit to, that does not lessen the cultural gap between school and home: because they do not admit to viewing similar programmes to their pupils, they do not use that experience in their teaching. We believe that to a much greater extent than we can yet show, teachers thus not only deny their pupils' culture, they also deny their own. However, whether it is or is not so that what teachers actually watch has much in common with their pupils' viewing habits, they do also watch more of the 'higher culture' of the ABC than do lower-class pupils. They are also more likely to use what they saw on the ABC in their classrooms. Thus there are differences of social class which put the middle-class child at a distinct advantage: whilst the lower-class child has been watching *Cop Shop* or *Prisoner*, more middle-class children and teachers have been watching *Nationwide* or *The World Around Us*. If one of those children or teachers mentions television, they will have a basis for interaction denied to the other child. In other words the lower socioeconomic classes are those with the least appropriate cultural capital, and thus they will be the most disadvantaged in school.

This contention may be supported by evidence from two different sources. First, it accounts for the well-established correlations between heavy television viewing and low aspirations and self-image in North America (Gross and Jefferies-Fox, 1978), and in Australia (Edgar, 1977). If what occupies the majority of children's out-of-school hours is denigrated and disallowed in school, those children are not only deprived of the security of school–home reinforcement of values, but are themselves denigrated: if what they enjoy doing is not worthwhile, they cannot be worthwhile people. As lowered self-esteem also correlates with under-achievement (Vander Zanden, 1980), as do high levels of anxiety (which are caused by conflict amongst other things – Docking and Thornton, 1979), we have an alternative explanation of how and why the scholastic achievement scores should be adversely affected by high television viewing.

The problem then is this: if so much of a heavy-viewing child's cultural experience is at odds with what is valued by teachers, why are the effects measured on scholastic performance so minute? The most obvious explanation is the 'ceiling effect' again. One can reasonably suppose that the basic scholastic skills being measured in the effects research are, to a greater or lesser extent, being 'overtaught' in schools. That is, teachers concentrate upon them, giving remedial help when required, until all but a very few children achieve a satisfactory standard, despite the displacement of homework and reading by television viewing. Further, as the basic skills are generally taught in a formal way regardless of individual interests, most children meet the requirements. The cultural effects would not appear in the content of such tests, simply because they are intended to be 'culture fair' tests of 'the basics'.

On the other hand, IQ would be a major determinant of achievement, which explains why the differences due to the amount of television watched tend to disappear when intelligence is taken into account. Better indicators of the effects of differences in the amount of television viewed on school performance are the age at which pupils leave school, and their career aspirations. Gross and Jefferies-Fox (1978), and Christiansen (1979), found just such relationships: high viewers leave school earlier, but their career aspirations are unrealistically high, which indicates that whilst they are less successful at school, they read themselves into occupational roles presented by television, rather than the ones which the educational system has selected them for.

Finally, the question as to what makes teachers denigrate television may be explained in two ways. Bourdieu (1980) has pointed to the close affinity that the purely academic culture has to the culture of the politically powerful, arguing that the role of the academic culture is both to select what is to be considered tasteful, interesting, consequential and valuable, and to teach it primarily through the school curriculum. The consciousness and behaviour of teachers in this account are structured by the very system of power relations of which they are the necessary agents, so that teachers will be more or less unaware both of what they do and why they do it. Teachers usually appeal to cognitive and academic reasons for excluding rather than appropriating television, but typically they do so with a vehemence that does not gainsay the analysis, but supports it. Teachers' reasons, which we have seen are without any solid empirical support, may be seen as rationalizations of viewpoints inherent in the structure of dominant culture, and hence determined by that structure in the first place. Although Bourdieu's work has been criticized in some respects (Giroux, 1981b), the central claim about the relationship of teachers to an elite curriculum remains sound. Differences in the teachers' judgements of the worth and appropriateness of the high-viewing child's cultural experience can legitimately be seen as the product of differences between the culture of the school and the ability of the child to utilize it. That ability is undoubtedly strongly affected by the cultural background of the home, which is in turn influenced by social class.

A second explanation for teachers' wariness of television is in terms of power and control in the classroom. To a great extent teachers maintain discipline in their classrooms by the respect of their pupils. One means of establishing that respect is by knowing more than their pupils do about what is considered important. If teachers know less about the more popular shows, they have an obvious interest in claims that these shows are unimportant, or better still, positively harmful. They thus have good reason to denigrate what they themselves do not watch.

Thus the large differences in quantity and kind of television viewing (which are as clearly demarcated as such differences ever are in a pluralistic society), and the epistemological differences between school and television learning, constitute as severe an obstacle as any to lower SES children in terms of eventual certification and hence their own SES potentiality. Teachers who blame television for lack of scholastic performance are probably detecting through informal means pupils who are under-achieving in that they are achieving merely the basics, whereas they should be achieving much more beyond that minimum level. In that respect it is thus possible to argue that through exclusion of televisual experience from classrooms from the best of intentions, teachers actually produce the conditions under which the medium becomes one of the most obvious and effective mechanisms by which existing social class differences are maintained within and by the educational system.

Television as teacher

So far we have examined the way in which the school deals with television. We now want to look at the second part of our question. What does television tell children about school? We do not propose to repeat aspects of cognitive, scholastic and instrumental learning here, as these have been discussed earlier in this book and have already been well explored elsewhere (Hornik, 1981; Williams, 1981; Salomon, 1979). Neither do we want to examine the way in which schools as such are portrayed on television, although that is one useful approach. We want to deal with some of the more subtle cultural messages about school which are communicated in other shows which, although ostensibly about quite different things, nevertheless can be seen to relate closely to the culture of the school. Our exposition will be as non-technical as we can make it, at this point, because our concern here is with messages which should be easily accessible to the average classroom teacher, and which can connect readily with widespread classroom practices. We will illustrate this general case by reference to two particular shows: quiz shows, which have one kind of relationship to the aims, purposes and conditions of schools; and to the popular Australian serial *Prisoner*, which is an example of another kind of bearing on schools and schooling.

Quiz shows and classrooms

We gained the first insight into how television relates to the hidden curriculum from an interview with a 13-year-old pupil in a quite different study. Here is an extract where the interviewer is trying to force the student to re-examine some of his assumptions about school knowledge:

Interviewer: What um, . . . is any of it any use to you? To learn all that stuff? [Industrial revolution.]
Ashley: Yeah . . . say if you want to be a teacher or something.
Interviewer: Yeah, but do you want to be a teacher?
Ashley: No.
Interviewer: No? What would you want to do?
Ashley: Welding and . . .
Interviewer: Do you? Well, what's the good of learning all about how factories used to be, or what they used before the seed drill was invented or something, if you want to weld?
Ashley: Don't know . . . just . . . have to go there [school] don't we?
Interviewer: Right . . . um . . . does it make any difference whether you learn it or not?
Ashley: Yeah.

Interviewer: Does it? What sort of difference does it make?
Ashley: Um . . . [pause] don't know . . . um . . . [pause]
                if we . . . um . . . like . . . you have to know all the
                things if you go on *Sale of the Century*, or something
                like that.
Interviewer: Right.
Ashley: If you don't go to school you're not going to win that
                are ya?

Most people would have expected children to hold the opposite
priorities: that quiz shows were good because they helped you do well
at school, not that school was worthwhile because it helped you with
television quiz shows. But in that quiz shows have a number of
important similarities to schooling and so the two are closely related,
Ashley is right.

First, there is the question of how school knowledge relates to real
life. Many parents, pupils and teachers have sensed for a long time
that most of what is learned at school is quite irrelevant to most other
aspects of life. Children learn, for instance, that light travels in straight
lines; they read 'classic' novels such as *Great Expectations* or *Moby Dick*;
they learn about the Eureka Stockade or the Boston Tea Party: they
learn how to calculate which of two cars travelling at what speed
starting a journey will arrive before the other. They pass examinations
if they can get half or more of it right. As one Year 10 boy said, 'What's
the point of learning all this stuff [climatic regions of India], I won't
need it to become a truck driver.' In that sense, almost all learning
beyond the elements of numeracy and literacy are irrelevant to most
pupils.

Yet there is another sense in which it is vitally relevant. As another
Year 10 boy said, 'I'm doing this so's I get a better certificate so I'll
get an apprenticeship.' It is not so much what is learned that is
important, but one's ability to learn it. Children can perceive that
school learning is useful because it enables you to go on to other things.
On the other hand, there are many pupils who know that they will
not be going on to things which are in any way affected by their school
performance: for many children, they know that if they get a job it
will be in spite of their failure at school. Yet day after day these pupils
have to continue learning school knowledge. These students often
become alienated from school and in a period of increased competition
for jobs and an increasing necessity for certification, the number of
such pupils grows (Fensham et al., 1985).

Another challenge to the value and purpose of education comes from the apparent contradiction that those who do best at school and continue in education do not necessarily come first in the income stakes. The obvious example is the teachers themselves. They have generally done well at school, and must appear to their pupils as being good at school learning, yet they are 'only' teachers. They currently earn less than skilled tradesmen and less than unskilled labourers in dangerous jobs. It is clear to many children that there are all sorts of skills which enable one to be a success in real life other than the ability to read and write well and to absorb factual information. The traditional notion – that those and only those who do well at school have the greatest access to the material rewards of our society – is becoming increasingly untrue, and in some respects schooling is becoming less, not more, relevant as the youth unemployment figures rise.

How do quiz shows and schooling relate in these respects? First, and most obviously, the shows look very much like classrooms. There is a quizmaster (teacher/schoolmaster) who tells the competitors (pupils) what to do, and how and when to do it. He judges the correctness and adequacy of their answers, and awards points (grades). The quizmaster faces the competitors, who sit in a row and generally have to answer individually. As soon as one right answer is received, they move onto the next question. If a wrong answer is given, someone else is allowed to try. Most important the questions tend, as in most teaching, to be purely factual; and, like school, they are 'pseudo' questions (Barnes, 1975) in that the quizmaster knows the answers before he poses the questions: he does not want to know the answers himself, he wants to know if the competitors know.

Then there are 'guess-what-I'm-thinking' sequences so beloved of teachers where the information is released incrementally, and competitors have to be the first to complete what the quizmaster could say himself if uninterrupted. It is not so much what the competitors actually know which is the criterion of success, but whether they can produce it on demand: speed of recall and skilful guessing are the abilities which win. There are also clearly articulated rules which have to be adhered to. Competitors who break them are punished by losing points or being excluded for that question or round. Quizzes are games, but they have much in common with the learning games played in school.

Because television quizzes and schools are structurally so similar, it is hardly surprising to find similar ideologies operating. As Fiske (1983) pointed out, quizzes encapsulate demonstrations of the ideology of competition and success in an advanced consumer society.

Education is, of course, intrinsic to that ideology. It may be summarized thus: anyone may enter, and everyone has an equal chance to be a winner; but only the best actually win. They win because they have the greatest personal endowments, and they make the best use of them. They are then rewarded with easier and greater access to the most desirable material goods produced by our society. There is an element of luck in it, but that is reduced as far as possible by the random assignment of turns and questions, and rules which prevent favouritism (sexism, sponsorship, patrimony). What luck remains is the luck inherent in life: the luck of the draw, being in the right place at the right time, just happening to have come across something before.

We can compare that ideology to the ideology of free comprehensive education: everyone can go to school; at school the most able do best; they go on to get the best jobs; they are thus entitled to more of the luxuries of our society. This is a powerful message of the hidden curriculum that our children have to learn in and about schools. Although the journey from pre-school to a well-deserved, well-paid job is collapsed in a quiz show into a single half-hour, the route, the means and the effects are all the same: an ability to learn facts and trot them out on demand entitles one to the good life.

In schools and quiz shows the facts themselves are as intrinsically worthless as the paper a banknote is printed on; but once acquired they may be cashed for real goods. The severance between school learning and the real world is thus stitched together by the quiz show as market place: school learning is bartered for an enhanced way of life. That the transaction is immediate does not invalidate the analogy, it merely clarifies, dramatizes and emphasizes it, and in so doing serves to legitimate schooling. Quiz shows make school seem worthwhile to Ashley; they postpone, if not prevent, his rejection of school and school learning. He sees knowledge as power, but it is power which pupils may attain without all the further transformations necessary in real life, such as achieving success in a job. In that sense it is a deceit, but it is the attractive and socially accepted deceit of the myth of schooling. Thus the crucial interaction between schooling and television may be seen as cultural and indirect. Consequently it is vital in the long term because it operates through an attitudinal effect which seems to us to be more important than the relationship between the amount viewed and performance in the basic skills. Furthermore, because it affects high and low viewers alike, it provides a further explanation for the minimal differences due to the amount of television watched.

Pupils and prisoners

To illustrate another kind of television show from which pupils learn, we have chosen a 'soapy' which was very popular with Australian children when we were doing our research. *Prisoner* is an Australian-produced series set in a woman's prison, which illustrates a very common genre of television serials throughout the Western world – that based on an institution. Other kinds of institutional life to be dramatized in this way are, for instance, police departments, corporations, hospitals, and religious organizations. So although we have based our analysis on a single example here, many of the points made apply in various ways to other such shows.

As with quiz shows, we can begin a number of structural parallels between the serial *Prisoner* and schools which indicate another powerful interactive relationship. The teachers reported that their pupils often said that school is like prison, and, of course, in some respects that is true. But it is true in structural rather than actual terms, and schools are not so much like actual prisons as the way in which prison as portrayed in *Prisoner* is like school. This is not remarkable, because both are institutions and have much in common with what Goffman (1961) termed a 'total institution':

> First, all aspects of life are conducted in the same place and under the same single authority. Second, each phase of the member's daily activity is carried on in the immediate company of a large batch of others, all of whom are treated alike and required to do the same thing together. Third, all phases of the day's activities are tightly scheduled, with one activity leading at a pre-arranged time into the next, the whole sequence of activities being imposed from above by a system of explicit formal rulings and a body of officials. Finally, the various enforced activities are brought together into a single rational plan purportedly designed to fulfil the official aims of the institution.

Schools and prisons are structurally very similar in all these general features, though they do realize some of them in different ways. Authority, grouping, regimentation, routines, enforcements and specific aims are common to both institutions. To take one of these by way of example, 'enforcement' is achieved in similar ways in both places. In fact the means are surprisingly similar. The most often used means are simple verbal utterances from commands to insults, sarcasm and threats. Isolation and confinement, whether in cells for weeks or in classrooms during recess, are more overt forms of coercion. Both prisoners and pupils are given unpleasant jobs such as scrubbing floors or litter-picking, and in some respects punishment in school is more severe than in prison: there is no officially administered corporal punishment in our prisons.

From our own research there were some indications that Australian children do perceive the parallels between prison and school, and that the programme *Prisoner* is naturally inserted into such a scheme. When 96 children aged 11–13 were asked in class if they thought schools were like prisons, there was overwhelming agreement. When asked why, they produced the following similarities:

1. pupils are shut in;
2. pupils are separated from their friends;
3. pupils would not be there if they were not made to be;
4. pupils only work because they are punished and it's less boring than doing nothing at all;
5. pupils have no rights: they cannot do anything about an unfair teacher;
6. some teachers victimize pupils;
7. there are gangs and leaders amongst the pupils;
8. there are silly rules which everyone tries to break.

In every class, *Prisoner* was volunteered as being 'Just like school'. Whilst this is insufficient to prove the point, it is difficult to see where all the ideas about prison (especially 5 and 7) came from if not the show in which they are key causes of the action.

There is one aspect of the school–prison parallel which is potentially very illuminating about the relationship between schooling and society, which is a major part of the hidden curriculum: staff–inmate relationships. First, the 'them and us' division as revealed in *Prisoner* is similar to schools in several ways. The warders are shown as being rational, and conducting themselves as responsible adult–parent figures. They appeal to reason ('If you don't do this, then that will follow'), and the prisoners respond as children ('Shan't. Won't. Don't want to . . .'). This interaction is present in all spheres of activity from doing things like making beds to working in the laundry, where it has perhaps the greatest significance. Children in schools work, not because they enjoy the work, choose and want to do it, but because the teacher is there to make them. In the laundry the prisoners work when a warder is there, but as soon as she goes out they stop for a chat or a smoke. They have spies in the corridors to warn of the approach of a warder when they are not doing what they are supposed to.

Second, in both institutions the staff are there by choice, the inmates not; but once the staff have chosen to work there they are under the same authority as that of the inmates. Staff are, for instance, not allowed to smoke in certain places at certain times. Neither inmates nor staff have rights of ownership to parts of the institution, and its facilities. Staff do not own their rooms, chairs or routines, and nor do the inmates. It is another important feature of the respective institutions that people in both groups compete amongst themselves within the group, and, as a group, against other groups in order to establish and maintain rights over space, goods and routines. Success in this competition gains them an effective position of ownership, in spite of the fact that under the authority they seldom have even the rights of a tenant.

Third, both groups develop rules and mores of conduct which govern how they interact with each other and their peers. The inmates have general practices such as, 'You don't do what you're supposed to do if you can do otherwise and get away with it', and the very complicated rules governing just when it is permissible to tell on a peer. Similarly, there are complex rules about how distance between the groups is maintained, and how much of what kinds of contact are necessary and allowable. For instance, favourites are not allowed, and familiarity is always exploited. Both groups talk about each other behind their backs, and each has a mythology about the other group and particular individuals within it. Nicknames abound, and are used to provide solidarity and to challenge authority.

One composite scene in *Prisoner* will suffice to illustrate most of these features.

> Cut to women chatting in the laundry. Spy runs in from the corridor, 'Vinegar Tits is coming.' Women begin to work so that when Vera (an unpopular prison warder) enters there is a hum of activity. She has a letter for Lizzy (an old lag, a popular 'character' among the prisoners). Vera knows it contains something to make Lizzy unhappy. She holds it in front of her without giving it to her, teasing her with it, 'Letter for you.' Bea (the unofficial leader of the women prisoners), calls across the room from her position as the symbol of authority, the iron: 'Oh, I didn't know you were the mail BAG.' All prisoners laugh. Vera glowers, throws down the letter, spins on her heel and exits. The in-group gather closely round Lizzy as she opens it, the others look on over their shoulders. Lizzy reads letter and cries, 'Oh no'. 'Bastard', says Bea.

Bea's carefully calculated joke insults the warder in such a way that the warder cannot punish her without herself looking foolish. It forces her out of the room and the group's caring solidarity takes over. Bea, the leader, expresses the feelings of all of them. The scene could well have come from any school-girl story.

Finally, the sexual relationship between staff and inmates is precisely that paralleled in the institution. Sexual relationships do occur in *Prisoner*, and have provided the plot for many episodes. Some warders object to any men being employed in the prison at all, and one constantly makes insinuations and accusations about the male deputy governor. It is an aspect of the way in which the prisoners are transformed into children: sexuality is either denied, or it becomes deviant according to the very rigid interpretation of what are held by the authority to be the social norms. Sexual relations are possible only by breaking the rules: there is no way in which they are sanctioned in either institution. Again, when watching *Prisoner*, adolescents see adults engaged in working out what are essentially adolescent problems.

Another important area of concern is the way the institution itself articulates with other spheres of life outside it. Young children often believe that the teacher lives at school, that they do not have an existence and other roles outside of it. A teaching mother recently reported to us that her 4-year-old son thought his teacher lived in the school, in spite of the fact that he knew his Mum was a teacher and she lived at home with him. The reason for such belief is probably the child's lack of access to the continuity of adult lives: children only see their teachers at school. They are there when they arrive, and remain when they leave. They do not see them at home doing the washing too. Yet children have ample grounds to suspect that teachers are normal people with families, people who have affairs and fights; who can dance or fall in love; who go swimming, shopping and to movies; who have grandparents and children, and who were themselves children once. One of the effects of *Prisoner* is to offer the child a kind of god-like view and understanding of the continuity of the lives of those who play roles and occupy positions in an institution such as school.

In the serial, we follow the warders home to their empty flat, their clandestine appointment in the pub, to their families, their problems and joys. We see how what they do at work is both a separate part of their existence and at the same time integral with who they are and what they do at other times in other places. What happened at work is never entirely left behind them when they leave, and sometimes it continues unbroken as a relationship with the husband or boyfriend of a prisoner, a quarrel or affair with another warder, or as an out-of-work meeting to plan something particular for work. Children do, no doubt, often wonder what it would be like to have their teacher as a parent, friend or lover, and speculate as to how the person would behave elsewhere or in another relationship – as teacher, or as someone quite different? How much of being a teacher is pure acting? In *Prisoner* they can see such questions worked out; not only worked out in terms of what happens, but more importantly in terms of why it happens: motives and contributing factors are clearly and explicitly articulated. In contrast to many shows explicitly about school such as *Welcome Back, Kotter*, this domestic life is not always a warm reassurance of the teacher's essential humanity.

Prisoner puts another important issue on the agenda concerning the limits of the powers of the powerful. Children have ample reason to suspect that their teachers have to do what they are told by the principal, who may also have to do what he is told by those men in dark suits who descend annually after a period of frenetic orderliness in the school. In *Prisoner* this process is overtly displayed; the governor herself is subject to control from above. In one episode she is about to pass sentence upon a prisoner in her office when the phone rings. She listens for a moment before saying, 'Yes, sir', and puts down the phone. The prisoner is then mysteriously ushered out unpunished. Later we find that the governor was following instructions from her superiors who are, significantly, always men. To misquote, 'Little fleas have bigger fleas . . .'. The complex operations of power in the school, and by analogy, society, are thus exposed by dramatization in a way that every student can readily understand.

Conclusion

Our point, in our discussion of these two shows, is not that these meanings are the only ones children gain from them, or that these shows have a peculiar excellence or specific ideological effects. All we argue is that meanings of this kind do exist, and are thus highly accessible to all meaning-making people, which must include both students and teachers. We chose these two types of shows because both bear on the ideology of school, but represent basically different viewpoints. Quiz shows mystify the education system, glamorizing it, justifying it in facile terms. A show like *Prisoner* provides a powerful metaphor for demystifying authority as exercised in schools, offering a basis for generalizing about the operations of power in society. Our point here is not that television as a whole gives children a higher truth about school; on the contrary, the two shows carry contradictory values. What we draw attention to is the importance of issues that are implicit in popular television programmes which are largely ignored and condemned by teachers, and excluded from the curriculum. If 'reading television' were an unvarying activity, always operating at the same low level for all viewers of all programmes, and ceasing immediately the television set was turned off, then the attitude of most teachers would be justified. But if, as we argue, reading television can draw on and mobilize a whole range of cognitive abilities, deployed on issues of major importance to young and old and circulated through primary networks of discourse, then educationalists surely have a responsibility to take account of the processes involved. Unsurprisingly, those who lose most from the exclusion of television from the school curriculum are those who are channelled by innumerable other features of that curriculum into low-paid, menial positions in the workforce, a position from which come those who habitually watch the most television.

Chapter 7

The violence debate

A crisis in media studies

A Kuhnian perspective

Research is never carried out in a social, scientific, or historical vacuum, and ours is no exception. In the Introduction we referred to some fundamental issues that divide people studying children and television, and we suggested that there is an important shift taking place in this field of study. This shift, its causes and its implications, is we believe interesting and worthy of attention in its own right, for the light it throws on research in the social sciences. At this point in the book we want to step back from our specific arguments about children and television, and give a background and context to the field itself. Disciplines and fields of study, like people, have a history. They have rhythms and cycles, shifts and trends. By understanding these broader patterns we can not only come to terms with the past, but we can hope to act more constructively in the present and in the future.

In this chapter we will be looking particularly at the history of one topic – the issue of televisual violence and its effects on children – as a topic of strategic importance in the field of study of children and television, as that field is situated in a number of larger contexts. In this history we will be drawing on the theories of T. S. Kuhn, the historian of science whose theories of what constitute a 'crisis' and a 'revolution' in a field of science seem to us illuminating about what we see as a crisis in this field. His ideas also seem to us potentially very constructive, suggesting positive ways ahead for researchers in this field. (For other applications and critiques of Kuhn's theories, see Barnes, 1982; Giddens, 1976; and Hodge, 1978.)

Fundamental to Kuhn's view of the nature of the progress of scientific knowledge through research, are three concepts: 'research paradigms', 'normal science', and 'revolutionary science'. The first of these notions, paradigms, is used by Kuhn (1970) in a number of different ways. At the most general level Kuhn says that paradigms are 'particular coherent traditions of scientific research' and that there are 'universally recognised scientific achievements that for a time provide model problems and solutions to a community of practitioners'. Kuhn's notion of a scientific paradigm includes the models, theories, methods and priorities for research in a particular area for a particular community. In the case of research on television and its effects on children, we will call the relevant paradigm the 'effects paradigm'. 'Facts' are not part of a paradigm, but are the result of the application of the paradigm, and as such are necessarily evaluated and interpreted according to the paradigm. Kuhn therefore sees science proceeding not by the simple accumulation of facts, but by the constant extension and revision of theories in a particular paradigm.

Needless to say, this view of science was itself revolutionary, and began, over two decades ago, a continuing debate about the nature of science itself. One of the effects of this debate has been to question the assumptions upon which all current paradigms of research rest. Perhaps the aspect of the sciences to have received most attention in past years is the 'received view' which holds that science is an orderly and logical process, based upon such assumptions as: that there is an ultimate order of things which is or may be made intelligible, and that any event can be defined as the result of particular causes. These assumptions have been strongly attacked in both the social and physical sciences (Giddens, 1976).

In attacking the notion of science as being an orderly accumulation of facts, Kuhn suggests that there are different kinds of activities taking place at different stages of our understanding of particular areas of knowledge. The first of these phases Kuhn refers to is 'normal science', by which he means 'research firmly based upon one or more past science achievements, achievements that some particular scientific community acknowledges for a time as supplying the foundation for further practice'. He goes on to say that the achievements of normal science are those that tend to be recounted by science textbooks. In a phase of 'normal science' the research paradigms are taken for granted: the current problems and theories are extended, and research is continually replicated to check previous verifications and to obtain ever more precise results. 'Normal science' is what most researchers spend most of their lives doing. Their work is to check previous findings, to reduce crude effects to more and more sophisticated variables, to re-synthesize existing knowledge within the field. Such a period is one of relative certainty that the right questions are being asked and answered.

However, periods of 'normal science' move into a phase of crisis, which is largely the result of the accretion of anomalies and conflicting results which are not explicable within the existing dominant paradigm. The crisis phase is characterized not so much by proving existing facts wrong, but by the generation of endless studies which appear to complicate rather than simplify the issues. In fact the research fails to account for many of the complexities which are encountered when the conglomerate 'main effects' are broken into their component variables.

When the crisis becomes widespread in a field there begins a revolution in which the existing paradigm is attacked both through a reconsideration of assumptions, and an increased willingness to try entirely new approaches. In science the period of revolution is not a battle beween polarized extremes; it is an attempt to deploy radical questioning and fundamental debate to relocate existing knowledge in a paradigm where it is more consistent and more amenable to reinterpretation, and where it can be used to indicate new ways of developing research.

Thus Kuhn sees the progress of science as a cycle in which each 'current view' is utilized until it proves too limited, and the ensuing crisis is resolved by a revolution out of which comes a new current consensus, which is a reclarification of the whole area of the research, a new alignment providing a new sense of purpose and direction. The new paradigm then makes sense of what were anomalies in the old paradigm, and provides new criteria by which to judge the value of existing research and priorities for the future. What triggers the revolution is not too few facts, but the difficulties encountered in fitting existing facts together.

We do not wish to apply Kuhn's ideas directly and uncritically to this field. Normally, theories as global and neat as Kuhn's turn out to need some modifications when applied to specific instances (Lakatos and Musgrave, 1970) and these discrepancies often raise important issues. In relating to children and television there is another point to stress. Kuhn projects a paradigm as a relatively self-contained entity, especially in the 'normal science' phase, which organizes the activities of a stable community. The study of television and children is not a 'paradigm', in this sense. It is more a topic than a discipline. There are no departments devoted to it, no professional associations carefully controlling methods and accreditation. Strictly it is part of a 'discipline' that is termed 'media studies' or 'communication studies', a part concerned with one kind of viewer (children), one kind of media (television). Media or communication studies itself is not indisputably a fully fledged paradigm. Its subject-matter is relatively new, and it has been colonized by a number of different disciplines concerned with aspects of the media, which have organized themselves earlier and more strongly than media or communication studies: especially psychology, sociology, and economics. So 'media studies' is an 'interdisciplinary field', which is to say that it is a field where established disciplines compete for this position in a new synthesis which is still to be settled: a pre-paradigm situation, in Kuhnian terms.

The way problems and methods are defined in the area of children and television is clearly dependent on the broader area of media/communication studies, and is also affected by events in those component/competing disciplines. In so far as these contributing disciplines are affected by the politics of higher education in different countries, and these in turn by economic and political forces in those countries, we would not expect the history of the field of children and television to make any sense, much less a Kuhnian sense, in its own terms. So what is interesting and surprising is the extent to which it does follow the Kuhnian pattern rather closely, while clearly being affected by a host of external forces, with the issue of violence-viewing playing a crucial role.

The history we are looking at is conveniently short. Research on television only began in the late 1940s when television first became widely available. There were a number of basic questions that people asked about the new medium: among them, whether television was likely to have any harmful effects, especially on children. The work of people such as Schramm (1954, 1964) and Himmelweit et al. (1958) in the 1950s addressed these important questions with a reassuring competence that established a confident basis for a new paradigm. The consensus on the effects of violence-viewing was a qualified seal of approval, in Schramm's authoritative view. Television viewing for most children, under most conditions, would do little harm, and some good. Schramm demolished the so-called 'bullet-theory' of communication, the simplistic model which conceives of the message as like a bullet fired at the helpless receiver, with unerring and inevitable effect. However, this act of demolition, according to Wartella (1982), was largely a symbolic or mythic act. In her study of American research into children and the media over this century, she was unable to find any stage when the bullet paradigm was dominant, or held by the majority of researchers. Certainly no bullet theorists had time to fire their shots about television before the dominant orthodoxy, the effects paradigm, claimed the field. The history of the paradigm has been rewritten in a classic Kuhnian fashion, to create a mythic enemy, a mythic struggle and a definitive victory that established the right of the new paradigm to rule.

The effects paradigm in the 1950s and 1960s settled down as a successful 'normal science'. The success was measured not by actual achievements, but by the feeling of confidence that research was on the right track: the effects of television, on children and others, would in time be exhaustively understood. But not too quickly, of course. The task could be safely parcelled out to large numbers of researchers, who needed an open-ended set of worthwhile projects to keep them employed, not a once-for-all solution. So a steadily increasing range of different responses was measured ever more precisely, controlling for another increasing range of variables based on mental, physical or social attributes such as sex, age, IQ, class, race, viewing habits, and viewing situation. Superficially there were all the hallmarks of progress through refinement and cumulation.

However, beneath the smooth surface of the 1960s there were some shifts under way which were to have important consequences. One was a shift in the balance of power between sociology and psychology, especially from the school of psychology which had developed out of 'Behaviourism'. This school mounted the strongest of claims to being a 'science', emphasizing methodological purity and controlled laboratory experiments. (For a defence of the achievements of this school in the field of media studies, and specifically on the topics of violence and sex, see Eysenck and Nias, 1978.) From this period came a series of classic laboratory studies (e.g. Bandura et al., 1963) which seemed to show, in carefully controlled laboratory conditions, that violence-viewing did have effects after all. These studies were eminently compatible with the governing paradigm, but they seemed to demonstrate, with impressive elegance and ingenuity in their experimental design, an effect that had eluded the broader grained work of pioneers such as Schramm and Himmelweit. This development had two consequences. First, it put the 'violence effect' back on the agenda, as an issue that was not yet resolved after all. Second, it created a situation where there were academic rewards for adjusting the research microscope sufficiently finely to detect 'violence effects', even if those effects might not loom large in the overall effects of television.

The culminating moment in this trend came with what should have been its greatest opportunity. The public concern in the USA over the possible effects of violence viewing on children finally created

gh momentum for a large-scale government enquiry to be set
The results of this were published by the Surgeon General, as
ision and Growing Up: the impact of televised violence (1972). The
significance of this report is that it articulated a major public demand
for answers from researchers to questions to which the public wanted
answers. The issue it focused on was television violence, and its alleged
effects on behaviour. It funded its own research – 23 projects, involving
60 researchers – as well as reviewing the work of others. After an
investment of money and effort on such an unprecedented scale, the
results were disappointingly inconclusive:

> Thus, there is a convergence of the fairly substantial experimental
> evidence for a *short-run* causation of aggression among some
> children by viewing violence on the screen, and much less certain
> evidence from field studies that extensive violence viewing
> precedes some *long-run* manifestations of aggressive behaviour.
> The convergence of the two types of evidence constitute some
> preliminary indication of a causal relationship, but a good deal
> of research remains to be done before one can have confidence
> in these conclusions.

Such caution is exemplary even if it was disappointing to those who
hoped for something more definite. As we argued in chapter 4, the
simple bullet theory case about the effects of 'violence viewing' is
riddled with problems. We can see that far from being a mythic
opponent from the past, the bullet theory was a claim from the present
and the future that Schramm was trying to neutralize in advance.
But this inability to provide the definite answers that had been asked
for was troublesome to researchers in the field. In the decade that
followed the Surgeon General's report there was an explosion of new
work in the field. A 1982 follow-up report by the US Dept. of Health
and Human Services, estimated that '90% of all research publications
on television's influences on behavior have appeared within the past
10 years'. The question we must ask is this: does this explosion show
the vigour of the old paradigm, or is it the frenetic activity which,
for Kuhn, is the typical symptom of deep crisis?

A sense of dissatisfaction with the dominant paradigm comes
not only from outside – from governments and members of the
public who ask for bread and receive small pebbles – but from within
the paradigm itself. Here is George Comstock, former chairman of
the Surgeon General's advisory committee, perhaps the most
influential and authoritative figure in the field, in a (1975) paper on
the topic: 'The effects of television on children: what is the evidence?'

A polling of the conclusions would lead one to accept the proposition that under at least some circumstances, viewing violence increases the likelihood of some forms of subsequent aggressiveness. Nevertheless, it is also difficult to escape the impression that there are wide differences in the acceptance of the findings. In fact, when one rehearses the various statements, one finds the term 'cacophony' appealing.

Comstock gave several examples to show how previous reviewers' conclusions range from 'the effects of television violence on aggressive behaviour in the ''real world'' seem slight', to the statement that 'laboratory studies, correlation field studies, and naturalistic experiments all show that exposure to television can, and often does, make you significantly more aggressive'.

At the conclusion of this short, though penetrating, analysis, Comstock makes two recommendations, the second of which is:

> That analysis be refocused on the implications of the alternative conceptual schemas available for evaluating the evidence, and their implications for the emphasis of the conclusion.

What Comstock is urging here is, in effect, a paradigm shift. Alternative 'conceptual schemas' (not just different hypotheses or theories) are to be called into play to explain the evidence. It is no longer a lack of 'facts or evidence' that is the problem, but, as we showed in chapter 6, it is the more profound incapacity to explain the overwhelming mass of data.

In understanding the forces that have affected the shape of the field, we must not forget the play of material interests, or fail to see that the Kuhnian pattern may be a typical effect, rather than a cause. The Surgeon General's report opened up an interface between social forces and the field of study. Public opinion had been partly mobilized by current research, but then, mediated by various public bodies, itself had led to attention and money supporting one line of research, and predisposing towards one research answer. However, where the stakes are raised, as was done by the Surgeon General's report, the chances of harmonious resolution recede, as other interest groups fight back. In the case of a government-endorsed report which might lead to legislation, the standards of proof had to be raised, and even the criteria of proof were liable to be called into question from outside a specific paradigm.

A distinguished psychologist of the behaviourist school, H. J. Eysenck (Eysenck and Nias, 1978) in fact strongly criticized the report for going 'soft' on effects of television violence and sex. They point out, perfectly correctly, that American governments defer to pressure from media corporations, and in this case pressures were undoubtedly brought to bear. The caution of the final conclusion is due in part to that pressure, applied in many subtle ways. The same thing has happened with reports (or government action) on such lucrative but problematic commodities as cigarettes and white sugar. So the Eysenck–Nias case has much to be said for it. But where they are inconsistent is in seeing the effects of such pressures on research in other paradigms which comes to other conclusions, but not in their own, which they see as value-free, a pure form of science that is disinterested in its pursuit of the truth. This is a claim that would have been more effective in the 1960s than it is now. The 1970s saw the development of a powerful critique of the self-confident empiricism of American and British psychology, sociology and education, a critique of their refusal to re-examine their theoretical assumptions, and the ideology which underpinned them (Cronbach, 1975; Giddens, 1976; Phillips, 1973; Gouldner, 1976). Gouldner (1976) coined the term 'crisis of sociology', and this sense of crisis has permeated the component disciplines of media studies, and the sub-field of children and television. So much so that a researcher as distinguished and academically powerful as Eysenck could feel that he is now a lone voice of reason, disregarded by those who are not qualified, in terms that he accepts, to disregard him. This is a case where events outside the 'paradigm' of children and television clearly have affected fundamental thinking within it; yet the ultimate effect is still a recognizable Kuhnian crisis within the field, which has its own effects outside. The case of children and television therefore enables us to see, in this instance, the complex interaction between internal and external pressures that shape the conditions of academic work: more complex than Kuhn's theory suggests, yet made more comprehensible by the application of that theory.

We do not wish to exaggerate the sense of crisis in the field as yet. No specialists on children and television have hurled themselves in despair from high buildings. Comstock himself, with others, prepared a major review of television and behaviour in 1978. In this work, though he points to a number of problems of research method, he appears to take the view that the methods and assumptions are basically sound and have generally been employed with diligence and honesty, and that, given time and ingenuity, the existing methods will become sufficiently refined to provide the answers to our questions about the relations between television and children's behaviour. The Surgeon

General's 1982 review similarly is guardedly optimistic. On the topic of violence and aggression it feels able to claim 'it can be said that the evidence for a causal relationship between excessive violence viewing and aggression goes well beyond the preliminary level', though in the section on violence and aggression (chapter IV), it is unable to announce the desired certainty. The other significant change from the 1972 report is the shift of emphasis. The 1982 report has only one chapter out of 10 on television and aggression, compared to the exclusive concern of the 1972 report with that topic. This is in spite of the amount of research still devoted to it. Comstock et al. in their 1978 review estimated that 80 per cent of work in the field was concerned with violence and aggression. One senses both an obsessive concern with this intractable problem, and also a desire to leave it be, to tackle other problems that will prove less resistant, using a conceptual framework that will produce results. A major shift, a quiet revolution, is already under way, it seems to us; but if it is unacknowledged, not debated, untheorized, it will lack the overall coherence, scope and sense of purpose that Kuhn claims is essential for the emergence of a paradigm.

The position of media studies in the UK is rather different, as are the ways in which the topics of violence and its effects on children are treated. There has been a regular flow of important work done on the media that is influenced to different degrees by a critical social theory and by semiotic principles. Our own work is deeply indebted to this body of work. A key figure here has been Stuart Hall, along with the Birmingham Centre for Cultural Studies, of which he was the director. The topics of violence and youth are important for British researchers who broadly share this perspective, but they tend to be constructed differently from what prevails in America. These researchers have been concerned especially with high-modality programmes aimed at adults; justifiably, in our view, since it is high-modality programmes, such as news, which most directly affect attitudes and beliefs. For this critical British research, violence is not important in isolation, but as part of a larger structure of representations whose value depends very much on who is represented as using violence, and why. Media emphasis on violence by picketers, it is assumed, will influence the public against the strike concerned. Police violence, on the other hand, will seem justified or not depending on judgements that are implied about the recipients of the violence, and on the positioning of the audience in relation to the struggle. There will be one response to what is represented as legitimate violence against the brutal (and foreign) sailors of the *Belgrano* threatening the life of the innocent Falklanders: another to a representation of the same event which emphasizes that 368 sailors died in the sinking of a ship which was outside the war zone and heading away from the action to a home port. The obvious political issues at stake shift the centre of the debate: whose interests are served by either representing or concealing violence? The political and ideological issues surrounding violence are so complex, from this point of view, that the question of whether there should simply be more, or less, violent content on television appears meaningless, if other questions are left out of account.

Such research perspectives have productively addressed many issues in the field of media studies, employing a variety of methods: political economy and media ownership (cf. Murdock, 1975; Bonney and Wilson, 1983) production ideologies (Buscombe and Alvarado, 1974) and content of news (cf. the Glasgow University Media Group). Of particular interest in the study of children and television is Tulloch and Alvarado's book (1984) on *Dr Who*. But one recurring weakness, especially with researchers who emphasize ideological effects, is a tendency to assume that the predicted effects will follow automatically along the lines of their ideological/semiotic analyses, without attempting to establish by any empirical means how consumers or readers actually interpret and use such texts.

There has been something of a stand-off between the critical tradition and what some of its practitioners often dismissively label as the 'positivistic' empiricist tradition dominant in America. Both approaches could have gained from a more charitable attitude to the other. As one instance, close to home, we can cite the Hodge–Kress form of linguistic analysis from which we have drawn extensively in the present book. This theory as applied to newspaper articles assumed that the structures of meaning uncovered in analysis would automatically have certain predictable effects on an audience, but Hodge and Kress did not in fact investigate, with a range of actual readers, whether these meanings or effects occurred. This lack of empirical research on responses was not given any strong justification in terms of their overall theory, and in some respects was inconsistent with it. However, two American researchers (Fry and Sigman, 1984) did go on to carry out some of the relevant empirical work. Taking two newspaper treatments of the same event, a riot, they predicted who would be held mainly responsible for the violence, following the Hodge–Kress method of analysis. They then used different groups of readers to test the hypothesis. The hypothesis was mainly confirmed, but not in all respects. In the light of this work the Hodge–Kress theory can be profitably modified and refined. It is only with research like this that semiotic analysis can reliably give what some proponents naively assume it already to guarantee: an understanding of how specific classes of social agent will interpret and act on types of message.

The British 'cultural studies' tradition, however, has one kind of problem which sets Kuhnian accounts in perspective. With few exceptions this tradition has been effectively marginalized in the tertiary sector. Courses structured according to these principles are more often in polytechnics than universities. Some of the most able researchers find it difficult to gain employment, and government agencies and media institutions denigrate and ignore significant works. Everywhere this form of media studies is a site of struggle. Kuhn encourages one to think in terms of a 'rotten door' theory of scientific revolutions: once the scientific community recognizes the inadequacy of its former paradigm its confidence will collapse, and it will welcome the new victor with open arms. In the British version, where the crisis is in the society itself, forces can be mobilized to hold in check the effects of a destabilizing crisis in a particular academic field.

New models for old

The Kuhnian framework we have used leads us to expect an immensely exciting, creative and strenuous period in which a new paradigm will establish itself. Typically, according to Kuhn, concepts, methods and models from adjacent but hitherto unrelated fields will be drawn into the new synthesis, along with portions of the older paradigm. But we can try to be more specific than this about where to look for what the new paradigm will need, and what its general shape might be. An obvious starting point is the shortcomings of, and the gaps in, the old paradigm, and the demands in the face of which it is collapsing, to see what existing fields of knowledge might prove useful. The quotation from the Surgeon General's report is a beautifully dense and comprehensive instance of the assumptions of the dominant paradigm, so we will use it as an illustrative text:

> it can be said that the evidence for a causal relationship between excessive violence viewing and aggression goes well beyond the preliminary level.

After the manneristic signifier of impersonality and caution, it starts with mention of experimental 'evidence', with the typical concern for proof, rather than discovery, and with demonstration, rather than insight or understanding. This orientation is adapted to use in polemical situations, in public debate; but without discoveries, without explanations which are illuminating beyond common sense, proofs and demonstrations ultimately lose their credibility. The passage continues with a typical concentration on causal relations. Causality is about power, so explanations of causality always matter, to parents and citizens as well as to politicians. A new paradigm must not renounce a concern with causality. It must on the contrary satisfy it more fully. The failure of the dominant paradigm is precisely its unsatisfactory account of causes and effects, not its interest in them. It is unsatisfactory partly because it works basically with a mechanistic kind of causality, instead of the more appropriate semiotic causality: actions are performed because of what people think and believe, not because of any quasi-physical force acting on them.

The limited success the Surgeon General's committee claimed was with 'short-run' causation, under experimental conditions. This is the controlled but atomistic and myopic kind of understanding which is especially associated with the one school of psychology, Behaviourism, an understanding not related to a grasp of large-scale processes over time or across society and culture. In their more confident phases, psychologists in the Behaviourist tradition have extrapolated from controlled laboratory experiments to large-scale phenomena; but when there is a widespread doubt that they have a theory that can relate large-scale to small-scale phenomena, the legitimacy of these extrapolations is called into question as mere speculation.

Finally there is the crucial problem of value-judgement, which social scientists have often tried to pretend they can transcend in their function as 'scientists', but which politicians and parents know cannot be avoided. The key term here is 'aggression'. The problem with aggression is that it is essentially a social act which can only take place in a social context, subject to judgements by various social agents, including the so-called aggressor. 'Aggression' is an ideologically loaded term. It implies violence which is physical, and probably unjustified (though not when used of an 'aggressive' marketing policy). However, not all actions labelled 'aggression' are the same in kind, differing only in degree. Not all aggression is undesirable, though this is the strong impression given by many researchers, and even more by people who use that research. Some aggression – the capacity to defend oneself, for instance – is essential to survival. A government programme aimed at eliminating aggression from the entire populace would be viewed with deep suspicion, as the equivalent of a universal lobotomy. When researchers take this kind of factor into account (e.g.

Berkowitz and Rawlings, 1962) they find that television violence that is represented as 'legitimate' leads to greater expression of aggressive feelings. This would be worrying if all aggression is regarded as bad. It would be encouraging if legitimate aggression is seen as valid; but if the very concept of 'legitimacy' was seen as immensely problematic, then nothing follows automatically from the study.

To summarize, then, the inadequacies of the dominant paradigm come from its biases: towards proof rather than insight: towards pseudo-mechanical rather than semiotic causality; its concern with behaviour rather than meaning, and with short-term, small-scale explanations. It fatally lacks an explicit account of broader political and social processes in which to situate the behaviour it studies, or its own practice as a discipline. It equally lacks a powerful theory of mind and meaning, to decode meanings and to trace thought processes into the inner recesses of the mind, and study the formation of structures of thought and feeling as they evolve over a lifetime. The Marxist tradition of cultural studies, with its account of ideology and class structure as well as its well-honed critique of positivist social science, is an obvious place to look to fill the first need, and in Britain especially there is now a flourishing group of researchers opening up the field of media studies. For the other area of need, this book has indicated some of the main traditions that must be considered for the new synthesis: Freudian theory, cognitive and developmental psychology (including Piaget and his followers), psycholinguistics, linguistics, semiotics and structuralism. It must be stressed, however, that what is needed is not an old list, but a new synthesis, which may link different components of different traditions in surprising and powerful ways. The new paradigm, at least in its initial scope, will offer the hope of asking and answering a whole new array of questions that will seem of immense importance to a new community.

Classic texts revisited

Although terms like 'revolution' emphasize discontinuity between successive paradigms, it is also important to recognize continuities. Kuhn stresses the point that the same element, even the same 'fact', alters its significance when it finds a place in a new paradigm, and the point is worth stressing for those who do not notice such effects. However, work done in the previous paradigm does not automatically become worthless or unusable for the new paradigm. In Kuhn's account some findings do become unavailable, waiting for further paradigm change in order to be comprehensible again, but a major activity of a new paradigm is to incorporate as much as it can of its predecessor. Kuhn's theories can encourage a dangerous tendency in members of a 'new paradigm' to ignore all previous work as intrinsically incomprehensible, because of its different paradigm assumptions. Such an attitude owes more to arrogance and laziness than to theoretical rigour, and we would argue strenuously against such an attitude – among Marxists or Semioticians as among Behaviourists or Chomskyans.

In current research there are many people whose work seems to be tending towards what we argue will be the new paradigm. Much of this work follows lines of research that stretch the previous paradigm without overtly breaking with it. Sometimes this is done by pursuing lines of research which strategically ignore the whole violence issue in favour of other kinds of effect which are different in principle (cf. Delia, MacLeod, Wartella, Salomon, Collins and Anderson). Some work deals with effects issues, and even the problem of violent content, but in radically different ways. Here the work of George Gerbner and his associates is especially instructive, because initially it seems to support the dominant paradigm in both methods (careful empirical work using a broad sample, statistical methods, etc.) and conclusions attributing an antisocial effect to violence-viewing. On closer inspection, however, his reasoning subverts some of the major features of the effects paradigm. Gerbner has both a semiotic theory and a theory of society underpinning his research. Semiotically he does not assume that violence on the media is automatically translated into violence (or its opposite) in real life. Instead he is concerned with the structures of belief slowly created by a lifetime of viewing, as calibrated against more objective versions of those objects of belief. He does not assume that simple imitation is the only possible effect/response. A belief that the world is a violent place, he reasons, could lead to a kind of passivity, which is the opposite of violence: though it could also lead to a kind of violence which is not imitation, but pre-emptive violence as a rational response to how the world seems to be. As we have suggested earlier, the correlations he has obtained are disappointingly small. Our own work indicates that a stronger theory of modality needs to guide Gerbner's analysis of 'violent content', and the structures of belief produced by television. However, there is a clear place in his work for such a theory, which can be seen as simply the fine-tuning of a hypothesis that is a normal paradigm activity. His overall framework, the 'cultivation hypothesis', can be legitimately seen as an interesting large-scale investigation of ideological effects of television over time: an investigation which has not yet proved conclusive, but which provides promising methods and models for the future.

However, as well as noting these growth points in recent work, it is just as important to look back, with respectful but critical eyes, at some of the classic studies of the previous tradition, to see whether they have something to offer when looked at from a fresh angle. The laboratory experiment was the signature of the old paradigm. Its limitations must be recognized; see for example Noble's wry observation:

> Do we want to know with certainty what will happen in a highly specific set of circumstances, or do we want to know what is more or less likely to happen when media violence is seen 'in natural, everyday viewing situations'? (1975: quoted with disapproval by Eysenck and Nias, 1978).

Noble opposes certain but irrelevant knowledge to uncertain but relevant knowledge. He has a point, though in some ways his objection is over-neat. The artificiality of laboratory experiments is generally acknowledged, but they can still be justified as a means to an end. Laboratory experiments aim to abstract and magnify causal relationships that are too small to be detected and studied in everyday contexts. They are concerned with micro-structures. We can distinguish the structures studied by a putative science into three levels: micro-structures (structures which are too small to be observed easily by normal processes of observation), macro-structures (those that are too large to be readily open to direct observation), and meso-structures (human scale structures). Historically, science has typically proved its credentials by revealing micro-structures or macro-structures to an unsuspecting lay public. Some of its spectacular successes have been macro-structural (e.g. theories of the solar system, or evolution, or continental drift), but others have been micro-structural (e.g. the role of bacteria, or atomic and molecular structures). Micro-structural discoveries can be of very great importance in explaining major causal processes, even though they are definitionally small and inaccessible. In semiotics the most important single achievement was the structural analysis of the phonological system, a micro-structural analysis that was then applied to macro-structures and meso-structures. Noble is right to insist that, to be seen as important, scientific discoveries must have relevance to everyday situations, to meso-structural levels. But that application need not be immediate. Micro-structural understanding is important in its own right, even if not sufficient in itself.

If the old paradigm is to have anything to pass on to the new it must be from experiments, especially laboratory experiments. It is these, then, which most need to be subjected to critique and reconstitution.

For purposes of illustration we want now to look at two classic experimental models that have been influential in the field. First we will take the Bobo-doll experiments of Bandura and his associates (Bandura et al., 1963; Bandura, 1965; Hanratty et al., 1969). The basic format of this influential experimental model is to show subjects (usually children) a film and then put them in a situation where they may or may not imitate behaviour seen in the film. The variable is whether the viewers have seen the film or not, and the measure of aggression is the number of imitative acts performed, as judged by observers.

In one of these experiments (Bandura, 1965) nursery-school children were used as subjects. They were exposed to one of three 5-minute television portrayals of a man attacking a Bobo-doll. In one of these he was rewarded, in another he was punished, in the third he was not either punished or rewarded. The children were then put in a situation where there was a Bobo-doll and various things which had

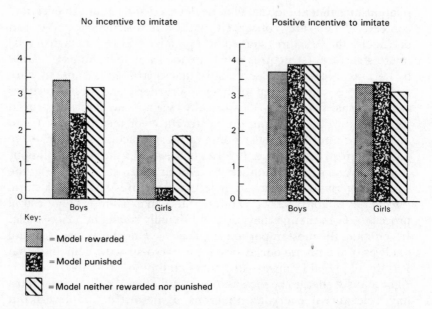

Figure 21   *Mean number of acts imitating television portrayal under different conditions of reward for model and different conditions of reward for imitation (adapted from Bandura, 1965).*

been used in the film. The second part of the experiment took the same children and asked them to demonstrate as much as they could remember from what had been displayed in the film, with the offer of an incentive. The results are as in figure 21, taken from Comstock et al., 1978. From this figure it is clear that boys are always more likely to imitate aggressive action than girls. Secondly, when there is no incentive to imitate, boys will imitate less often when the model was punished, but they will still imitate in that situation more often than girls when the model was not punished.

If this experiment is interpreted in the normal terms whereby an effect appears or not in response to a stimulus, this experiment will help to support the contention that viewing of violence leads to, causes, aggressive behaviour. However, if we reinterpret this experiment in terms of a model with a semiotic dimension, which can take account of how various situations are interpreted by the subjects, and how what they do needs to be interpreted in the light of understanding of general communication models and ideological forms, the experiment may lead to different conclusions.

For imitation to occur, the film itself must be interpreted in terms of overt syntagms of the form x *does* y *to* z *with* i. Imitation can only occur if classes of entity to which x, y, z, and i belong are repeated in the new situation. In this particular experiment type, z and i are repeated not as classes but as identical items. There is no need for the child to extrapolate to understand z is a class of object, i is a class of instrument. The child is given both object and instrument. The extrapolation for the child then is to decide whether he or she qualifies as an agent of class x, able therefore to perform action class y. As we noted in chapter 4, we need to know how the child classifies its own action: as serious, as play, or even both.

The experiment shows that different kinds of agent behave differently in different kinds of situation. This can be interpreted as a gap between acquisition and performance. Another possibility, however, is that for the different classes of agent, boys and girls, there is a different message contained in the initial stimulus. The boys imitate, the girls tend not to. For the boys we can suggest that there is a covert syntagm, either an imperative ('do y or be x') or at least a permissive syntagm of the form ('if you wish to you may do y'), and for the girls a corresponding covert syntagm, a prohibition ('do not do y'), which of course cancels the permission to do y or to be x. An analogue of what might be happening here from normal language use can be seen in the common situation whereby a teacher says 'children, the door is open', and children immediately move to shut it. They take a statement that the door is open as a covert command. Or more specifically, a teacher might say 'Johnny, will you shut the door?', which has the overt form of question but is interpreted as a covert order. If a child said 'the door is open' in the presence of a teacher, the teacher would not interpret this as a covert command, but perhaps as a request for permission to shut it, so the behaviours which follow would be very different. The difference would be comprehensible not in terms of a stimulus–response model with a surface stimulus, but in terms of a different covert message which is present in an apparently identical surface utterance.

In this form of the experiment the doer of the action is rewarded, punished, or left alone. Each of these can be translated as equivalent to an instruction such as 'do this', 'don't do this' or 'decide what to do'. That is to say, what we have called a covert syntagm, a covert imperative or prohibition, is overt in this form of experiment, and it is clear that it does have a significant effect. However, we also notice that boys much more than girls still do the action even when there is a prohibition overtly built into the message. That is, for boys it seems that the overt 'don't do' can be cancelled out by the covert 'do'. Or another way of putting it, the overt 'don't do' is ambiguous. It can be interpreted by boys as an instruction to do, but not by girls. Similarly girls who are in effect instructed to 'do', by an overt instruction which should cancel out the 'don't do', still don't perform the forbidden actions as frequently as boys. That is, there must still be an overriding negative which they are responding to.

All we have in this experiment is behaviour, which is in effect a single, simple surface form realizing two potentially contradictory classes of statement; what the children understand, and what they choose to do. It is possible that girls are at this age less able to abstract the initial syntagm, *x does y to z with i*, in order to act on it, but studies of girls' and boys' relative linguistic and cognitive development provide evidence to the contrary. A safer supposition would be that the differences in behaviour are a function of what children understand and what they wish to do with what they understand: or more generally, they proceed from a difference in the totality of what they understand, about the experiment and about the world. Rather than thoughtless imitation, the experiment shows aspects of the complex interaction between the structure of authority and other authoritative but oppositional counter-messages.

There are a number of important observations suggested by this experiment. One is that the dominant tradition, precisely by being blind to the semiotic richness of the total situation of the 'stimulus', has been incapable of controlling this whole dimension. But this blindness is not intrinsic to the experimental method. There is no reason why someone like Bandura should not read deeply into semiotic theory and theories of ideology, and redesign his experiments accordingly. It is not even the case that these semiotic structures are unavailable to consciousness. Noble (1975) reports the example of a young girl on her first laboratory visit, 'Look, Mummy, there's the doll we'll have to hit.' It would be interesting, for instance, to repeat the Bandura experiment on a small group of children, half boys and half girls, and then ask them what meanings they attached to the various elements of the major syntagm, building up the basic paradigmatic structures of both boys and girls. It is the discovery of these paradigmatic structures, internal and larger in scope than any unit of spoken discourse, that will be the genuine scientific advance enabled by such an experiment. Even so, this analysis points outside of the situation for any explanation of causality. The two covert syntagms that we have posited for boys and girls respectively are clearly ideological structures which are perceived in the situation and acted on accordingly. But this is not a causal explanation. Why do these syntagms have the hold they do? What is the energy they draw on? How have children acquired them? These are the important causal questions. They cannot be asked without the kind of semiotic analysis we have done, but they cannot be answered solely in terms of meanings and semiotic systems.

A second very influential class of experiments purportedly proving the same effect from the same cause as in the previous class of experiment turns out on examination to be very different. In this class of experiment (e.g. Walters and Thomas, 1963; Hartmann, 1965; Feshbach, 1972) subjects are typically shown either a violence film or a non-violence film or alternatively a violence film and nothing, and then are given the opportunity, in simulated conditions, either to hurt or not hurt experimental subjects. Walters and Thomas (1963) have a typical experiment of this form. They exposed their subjects to a knife-fight scene or to an educational film. These subjects then were asked to 'assist' the experimenter in a learning experiment. The assistance took the form of electric shock, which we are led to believe subjects believed caused real pain to the learner. Subjects were free to determine the intensity or duration of the shocks they administered, and these were the dependent variables which were the semiotic signs of aggressive behaviour.

In most of these experiments an equation does seem to be established between violence-viewing and a tendency to hurt, as indicated by a tendency to cause more pain to the ostensible learner through administering a greater number or intensity of shocks. However, in chapter 4 we discussed one experiment, by Feshbach (1972), which found the contrary effect. Feshbach used noxious noises rather than electric shocks, but that would not appear to alter the semiotic significance of his measure. What he altered was the modality, the way the subjects interpreted the imagined violence. Subjects were shown identical footage depicting campus riots. Feshbach had carefully constructed a film with ambiguous modality by editing together pieces of newsreel footage with scenes from a movie about campus life. He was then able to influence the modality assigned to it by simply informing one group that it was all news footage and the other that it was only a movie. Under these conditions he found that only the subjects who believed that the violence was real tended to press the 'hurt' button harder and longer.

Feshbach has all the qualifications for a mythic hero-figure of the new paradigm. Kuhn saw such processes of canonization as very common in the business of rewriting the history of the discipline that a new paradigm usually carries out. Feshbach did, heroically and almost single-handedly, resist the majority opinion in the field, upholding the 'catharsis theory' which proposed radical complications to the modified bullet theory. This experiment, along with some by Noble and others, carried out scrupulously in terms of the dominant paradigm, could not be dismissed out of hand. They prevented the closure that would have made the paradigm impenetrable in its inadequacy. It is true that there are some features of Feshbach's experiment that raise questions in the light of a more advanced theory of modality. We have not viewed the film he used, but a film composed of news footage plus movie footage could hardly have had a clear plot, and the contradictory modality cues from the different sources might well have made it seem weird (and hence, low-modality) to its viewers: and if this hadn't been the case, Feshbach might not have got such clear-cut results. His discussions of the role of fantasy seem to show no well-articulated theory of modality. Such cavils, however, do not lessen the importance of his achievement.

Feshbach's importance lies not in his championing an unpopular cause, nor in his focusing on a variable that others had not looked at, for testing different variables is the stock-in-trade of the experimental method. It is because he invoked, in an unobtrusively simple form, a radically new principle which challenges the very basis of what was previously regarded as sound method. He stressed the importance of taking account of the modality schemas that subjects bring to bear in interpreting the stimulus film. We can apply the same principle to the rest of the experimental situation. The measure, which indicates the response to the film, is in itself a sign: the action of pressing a button, in response to another visual image on a screen. The significance of pressing or not pressing a button can only be understood in the light of the structures of meaning assigned to it by individual subjects. This action follows the watching of the film, but it is part of a sufficiently complex situation, consisting of the 'learner' or other person they are supposedly watching on a monitor, plus the instructions they are meant to be following, plus the experimenter, the source of the instructions.

The action of pressing a button may seem simple, but the invisible mental operations that lie behind it are formidably complex. The majority of studies using a form of the 'aggression machine' have found a tendency to press the 'hurt' button more after what different experimenters defined as 'violence-viewing' (with normally no reference to its modality), so it would seem that there is an interaction between the schema used to analyse the experimental situation. The experimental situation that is part of the significance of the act of button-pressing becomes even more complex when the experimenter tries to provoke anger in the subjects in order to heighten the effects to be measured. In one experiment, by Berkowitz and Geen (1966), university students who were shown a boxing scene (from a film, Kirk Douglas in *The Champion*) were not more 'aggressive' than those who saw an athletics film (real-life coverage of Bannister versus Landy in the Commonwealth Games mile). Students were then divided into two groups, each performing a task with an accomplice of the experimenter. One group received seven times the number of shocks for 'poor performances'. They then had the opportunity to 'punish' with shocks the person who had given them shocks in the previous task. Unsurprisingly, those who had received many shocks were much more inclined to be 'aggressive' (or punitive) to their former tormentor than those who had received only a few. There was also a small tendency for those who had watched the 'violent' film to administer more shocks than those watching the athletics film. Again, the dimensions of meaning not taken into account and not controlled are so many that it is not clear what generalizations validly emerge.

Researchers using this class of experiment typically choose as films two complex texts which contrast in one feature that they are conscious of (violence/non-violence), but which also contrast in innumerable other ways that they are not conscious of, and have no principled way of recognizing and controlling. They also have no principled way of analysing the meanings assigned to the other part of the experiment, the chain of events involving the 'hurt' button. Conclusions that are based on the relation between an uncontrolled and partially understood stimulus and an uncontrolled and partially understood response are clearly most unsafe. Virtually all of these experiments are invalid for this reason (which is not, of course, to say that the viewing of violence in films will never give rise to aggressive, angry responses – like giving punitive accomplices of an experimenter their just desserts). Interestingly, Feshbach's form of this experiment is the soundest of the whole group, since as a stimulus for his two groups he used an identical film, changing only the experimenter's instructions. The stimulus was carefully constructed, and the feature altered was strictly controlled, unlike what usually happens in this dramatic, ingenious but generally unsatisfactory class of experiment.

These two classes of experiment (the Bobo experiments and the aggression-machine experiments) are usually treated in the literature as different ways of proving the same thing: the effect of violence-viewing on subsequent aggression (with Feshbach as an anomaly waiting to be fitted in, or crushed by weight of numbers). It would be more accurate to see them as two different ways of failing to prove a random set of different things; but this is not to say that the experimental method itself is unusable in the new paradigm, though semiotics provides such powerful analytic tools for the study of micro-structural phenomena that laboratory experiments may occupy a less significant place. Nor is it the case that all the conclusions that those researchers believed they had demonstrated can now be said to be wrong. What our study does show is that work that is accepted as thorough and sound in terms of the principles of one paradigm can seem chaotic, trivial, confused and inconclusive from the perspective of another paradigm.

The converse, of course, is also likely to be the case, and so we have few illusions about how our present work must appear to some other researchers. Kuhn would predict radical incomprehension between 'normal' members of different paradigms. As researchers who have tried ourselves to communicate across paradigm boundaries, we have experienced some such phenomenon at first hand many times. It is usually not exactly incomprehension: more a refusal to accept that ideas produced by different means and supported by a different kind of argument and evidence could or must be taken seriously. We are also sceptical of an explanation that attributes effective power to something as abstract as a 'paradigm'. There are good pragmatic reasons for narrow-mindedness in academic disciplines. Paradigm allegiance is usually rewarded by the senior figures who normally have great influence and/or vested interest in the existing structures of knowledge. Paradigm expertise is often the major commodity an academic has for sale. Open-mindedness and interdisciplinary range are not nearly as attractive, when the major potential buyers are operating an effective closed system. As Kuhn points out, it is only at times of recognized crisis that this set of controls and brakes is relaxed, and there is more open, unstructured communication between different paradigms and traditions of knowledge; an exchange of ideas and methods and people. These have often proved the most fruitful and exciting periods in various branches of science. We believe that the field of media studies may be approaching just such a creative period, and children, hopefully, will be among those who benefit from this new understanding.

Conclusion

In this chapter we have addressed two issues. One is fairly specific, the issue of violent content on television and its effects on children; the other more speculative, our ideas on where the study of children and television has been and where it is likely to go. On the issue of violent content, our brief history shows that knowledge does not simply advance by slow steady steps. The position of Schramm and Himmelweit on the effects of violent content in mainstream television on the majority of children, though enunciated several decades ago, is still sound and judicious enough. However, though they were right enough about the effects, it was not clear exactly what was happening, and why they were right – and therefore, under what possible circumstances their conclusions might be wrong. This nagging uncertainty fed into the research effort of the 1960s and 1970s, which aroused unjustified anxieties that violent content on television might have certain specific and dangerous consequences for any and every viewer, and hence saw television as a virtually autonomous agent of social change. We believe that that anxiety has had more than enough time and money and expertise devoted to substantiating it, and the attempt to do so should now be regarded as discredited. We come down on the side of the view which sees the effects of television, including violent content, as a kind of 'catalyst', acting to enhance or inhibit the operation of other forces to produce a range of different, sometimes contradictory, effects. It is not helpful to see any aspect of television content as an autonomous cause with consistent effects irrespective of the social conditions of the viewer. Violent content is not intrinsically good or bad, any more than violence or aggression in social life is always equally reprehensible. This does not mean that violent content in television is unimportant or without effects. It does indicate, however, that any attempt to achieve a consistent effect among children by controlling levels of 'violent content' on television is at worst impossible, at best fraught with too many difficulties.

On the question of the field of media studies itself, we have more a plea than a conclusion. The topic of children and television should matter to everyone, because television is so pervasive a medium, and a society's children are its future. We see signs of a new openness, and more powerful and productive methods of enquiry in this field, and we hope that this is indeed where things are heading. We can outline the shape of this future, and say where we think it should move; towards a social semiotic synthesis, with a strong and diverse empirical basis, to encapsulate it in labels. But we are not prophets, and we do not pretend to be impartial observers. The function of this chapter has been to stress the need for a tolerant, broad-based interdisciplinary approach to this area of studies: not to stress any one approach, or argue one-sidedly for any single conclusion.

Chapter 8

Conclusion
Ten theses on children and television

Our project was not set up to prove a single point or a set of closed
conclusions. Rather, it was designed in an open-ended way to explore
and perhaps explicate some aspects of the interlocking set of structures
and processes that together constitute the field of study of children
and television. We have looked at children's developing powers of
mind, and their strategies for making sense as they interact with the
complex levels and structures of the television message, in potentially
determining social contexts and sets of relationships. We have assessed
how this whole complex has been interpreted and used in an
institutionalization of knowledge that is a powerful force in shaping
public beliefs and public policy. This is our sense of our brief, in this
book. We hope we have done some justice to it. At various stages,
however, people have quite rightly pressed us to say what follows,
for certain practical purposes, from our study. 'Practice', of course,
is not a single simple outcome: what a parent will want to know and
do will be different from the interests of, say, a teacher or a producer
of children's television. So to meet this kind of request we will conclude
this book with a set of ten propositions, ten theses about children and
television, the plausibility of which we believe our study has helped
to establish. In the process we will address in an informal way some
major implications these theses may have for various people concerned
with children and television: parents, educators, concerned citizens,
government agencies, media professionals, researchers and students.

  1   Children typically have the capacity to be active and powerful
      decoders of television, and programmes watched by them are
      potentially rich in meaning and cultural value; though not
      all programmes and ways of viewing are of equal benefit for
      all children.

Children's semiotic powers, and the complexity of the meanings they construct and consume make up the central premise of our whole argument. This premise is not a blanket excuse for anything on television that children watch. It is not the end of discrimination in this area, but the rational basis for a beginning. We do not see all children as equally active and adequate 'readers' under all circumstances; nor do we see all programmes as equally dense in meaning or culturally valuable. Media professionals should not underrate children's ability to handle great complexity, nor should they under-provide for that need of children for relevant complexity. Lobbyists are very important in maintaining high production standards. Children's television is notoriously given the smallest budgets and least attention, and economic reasons are too often justified by reductive assumptions about children's semiotic abilities. It seems better to give them good programmes made for adults than cheap, insubstantial programmes whose main claim to be tailored to children's needs appears to be the fact that adults would not watch them with enjoyment. Educationalists, parents and researchers alike should take this generally despised area of children's lives and development more seriously and with greater respect for its actual and potential value. However, there can be too much television watching by children. Though television is functionally redundant up to a point, there will be a decreasing return from heavy viewing as more of the same kind of viewing displaces other important activities. So it is generally more important for adults to limit the total time spent viewing than to select the programmes viewed.

2   Children's cognitive and semiotic systems develop at least up till the age of 12, so that they not only prefer different kinds of programmes from adults, they also respond differently to programmes, and interpret them differently: but from the age of 9 they are capable of their own kind of understanding of most mainstream television.

It is impossible to capture in a few short sentences the nature, scope and implications of children's growing powers of interpreting and understanding television. For media producers the concept of multilevel 'family' programming, capable of being 'read' in different but appropriate ways by different age levels, is a valid one, better we would suggest than an attempt to match specific levels of development with programming targeted to very specific age ranges. In general children enjoy and can learn much from some programmes that are regarded by many adults as 'too old' for them, though they will be responding in their own distinctively 'childlike' way. We believe that there is a parallel in children's developing ability to handle complex television messages, with the idea of young children not being imperfectly socialized miniature adults, but well adjusted to a social system which is different from that of adults, not necessarily inferior (Mackay, 1974). As with the development of language, it seems that children's systems increasingly approximate to adult systems as they are exposed to, and allowed to operate in, adult systems. This means that educationalists and parents need not be too concerned at children watching the most popular adult shows.

3   Children's television typically carries dominant ideological forms, but also a range of oppositional meanings.

This mixed content of children's television (and other television and other media) and the typical contradictions of response to which it gives rise, is, we believe, the crucial content issue for children's television. Media producers should be, and mostly are, well aware that an excessive overbalance of the dominant ideology makes for dull and unprofitable children's television: though producers sell programmes to advertisers and networks, rather than to children, and these corporate bodies tend to have a different attitude towards the dominant ideology. Different programmes give different amounts of space to oppositional readings, and recuperate the dominant ideology with different degrees of effectiveness. However, since these components are so subtly intermixed, and since different ways of reading and conditions of reception can so radically alter the thrust of a programme, any attempt to use legislation to specify and control the ideological content of television programming is likely to be futile – and any such attempt would itself have to take sides on ideological issues. However, although tight legislative control of television content would prove ineffective, or else would remove much of the entertainment and stimulus value of children's television, there are other more constructive responses to the mixed ideological content of children's television. Parents and educators can recognize and use the contradictions of specific programmes to help to clarify some fundamental social issues, for children and for themselves. They should do this, not only by relying on children's active processing of the message, but also by making children more conscious and aware of what they are processing and how.

4   It has long been known that the reality factor – television's perceived relation to the real world – is variable, depending

on age, experience and social conditions. Indeed, it is a decisive factor determining the nature of media responses and media effects. But the ability to make subtle and adequate reality judgements about television is a major developmental outcome that can only be acquired from a child's experience of television.

Differences in modality judgements account for most of the reactions by children that most surprise and trouble parents: their apparent over-reaction, their impressionability. Parents are right to protect their children from over-stimulation when they are young, but they should not worry unduly about occasional 'modality mistakes' or over-reactions to specific programmes. These are indicative that learning is taking place, as children try to make things fit their scheme of the world by experimenting. Nor should parents be over-anxious at older children's seeming callousness, as if it were 'narcotization', when it is simply an accurate perception of the unreality of television.

The process of refining modality judgements – about television messages and other message systems – should be a major concern to educators, since it is of such obvious importance in equipping them to cope with the barrage of messages they will be confronted with as citizens in a mass-communications society. The processes of media production, as part of the necessary knowledge for a media modality system, should be part of everyone's school knowledge.

The pathological modality problems which do exist, for some children, should be seen as part of a more general social problem, and it is principally that problem, not merely its associated television symptoms, which should be the focus of attention by government agencies and other concerned bodies. Using television as a scapegoat is too often an excuse for inaction with regard to deeper causes.

5   All children need some fantasy programmes, such as cartoons for younger children. All children, particularly older ones, also need some programmes which touch more closely their reality.

Young children's liking for cartoons, so frequent a target for lobbyists and concern for parents, is a natural and healthy developmental phenomenon. Older children need programmes with the greater impact that comes from higher modality. Successful children's programmes utilize this, though they do not always seem to be explicitly and consistently aware of it. But people of all ages prefer a mix of modality types, to give the range of media effects, from relaxation to excitement. It is only by providing programmes with a range of modality values that children will experience a sufficiently rich modality environment to enable them to learn to distinguish one kind from another.

6　Media violence is qualitatively different from real violence: it is a natural signifier of conflict and difference, and without representations of conflict, art of the past and present would be seriously impoverished.

The issue of violent content cannot be considered apart from the modality value of media representations of violence. The strong move by lobbyists, especially overt in the USA but also effective in Britain and Australia, to limit the depictions of violence on television is therefore based on a radical misconception of how the media work. This said, it remains true that high-modality violence is likely to be disturbing to young children, who will neither enjoy nor learn well from such programmes. Furthermore the ideological meaning of some kinds of violence – as in some kinds of pornography or racism – must be sufficiently offensive to be banned on those grounds: not because of violence as such but because of the world-view they are proclaiming and legitimating.

7　Meanings gained from television are renegotiated and altered in the process of discourse, and in that form have social status and effect.

The activity of children in response to television does not stop with watching programmes, but continues with all sorts of other acts of meaning-making. Anyone concerned with the effects of television must follow up the sometimes tortuous course of this redefinition and appropriation. This is especially true for parents and teachers, if they want to engage constructively and directly with the real meanings at issue. That is, adults in their contact with children should take an active part in helping to mediate children's interaction with and ideas about television. Significant adults should be wary of blanket rejection of programmes which are avidly viewed by children, or which provoke strongly positive responses. They should also acknowledge the role of peer interaction, as vital for a child's normal development.

8　General ideological forms have an overall determining effect on interpretations of television.

Ideological forms in television can only confirm and replicate what is widely promulgated by other means. Television is often unjustly blamed for the breakdown of other ideological apparatuses by the Right, or attributed with the combined effectivity of all the rest by the Left. But television has too diffused and contradictory a content to have a single effect one way or another on its own: it has a social role to play, but only in conjunction with other forces and structures, and can never be singly and aberrantly determining.

9   The family is not simply a site for countering the meanings of television, it is also active in determining what the meanings will be.

The family remains a powerful agent of socialization in contemporary society. There are determinations of the family itself in a class society, and parental authority is contested by other sites of power, including school and peer groups. Whereas parents may feel powerless, or seek to exercise power by limiting their children's viewing, a more open and equal relationship over television could be an educative and bonding factor. Families need to think about and act upon the way in which they interact with their televisions, not simply try to control the quantity or kind of programmes viewed when and by whom. Such control will typically produce friction and struggle, as it usually combines arbitrary routines with ad hoc exceptions.

10   The school is a site where television should be thoroughly understood, and drawn into the curriculum in a variety of positive ways.

The suspicion of television by educators, the barriers that are set up between television and schooling, are, we feel, unjustified and wasteful of a potentially valuable resource. The common argument is that one should keep television out of the school because 'children spend too much time in mindless television viewing anyway'. This is in fact as good a reason for bringing television into the school curriculum as it is for excluding it. The less one knows and understands about the medium, the less one engages with it in a discriminating fashion. Television literacy and appreciation are obvious school subjects which seem to be making too little progress. Overall, television is a factor which modern education cannot simply deplore or ignore, but should come to terms with as part of its primary function of equipping students to be adequate citizens in the society in which they live.

References

Althusser, L., 1971. Ideology and ideological state apparatuses. In *Lenin and Philosophy and Other Essays*. London: New Left Books.

Althusser, L. and Balibar, E., 1977. *Reading Capital*. London: New Left Books.

Alvarado, M. and Buscombe, E., 1974. *The Making of Hazel*. London: London University Press.

Anderson, D. R., 1980. Watching children watch television. In G. Hale and M. Lewis (eds) *Attention and the Development of Cognitive Skills*. New York: Plenum.

Anderson, D. R., Levin, S. R. and Lorch, E. P., 1977. The effects of television program pacing on the behavior of pre-school children, *Television Communication Review*, 25, 159–66.

Apple, M., 1979. *Ideology and Curriculum*. New York: Random House.

Australian Senate Inquiry, 1978. *Children and Television*. Canberra: Australian Government Publishing Service.

Baggaley, D. and Duck, B., 1976. *The Dynamics of Television*. Farnborough: Saxon House.

Bandler, R. and Grinder, J., 1979. *Frogs into Princes*. Utah: Real People Press.

Bandura, A., 1965. Influence of models' reinforcement contingencies on the acquisition of initative responses. *Journal of Personality and Social Psychology*, 1, 589–95.

Bandura, A., Ross, D. and Ross, S. A., 1963. Imitation of film-mediated aggressive models. *Journal of Abnormal and Social Psychology*, 67, 601–7.

Banister, D. and Fransella, F., 1971. *Inquiring Man*. Harmondsworth: Penguin.

Barnes, B., 1982. *T. S. Kuhn and Social Science*. London: Macmillan.

Barnes, D., 1975. *From Communication to Curriculum*. Harmondsworth: Penguin.

Barthes, R., 1973. *Mythologies*. London: Granada.

Barthes, R., 1977. *Image–Music–Text*. London: Fontana.

Bateson, G., 1973. *Steps to an Ecology of Mind*. New York: Ballantine.

Berger, J. and Luckmann, T., 1967. *The Social Construction of Reality*. Harmondsworth: Penguin.

Berkowitz, L. and Geen, R., 1966. Film violence and cue properties of available targets. *Journal of Personality and Social Psychology*, 3, 525–30.

Berkowitz, L. and Rawlings, E., 1963. Effects of film violence on inhibitions against subsequent aggression. *Journal of Abnormal and Social Psychology*, 66, 405–12.

Berne, E., 1968. *Games People Play: The Psychology of Human Relationships*. Harmondsworth: Penguin.

Bernstein, B., 1971. *Class, Codes and Control*. London: Routledge & Kegan Paul.

Berry, J. W. and Dasen, P. R., 1974. *Culture and Cognition: Readings in Cross-cultural Psychology*. London: Methuen.

Bettelheim, B., 1960. *The Informed Heart*. Glencoe, Ill.: Free Press.

Bettelheim, B., 1976. *The Uses of Enchantment*. Harmondsworth: Penguin.

Biggins, B., 1981. Survey of teachers' perceptions of the impact of television on the children they teach. The South Australian Children's Film and Television Council.

Bigsby, C., 1976. *Approaches to Popular Culture*. London: Edward Arnold.

Birdwhistell, R. L., 1972. *Kinesics and Context*. Harmondsworth: Penguin.

Bonney, W. and Wilson, A., 1983. *Australia's Commercial Media*. Melbourne: Macmillan.

Bourdieu, P., 1980. The aristocracy of culture. *Media, Culture and Society*, 2, 225–54.

Bourdieu, P. and Passeron, J. C., 1977. *Reproduction in Education, Society and Culture*. London: Sage.

Brecht, B., 1964. *Brecht on Theatre* (translated by J. Willett). London: Eyre Methuen.

Brown, R., 1973. *A First Language*. Harmondsworth: Penguin Education.

Brown, R. and Bellugi, U., 1964. Three processes in the acquisition of syntax. *Harvard Education Review*, 34, 133–51.

Chomsky, C., 1969. *The Acquisition of Syntax in Children from 5 to 10*. Cambridge, Mass.: MIT Press.

Chomsky, N., 1957. *Syntactic Structures*. The Hague: Mouton.

Chomsky, N., 1965. *Aspects of the Theory of Syntax*. Cambridge, Mass.: MIT Press.

Christiansen, J. B., 1979. Television role models and adolescent occupational goals. *Human Communication Research*, 5, 335–7.

Collins, W. A., 1979. Children's comprehension of television content. In E. Wartella (ed.), *Children Communicating: Media and Developmental Thought, Speech, Understanding*. Beverly Hills: Sage.

Comstock, G., 1975. *The Effects of Television: What is the Evidence?* Rand paper series, P-5412. Santa Monica: Rand Corporation.

Comstock, G., Chaffee, S., Vatzman, N., McCombs, M. and Roberts, D., 1978. *Television and Human Behaviour*. New York: Columbia University Press.

Connell, R. W., 1971. *The Child's Construction of Politics*. Melbourne: University of Melbourne Press.

Connell, R. W., 1977. *Ruling Class, Ruling Culture: Studies of Conflict Power and Hegemony in Australian life*. Cambridge: Cambridge University Press.

Cronbach, L. J., 1975. Beyond the two disciplines of scientific psychology. *American Psychologist*, 30.

De Fleur, M., 1964. Occupational roles as portrayed on T.V. *Opinion Quarterly*, 28, 57–74.

Delia, J., and O'Keefe, B., 1979. 'Constructivism'. In Wartella, 1979.

Docking, R. A. and Thornton, J. A., 1979. Anxiety, achievement and cognitive incongruence. *Australian Journal of Education*, 23(3), 250–61.

Dorfman, A. and Mattelart, A., 1975. *How to Read Donald Duck: Imperialist Ideology in the Disney Comic*. International General.

Durkin, K., 1985. *Television, Sex Roles and Children: A Developmental Social Psychological Analysis*. Milton Keynes: Open University Press.

Eco, U., 1976. *Introduction to Theory of Semiotics*. Bloomington: Indiana University Press.

Edgar, P., 1977. *Children and Screen Violence*. St Lucia: University of Queensland Press.

Edgar, P. and Callus, U., 1979. *The Unknown Audience*. Melbourne: Channel 9.

Eimas, P. D., Signeland, E. R., Jusczyk, P. and Vigorito, J. M., 1971. Speech perception in infants. *Science*, 303–6.

Eysenck, H. and Nias, B., 1978. *Sex, Violence and the Media*. Adelaide: Mary Martin Books.

Fensham, P., Power, C., Tripp, D. and Kemmis, S., 1986. *Alienation from Schooling*. London: Routledge & Kegan Paul.

Fergusson, C. A., 1959. Disglossia. *Word*, 15, 325–40.

Feshbach, S., 1961. The stimulating versus cathartic effects of a vicarious aggressive activity. *Journal of Abnormal and Social Psychology*, 63, 181–5.

Feshbach, S., 1972. Reality and fantasy in filmed violence. In J. P. Murray et al., (eds). *Television and Social Behaviour*, vol. 2: *TV and Social Learning*. Washington DC: Government Printing Office.

Feshbach, S., 1976. The role of fantasy in the response to television. *Journal of Social Issues*, 32(4), 71–85.

Fineberg, S., 1977. The classroom's no longer prime time. *Today's Education*, 66(3), 78–9.

Fisher, E., 1982. Children's television viewing preferences. Unpublished manuscript from author and Murdoch University.

Fishman, J. A., 1972. Sociology of language. In P. P. Giglioli (ed.), *Language and Social Context*. Harmondsworth: Penguin.

Fiske, J., 1982. *Introduction to Communication Studies*. London: Methuen.

Fiske, J., 1983. Quiz shows and the purchase of cultural capital. Mimeo from the author at the West Australian Institute of Technology, Bentley, Perth.

Fiske, J. and Hartley, J., 1978. *Reading Television*. London: Methuen.

Fiske, J., Hodge, B. and Turner, G., 1984. Videoclips. *Australian Journal of Cultural Studies*, 2, 1.

Fodor, J. A., 1975. *The Language of Thought*. New York: Crowell.

Freud, S., 1960. *Jokes and their Relation to the Unconscious* (translated by J. Strachey). London: Routledge & Kegan Paul.

Freud, S., 1971. *Introductory Lectures on Psychoanalysis* (translated by J. Strachey). Harmondsworth: Penguin.

Fry, D. L. and Sigman, S. J., 1984. Newspaper language and readers' perceptions of news events. *Newspaper Research Journal*, 5(3).

Gerbner, G., 1972. Violence in television drama: trends and symbolic functions. In G. A. Comstock and E. A. Rubinstein (eds), *Television and Social Behaviour*, vol. 1: *Media Content and Control*. Washington DC: Government Printing Office.

Gerbner, G. and Gross, L., 1976. Living with television: the violence profile. *Journal of Communication*, 26(2).

Gerbner, G., Gross, L., Eleey, M. F., Jackson-Beeck, M., Jeffries-Fox, S. and Signorielli, N., 1977. *Violence Profile No. 8: Trends in Network Television Drama and Viewer Conceptions of Social Reality 1967–1976*. Philadelphia: Annenberg School of Communications, University of Pennsylvania.

Gerbner, G., Gross, L., Signorielli, N. and Morgan, M., 1980. Aging with television: images on television drama and conceptions of social reality. *Journal of Communication*, 30, 37–47.

Giddens, A., 1976. *New Rules of Sociological Method: A Positive Critique of Interpretive Sociologies*. London: Hutchinson.

Giroux, H., 1981a. Schooling and the myth of objectivity: stalking the politics of the hidden curriculum. *McGill Journal of Education*, XCVI(3), 282–304.

Giroux, H., 1981b. Hegemony, resistance, and the paradox of educational reform. *Interchange*, 12(2/3), 43–6.

Giroux, H., 1983. *Theory and Resistance in Education: A Pedagogy for the Opposition*. Hadley, Mass.: Bergin & Garvey.

Glasgow University Media Group, 1976–80. *Bad News*. London: Routledge & Kegan Paul.

Goffman, I., 1961. *Asylums*. Harmondsworth: Penguin.

Goldsen, R. K., 1971. M.C.B.'s Make-believe research on T.V. Violence. *Transaction*, (October), pp. 25–35.

Gouldner, A. W., 1976. *The Dialectic of Ideology and Technology*. London: Macmillan.

Greenberg, B. S., 1974. Gratifications of television viewing and their correlates in British children. In J. G. Blumler and E. Katz (eds), *The Uses of Mass Communications*. Beverly Hills: Sage.

Greenfield, P. M., 1984. *Mind and Media: The Effects of Television, Computers and Video Games*. London: Fontana.

Greenlee, D., 1973. *Peirce's Concept of the Sign*. The Hague: Mouton.

Gross, L. and Jefferies-Fox, S., 1978. What do you want to do when you grow up, little girl? In G. Tuchman, A. K. Daniels, and J. Benet (eds) *Hearth and Home: Images of Women in the Mass Media*. New York: Oxford.

Guttman, I., 1965. *Asylums*. Harmondsworth: Penguin.

Hall, S. (ed.), 1980. *Culture, Media, Language: Working Papers in Cultural Studies, 1972–79*. London: Hutchinson.

Halliday, M. A. K., 1976. *System and Function in Language*. London: Oxford University Press.

Halliday, M. A. K., 1978. *Language as Social Semiotic: The Social Interpretation of Language and Meaning*. London: Arnold.

Hanratty, M. A., Liehert, R. M., Morris, L. W. and Fernandez, L. E., 1969. Imitation of film-mediated aggression against live and inanimate victims. *Proceedings of the 77th Annual Convention of the American Psychological Association*.

Hartmann, D. P., 1969. Influence of symbolically modeled instrumental aggression and pain cues on aggressive behaviour. *Journal of Abnormal and Social Psychology*, 11, 280–8.

Hawkins, R. P., 1977. The dimensional structure of children's perception of television reality. *Communication Research*, 4(3), 299–320.

Hawkins, R. P. and Pingree, S., 1980. Some processes in the cultivation effect. *Communication Research*, 7(2), 193–226.

Himmelweit, H. T., Oppenheim, A. N. and Vince, P., 1958. *Television and the Child*. London: Oxford University Press.

Hodge, B., 1978. *Foreshortened Time*. London: Brewer.

Hodge, B. (ed.), 1981. *Communication and the Teacher*. Melbourne: Longman Cheshire.

Hodge, B. and Kress, G., 1983. Functional semiotics. *Australian Journal of Cultural Studies*, 1(1).

Hodge, B. and Kress, G., 1986. *Social Semiotics*. Cambridge: Polity Press (forthcoming).

Holz, J., 1981. The 'first curriculum': television's challenge to education. *Journal of Communication*, 31(1), 195–202.

Hornik, R. C., 1978. Television access and the slowing of cognitive growth. *American Educational Research Journal*, 15(1), 1–15.

Hornik, R., 1981. Out-of-school television and schooling: hypotheses and methods. *Review of Educational Research*, 51(2), 192–214.

Huston, A. C., Wright, J. C., Wartella, E., Rice, M. L., Watkins, B. A., Campbell, T. and Potts, R., 1981. Communicating more than content: Formal features of children's television programmes. *Journal of Communication*, 31(1), 32–4.

Huston-Stein, A. C. and Wright, J. C., 1977. *Interaction of Media, Cognition and Learning*. San Francisco: Jossey-Bass.

Jackson, P., 1968. *Life in Classrooms*. New York: Holt, Rinehart & Winston.

Jaglom, L. and Gardner, H., 1981. Decoding the worlds of television. *Psychology Today*.

Jakobson, R., 1968. *Child Language, Aphasia and Phonological Universals*. The Hague: Mouton.

Katz, E., Blumler, J. and Gurevitch, M., 1973. Uses and gratifications research. *Public Opinion Quarterly*, 37, 509–23.

Kelly, G., 1955. *The Psychology of Personal Constructs*. New York: Norton.

Kress, G. and Hodge, B., 1979. *Language as Ideology*. London: Routledge & Kegan Paul.

Kuhn, T. S., 1970. *The Structure of Scientific Revolutions*, 2nd edn. Chicago: Chicago University Press.

Labov, W., 1972. The logic of non-standard English. In P. P. Giglioli (ed.), *Language and Social Context*. Harmondsworth: Penguin.

Lakatos, I. and Musgrave, A., 1970. *Criticism and the Growth of Knowledge*. Cambridge: Cambridge University Press.

Lévi-Strauss, C., 1963. *Structural Anthropology*. New York: Basic Books.

Lévi-Strauss, C., 1969. *The Elementary Structures of Kinship*. London: Beacon Press.

Lévi-Strauss, C., 1972. *The Savage Mind*. London: Weidenfeld & Nicolson.

Lundgren, U., 1981. Education as a context for work. Opening address to the Australian Association for Research in Education, Sydney, 1980. *Australian Educational Research*, 8(2), 5–29.

Luria, A. R. and Yudovich, F. I., 1971. *Speech and the Development of Mental Processes in the Child: An Experimental Investigation*. Harmondsworth: Penguin.

Mackay, R. W., 1974. Conceptions of children and models of socialisation. In H. P. Dreitzel (ed.), *Recent Sociology*, No. 5. London: Macmillan. Revised in R. Turner, *Ethnomethodology*. Harmondsworth: Penguin.

Marcuse, H., 1966. *One-dimensional Man*. London: Routledge & Kegan Paul.

McCleod, J. M., Atkin, C. K. and Chaffee, S. H., 1972. Adolescents, parents and television use: Adolescent self report measures from Maryland and Wisconsin samples. In G. A. Comstock and E. A. Rubinstein (eds), *Television and Social Behaviour*, vol. 3: *Television and Adolescent Aggressiveness*. Washington DC: Government Printing Office.

McLuhan, M., 1964. *Understanding the Media: the extensions of man*, New York: McGraw-Hill.

Medrich, E. A., 1979. Constant television: a background to daily life. *Journal of Communication*, 30(1), 159–65.

Mills, M. and Melhuish, E., 1974. Recognition of mother's voice in early infancy. *Nature*, 252(5479), 123–4.

Morgan, M. and Gross, L., 1980. Television viewing, I.Q. and academic achievement. *Journal of Broadcasting*, 24(2), 117–33.

Morrison, S. and Gardner, H., 1978. Dragons and dinosaurs: the child's capacity to differentiate fantasy from reality. *Child Development*, 49, 642–8.

Murdock, G., 1975. The sociology of mass communications and sociological theory. *Australian and New Zealand Journal of Sociology*, 11(3), 27–30.

Murray, J. P., 1973. Television and violence: implications of the Surgeon General's research program. *American Psychologist*, 28.

Nash, R., 1973. *Classrooms Observed: The Teacher's Perception and the Pupils Performance*. London: Routledge & Kegan Paul.

Newcomb, H., 1978. Assessing the violence profile studies of Gerbner and Gross. *Communication Research*, 5(3), 264–83.

Noble, G., 1970. Film mediated aggressive and creative play. *British Journal of Social and Clinical Psychology*, 9(1), 1–7.

Noble, G., 1973. Effects of different forms of filmed aggression on children's constructive and destructive play. *Journal of Personality and Social Psychology*, 26, 54–9.

Noble, G., 1975. *Children in Front of the Small Screen*. Constable: Sage.

O'Toole, M., 1981. The plot structure of Tom and Jerry. Seminar held at Murdoch University, May. Unpublished.

Palmer, P., 1980. *TV Viewing in the Family Context. A Symbolic Interactionist Perspective*. Paper delivered at Active Eye Project Seminar, Murdoch University, Perth.

Phillips, D. L., 1973. *Abandoning Method*. San Francisco: Jossey-Bass.

Piaget, J., 1952. *The Origins of Intelligence in Children*. New York: International Universities Press.

Piaget, J., 1954. *The Construction of Reality in the Child*. New York: Basic Books.

Piaget, J., 1959. *The Language and Thought of the Child* (first published 1926). London: Routledge & Kegan Paul.

Piaget, J., 1968. *Structuralism*. London: Routledge & Kegan Paul.

Piaget, J., 1975. The stages of intellectual development of the child. In P. Mussen, J. Linger and J. Kagan (eds), *Basic and Contemporary Issues in Developmental Psychology*. New York: Harper & Row.

Piaget, J., 1977. *The Grasp of Consciousness*. London: Routledge & Kegan Paul.

Piaget, J. and Inhelder, B., 1956. *Child's Conception of Space*. London: Routledge & Kegan Paul.

Piaget, J. and Inhelder, B., 1970. The gaps in empiricism. In Lakatos and Musgrave, 1970.

Postman, N., 1979. *Teaching as a Conserving Activity*. New York: Delacourte.

Postman, N. and Weingartner, C., 1969. *Teaching as a Subversive Activity*. New York: Delacourte.

Potter, R. L., 1978. Understanding exceptionality through television. *Teacher*, October, 42–51.

Ricoeur, P., 1970. *Freud and Philosophy*. New Haven, Conn.: Yale University Press.

Salomon, G., 1979. *The Interaction of Media, Cognition and Learning*. San Francisco: Jossey-Bass.

Schramm, W. (ed.), 1954. *The Process and Effects of Mass Communication*. Urbana, Ill.: University of Illinois Press.

Schramm, W., 1964. *The Effects of TV on Children and Adolescents*. New York: UNESCO.

Schulman, M., 1973. *The Ravenous Eye*. London: Cassell.

Sharman, K., 1980. Television and school achievement. Report to Australian Council for Educational Research, in *Research Information for Teachers*, 2.

Smith, N., 1973. *The Acquisition of Phonology: A Case Study*. Cambridge: Cambridge University Press.

Smythe, D., 1953. *Three Years of New York Television*. Monitoring Study No. 6. Illinois: Urbana.

Snyder, B. R., 1971. *The Hidden Curriculum*. New York: Knopf.

Surgeon General's Scientific Advisory Committee on Television and Social Behaviour, 1972. *Television and Growing Up: The Impact of Televised Violence*. Washington, DC: US Government Printing Office.

Thompson, D., 1964. *Discrimination and Popular Culture*. Harmondsworth: Penguin.

Thompson, J. B., 1984. *Studies in the Theory of Ideology*. Cambridge: Polity Press.

Tripp, D. H., 1983. Co-authorship and negotiation: the interview as art of creation. *Interchange*, 14(3), 32–45.

Tripp, D. H., Hodge, R. I. and D'Amelio, S., 1984. *Television and Reality: One Child's Constructs*. Active Eye working paper presented at the Third National Child Development Conference, Perth, August.

Tulloch, J. and Alvarado, M., 1984. *Dr Who: The Unfolding Text*. London: Macmillan.

Vander Zanden, J. W., 1980. *Education Psychology in Theory and Practice*. New York: Random House.

Vygotsky, L. S., 1962. *Thought and Language*, edited and translated by E. Harfmann and G. Vakar. Cambridge, Mass.: MIT Press.

Wagner, D. M. and Vallacher, R. R., 1977. *Implicit Psychology*. New York: Oxford University Press.

Walters, R. H. and Thomas, E. L., 1963. Enhancement of punitiveness by visual and audiovisual displays. *Canadian Journal of Psychology*, 17, 244–55.

Wartella, E., 1979. *Children and Television: The Development of the Child's Understanding of the Medium*. Report prepared for the Federal Communications Commission, August.

Wartella, E. (ed.), 1979. *Children Communicating*. Beverly Hills: Sage.

Wartella, E. and Reeves, B., 1982. For some children under some conditions: A history of research on children and media. Paper presented at the International Communication Association Conference, Boston.

Watson, P. C. and Johnson-Laird, P. N. (eds), 1977. *Thinking: Readings in Cognitive Science*. Cambridge: Cambridge University Press.

Wegner, D. M. and Vallacher, R. R., 1977. *Implicit Psychology*. New York: Oxford University Press.

Whorf, B., 1956. *Language Thought and Reality*. Cambridge, Mass.: MIT Press.

Williams, R., 1958. *Culture and Society – 1780–1950*. London: Chatto & Windus.

Williams, R., 1974. *Television: Technology and Cultural Form*. London: Fontana.

Williams, R., 1976. *Keywords*. London: Fontana.

Williams, T. M., 1981. How and what do children learn from television? *Human Communication Research*, 7(2), 180–92.

Willis, P., 1977. *Learning to Labour*. Farnborough: Saxon House.

Winick, M. P. and Winick, C., 1979. *The Television Experience: What Children See*. Beverly Hills: Sage.

Winn, M., 1977. *The Plug-in Drug*. New York: Viking Press.

Witkin, H. A., Dyk, R. B., Paterson, H. B., Goodenough, D. R. and Kemp, S. A., 1962. *Psychological Differentiation*. New York: Wiley.

Witkin, H. A., Moore, C. A., Goodenough, D. R. and Cox, P. W., 1977. Field-dependent and field-independent cognitive styles and their educational implications. *Review of Educational Research*, 47(1), 1–64.

Wollheim, R., 1968. *Freud*. London: Fontana.

Index

aberrant coding 43
aggression
  in social context 200–1
  see also violence
'aggression machine' experiments
  207–8, 209, 210
alienation effect 103, 109, 112
alienation from school 180
Althusser, L. 23
Alvarado, M. 198
anchorage 24
Anderson, D. R. 62, 92, 202
anthropology 6
Apple, M. 172
appropriation of television 217
attention span, effect of television
  on 160
attitudes to learning 174
audience responses on soundtracks
  137
Australian Council for
  Educational Research 165
Australian Senate Inquiry 1, 100,
  101, 133
authenticity 122

Baggaley, D. 5
Bandler, R. 46
Bandura, A. 148, 193, 204, 207
Banister, D. 85
Barnes, B. 189
Barnes, D. 181
Barthes, R. 6, 12, 24

Bateson, G. 6, 12, 46, 134, 135
Batman 107, 170
Behaviourism 193, 200
Bellugi, U. 44
Berger, J. 6, 73
Berkowitz, L. 201, 209
Berne, E. 47, 48
Bernstein, B. 6, 12, 83, 84, 88,
  96, 97, 175
Berry, J. W. 46
Bettleheim, B. 32
bias *see* class bias; gender bias
Biggins, B. 160, 170
Bigsby, C. 4
Birdwhistell, R. L. 51, 147
Birmingham Centre for Cultural
  Studies 197
black children
  and language 49
  and television 49, 138–42
Bobo-doll experiments 115, 148,
  204, 210
Bonney, W. 2, 198
Bourdieu, P. 174, 175, 177, 178
boys
  imitation of aggressive action
    205
  interaction with girls 147–
    51
  response to gender bias on
    television 93, 95
Brecht, B. 103, 109, 112
Brown, R. 36, 44, 45
Bruner, J. 7

bullet-theory of communication
    192, 194
Buscombe, E. 198

Callus, U. 91, 133
Canavan 133
capacity to discriminate 9
Carry on Camping 156
cartoons 66, 71, 109
    children's interest in 91, 98,
        138
    complexity of 16
    criticized by adults 9, 17, 92,
        119
    and reality 110, 111
    role of in children's
        development 9, 32, 98, 130,
        216
    *see also Fangface; Godzilla; Scooby
        Doo; Spiderman; Tom and Jerry*
catharsis theory 102, 105, 208
censorship 64, 65, 66, 143
Chafee, S. H. 91
Charlie's Angels 169
children
    ability to perceive plot 22
    black *see* black children and
        television
    development of *see* development
    misconceptions of about media
        processes 118, 124, 126, 139,
        141
    semiotic systems of 214
    use of television by 45
    as victims of television 73
    viewing controlled by parents 1
    ways of thinking of 7
Chomsky, C. 6, 12, 43, 44, 45,
    46, 76
Christiansen, J. B. 177
class
    bias 74, 93
    consciousness 84
    inequalities 83
    and modality 126–9

portrayal of, on television 30,
    38
and thought structures 95–8
and viewing habits 176
codes 15, 17, 19, 49
    H-form 48, 49, 62, 63, 83
    L-form 48, 49, 62, 63, 83, 84
cognitive deprivation 98
cognitive theorists 7
Coleridge, S. T. 103, 137
Collins, W. A. 22, 23, 36, 37,
    161, 202
comedy programmes 138
comics 109
communication skills, affected by
    television 161
Comstock, George 102, 161, 194,
    195, 196, 197, 205
Connell, R. W. 82, 84
constructs 86, 88
content analysis 4, 85
contents of television 14, 49, 61
'cool' media 46
Cop Shop 169, 176
creativity affected by
    television 100, 131, 160
credits 109–10
'crisis of sociology' 196
crisis phase in science 191
Cronbach, L. J. 196
'cultivation hypothesis' 74
cultural capital 98, 174, 175
cultural studies 9
curriculum *see* hidden curriculum

Dallas 91
Dasen, P. R. 46
De Fleur, M. 74
Delia, J. 8, 202
development of children 75–95
    affected by television 99
    language 36, 75
    of modality structures 112
    perception 75, 83
    play important for 134
    of political consciousness 84

development of children *(continued)*
  of reality constructs 119–26
  stages of 81
  of thought 75, 78, 81, 83
diachronic 20, 21
diatopic 20, 21
Diff'rent Strokes 140
discipline in school 178
discontinuous syntagms 21, 22
Docking, R. A. 176
Doctor Who 137, 170, 198
documentary programmes 107,
  120, 170
drama 107
Duck, B. 5
Dukes of Hazzard, The 141
Durkheim 6
Durkin, K. 53

Eco, U. 6, 43
Edgar, P. 91, 133, 176
effects of television *see* television,
  effects of
ego-centrism 83, 90
Eimas, P. D. 78
elaborated code 83, 175
enculturation 173
escapism 131
Eysenck, H. 102, 193, 195, 196,
  203

family
  control of children's viewing
    by 1, 218
  socialization by 218
  viewing mediated by 176
Fangface research 15, 17, 23, 24,
  31, 50–71, 74, 93, 110, 111,
  115, 144–5, 151–3
fantasy 105
  effect 103
  value of 130, 216
fatigue caused by television 161
feature films 91
Fensham, P. 180
Fergusson, C. A. 48

Feschbach, S. 102, 103, 207, 208,
  210
field-dependence 83, 96
Fineberg, S. 160
Fisher, E. 91
Fishman, J. A. 48
Fiske, J. 7, 75, 92, 181
Fransella, F. 85
Freud, S. 6, 8, 12, 46, 47, 148,
  201
Fry, D. L. 198
functional irrationality 24

Gardner, H. 103, 119, 120, 124
gaze direction 149, 150
Geen, R. 209
gender bias 74, 93, 94, 95
  effect on boys 93, 95
  effect on girls 93
generative understanding of
  television 60
genre recognition 52
Gerbner, George 5, 74, 202
Giddens, A. 189, 190, 196
girls
  interaction with boys 147–51
  response to gender bias on
    television 93–5
Giroux, H. 23, 172, 178
Glasgow University Media Group
  198
Godzilla 91
Goffman 6, 183
Goldsen, R. K. 5
Gouldner, A. W. 196
grammar 41, 42, 43, 44, 45
  of television programmes 60
  of verbal language 46
Greenberg, B. S. 14
Grinder, J. 46
Gross, L. 74, 162, 163, 176, 177

Hall, Stuart 9, 197
Halliday, M. A. K. 6, 12, 44,
  45, 46, 49, 90, 104, 134
Hanratty, M. A. K. 204

Hartley, J. 7, 75
Hartmann, D. P. 207
Hawkins, R. P. 74, 102, 103
H-form codes 48, 49, 62, 63, 83
hidden curriculum 171–3
high-definition media 46
Himmelweit, H. T. 102, 192,
    193, 211
Hodge, B. 12, 44, 76, 84, 88,
    104, 134, 189, 198
Holz, J. 160, 162
Hornik, R. C. 159, 160, 162,
    163, 179
'hot' media 46
Huston-Stein, A. C. 37
hyperactivity 160
hypotactic structure 35, 44, 80, 89
hypotaxis 39

ideology 23
    children's response to 47, 75
    of quiz shows 182
    of television programmes 1, 10,
        22, 39, 61, 71, 157, 215,
        217–18
imagination 1, 100, 131, 160
Incredible Hulk, The 31, 52, 60,
    109, 139, 156, 157
information-deprivation 140, 141
    see also media production
    processes
Inhelder, B. 81
irrationality see functional
    irrationality

Jackobson 6
Jackson, P. 172
Jaglom, L. 119, 120, 124
Jakobson, R. 12, 44, 78
James Bond 139
Jefferies-Fox, S. 176, 177
Johnson-Laird, P. N. 81

Katz, E. 8, 78
Kelly, George 6, 7, 85, 86
King Kong 156

knowledge, diversity of children's
    and teachers' 170
Kojak 169
Kress, G. 12, 76, 88, 104, 134,
    198
Kuhn, T. S. 189, 190, 191, 192,
    193, 197, 199, 201, 202, 208,
    210, 211

Labov, W. 6, 48, 49
Lakatos, I. 191
language
    acquisition device 44
    development of 36, 75
    elaborated code 83, 175
    grammar of 46
    philosophy of 6
    restricted code 83, 96
large-scale structures 22
laughter
    canned 137
    as indicator of modality 106
    as indicator of subversive
        meaning 148, 149
Lévi-Strauss, C. 6, 12, 15, 24,
    29, 31, 32, 45, 51, 52, 76
L-form codes 48, 49, 62, 63, 83,
    84
linguistics 6
literary criticism 4, 5
Locke, J. 6
low-definition media 46
low self-esteem 8, 133, 176
Luckman 6, 73
Lundgren, U. 174
Luria, A. R. 45

Mackay, R. W. 215
MacLeod 202
McLeod 91, 102
McLuhan, M. 46
magazine programmes 91, 92
Malinowski 6
Marcuse, H. 24, 74, 98
Marvel comic 107
Marxism 8, 9, 201

meanings
  negotiated 56, 142–57, 217
  subversive 47, 54, 55, 61
  of television 2, 3, 4, 5, 40, 41,
    47, 61
  see also semiotics
media
  high-definition media 46
  illusions 123, 139
  low-definition media 46
  production processes, children's
    misconceptions about 118,
    124, 126, 139, 141
  studies 192, 196
Medrich, E. A. 161, 176
Mellhuish, E. 78
membrane between television and
  reality 119, 124
messages 8, 42, 49
meta-grammar 46
middle-class children 83
  viewing habits of 176
Mills, M. 78
Mr Ed 124, 125
modality 43, 104–31
  disorders of 134, 135
  judgements 109, 111, 117, 118,
    123, 138
  markers, redundancy of 111,
    130
  transformations 136–7
Monkey 124, 125
Morgan, M. 162, 163
Morrison, S. 103
Muppets, The 155–7
Murdock, G. 198
Murray, J. P. 5
Musgrave, A. 191
myth 15, 24, 25, 29, 45, 51, 52

Nash, R. 86
national consciousness 84
Nationwide 176
negotiated meanings see meanings,
  negotiated

Newcomb, H. 15, 74
news programmes 107, 120, 138,
  139, 170
Nias, B. 102, 193, 195, 196, 203
Noble, G. 5, 8, 102, 103, 203,
  207
'normal science' 190, 191

object-oriented perception 96
'one-dimensional mind' 75, 98
O'Toole, M. 36

Palmer, P. 91
parents see family
Passeron, J. C. 174
pathological reaction to
  television 132, 133, 134
peer interaction 217
Peirce 78
Personal Construct Theory 85
Phillips, D. L. 196
phonology 44, 78
Piaget, J. 6, 7, 12, 46, 76, 78,
  81, 82, 83, 84, 146, 201
Pingree, S. 74
Plato 100, 101, 111
'plug-in-drug', television as 74,
  98, 100
police shows 170
polysemy 32
pornography 217
Postman, N. 1, 160, 162
power 83
  of school hierarchy 187
primary oppositions 28
Prisoner 91, 169, 176, 179, 183–7
psychoanalysis 8
psychology 6, 8

quiz shows 179, 180, 181, 182,
  187

racism 217
radio 46
rank-shifting 90
Rawlings, E. 201

reading *see* television, effects of on reading skills
reading television 3, 56, 75, 159, 188
reality 9, 101
    criteria 125, 126
    judgements 121, 125, 130
    and television 110, 111, 119, 131, 215
reality-construction 74, 75
research 7, 10, 41, 43, 73, 75
    into children and television 2, 192, 197
    see also 'aggression machine'; 'Bobo-doll'; *Fang face*; triadic experiments
'research paradigms' 190
restricted code 83, 96
revolution in science 191, 199
'revolutionary science' 190, 201
rules, school 172

Salomon, G. 5, 37, 46, 161, 179, 202
Saussure 12
schizophrenia 134, 135
school 10
    achievement, related to television viewing 163
    alienation from 180
    compared with prison 183
    culture 172
    irrelevance of 180
    rules 172
    and television 159–88, 218
Schramm, W. 192, 193, 194, 211
Schulman, M. 1, 160
science
    'normal' 190, 191
    open-mindedness in 211
    as orderly logical process 190
    revolution in science 191, 199
    'revolutionary science' 190, 201
Scooby Doo 31, 51, 60
semiotics 5–7, 15–16, 17–23, 31–40

serials 91, 92, 98, 170
sex on television 113, 196
sex ratio on television *see* gender bias
sexism 55–6, 151–3
Sharman, K. 164, 165
Sigman, S. J. 198
sign 59
Six Million Dollar Man 109
skew of television *see* class bias; gender bias
Skinner 6
slow motion 109
Smith, N. 53
Smythe, D. 74
Snyder, B. R. 172
soap operas 170
social class *see* class
social construction of reality 73, 74, 75
social isolation 133, 136, 138
socialization of thinking 98
sociolinguistics 48
sociology 6
Sons and Daughters 91
soundtracks 62, 107, 137
Space 1999 170
Spiderman 170
Star Wars 92
subversive meanings 47, 54, 55, 61
Sullivans, The 169
Surgeon General's Report 133, 161, 194, 195, 197, 199, 200
symbolic annihilation 74, 99
symbolic modes of presentation 46

teachers 4
    attitudes of, to television 1, 4, 166–71
television
    ambiguity of 7
    amount watched 1, 2, 8, 74
    appropriation of 217
    as it interacts 8

television *(continued)*
  as bad influence 1, 73, 91
  black children and 49, 138–42
  class ratio on 74
  cultural value of 175, 213
  discussions about 143, 144
  effects of 2, 7, 160, 161, 202
    on attention span 160
    on communication skills 161
    on creativity 100, 131, 160
    fatigue 161
    hyperactivity 160
    on imagination 1, 100, 131,
      160
    on reading skills 1, 3, 160
    teachers' views on 166
  gender bias on 93, 94, 95
  generative understanding of
    television 60
  grammar of programmes on
    60
  as mindless, 'plug-in-drug' 10,
    73, 74, 98, 100, 159
  pathological reaction to 132,
    133, 134
  'reading' 3, 56, 75, 159, 188
  and reality 110, 111, 119, 131,
    215, 216
  research into *see* research
  and school 159–88, 218
  use of by children 45
  useful for cognitive growth 92
  viewing
    diversity of children's and
      teachers' 170
    isolation of 138
    mediated by family 176
    relationships 137
    and school 160, 163, 218
    social context of television 8,
      132–8, 142, 157
    of working class 8
Thomas, E. L. 207
Thompson, D. 4
Thompson, J. B. 22
Thornton, J. A. 176

Tom and Jerry 36, 102, 116, 124
transactional analysis 47, 48, 57
transformations 23, 32, 43, 60,
  61, 76, 77, 80, 90, 91, 92
triadic experiments 86, 93, 112,
  120
Tripp, D. H. 49, 130
Tulloch, J. 198

Vander Zanden, J. W. 176
verbal
  ability and television
    viewing 160
  channel 61
  code 62, 70, 71, 78
  language 24, 63, 64, 78, 79
violence on television
  children's perception of 112,
    117, 140, 141, 202, 217
  concern about 7, 9
  effect of 5, 97, 102, 103, 113,
    114, 115, 132, 193–7, 207,
    209, 211
  in fiction 101
  see also 'aggression machine'
    experiments; 'Bobo-doll'
    experiments; catharsis
virtuous errors 133
visual
  channel 61, 64
  code 70, 71
  cues 62
Vygotsky, L. S. 7, 12, 82, 83

Walters, R. H. 207
Wartella, E. 8, 192, 202
Watson, P. C. 81
weather reports 139, 170
Welcome Back, Kotter 187
westerns 170
Whorf, B. 78
Williams, R. 9, 22, 159, 179
willing suspension of disbelief
  103, 137
Willis, P. 172

Wilson, A. 2, 198
Winn, Marie 1, 74, 98, 99, 100, 160, 161
Witkin, H. A. 83, 96
Wonder Woman 91
working-class children

disadvantages of viewing habits 176
at school 172–3
World About Us, The 176
Wright, J. C. 37

Yudovich 45